Getting Started in

SECURITY ANALYSIS

SECOND EDITION

Peter J. Klein
with Brian R. Iammartino

WILEY

John Wiley & Sons, Inc.

Published by John Wiley & Sons, Inc., Hoboken, New Jersey.
Published simultaneously in Canada.

For general information on our other products and services or for technical support, please contact our Customer Care Department within the United States at (800) 762-2974, outside the United States at (317) 572-3993 or fax (317) 572-4002.

Wiley also publishes its books in a variety of electronic formats. Some content that appears in print may not be available in electronic books. For more information about Wiley products, visit our web site at www.wiley.com.

Library of Congress Cataloging-in-Publication Data:

Klein, Peter J.
  Getting started in security analysis / Peter J. Klein with Brian R. Iammartino.—2nd ed.
    p. cm.—(The getting started in series)
  Includes bibliographical references and index.
  ISBN 978-0-470-46339-0 (pbk.)
  1. Investment analysis. 2. Securities. 3. Portfolio management. I. Iammartino, Brian R.,
1978- II. Title. III. Title: Security analysis.
  HG4529.K565 2009
  332.63'2—dc22

               2009025141

Printed in the United States of America

10 9 8 7 6 5 4 3 2 1

For my son,
Jack Patrick Walsh Klein
Cui multum datum est multum quaeretur ab eo

— PJK

For my parents, Nick and Eileen Iammartino,
who helped make this possible,
and for my wife, Meredith Hamilton,
who helped make it happen

— BRI

Contents

Acknowledgments   vii

Introduction   1

PART 1
Tools of the Trade

Chapter 1
Accounting   17

Chapter 2
Economics   35

Chapter 3
Investment Mathematics   77

Chapter 4
Quantitative Analysis   97

PART 2
Fundamental Financial Security Analysis

Chapter 5
Equity Analysis and Valuation   119

Chapter 6
Credit Analysis   169

Chapter 7

Real Estate   203

PART 3

Portfolio Management

Chapter 8

The Investment Management Process   261

Epilogue   307

Appendix: Selected Tables   309

Bibliography   315

Index   317

Acknowledgments

There have been many colleagues that I would like to thank—those who served as a sounding board, de facto editors, and cheerleaders—who kept me going through this project. Primary among these is Brian Iammartino, without whose insights, indefatigable work ethic, and financial acumen this work would have suffered greatly. Watching Brian "grow up" over the last 15 years has been a thrill and I expect great things coming from his mind (and pen) over the next several years. Additionally, one could never ask for a better "partner" than Jane Voorhees—truly the best in the business. Also, the following have been instrumental in this work, as well as in my practice's day-to-day "financial thinking": Stacey Tucker and Robert Limmer of UBS Wealth Management, Adam J. Gottlieb of Ruskin Moscou Faltischek, PC, and John Curran of Tigris Financial.

Clients and business associates are also a valuable resource in an undertaking such as this; they often provide insights that others, especially those "in the business," may overlook. I would especially like to thank Dr. Robert Ross—the quintessential entrepreneur, and founder of the Ross University Medical School, Veterinary School and School of Nursing. Additionally, Don Hill of Sherman, Connecticut has been an invaluable resource over many years, as has been the Rosen family—Robert, Florence, and David—thank you for your efforts and enlightening debates. Jerry Sloane of Berdon LLP was instrumental in guiding me in many different areas, especially accounting, which is his profession. The late Claire Friedlander deserves special thanks for her never-ending trust and appreciation for my work. Though she is missed each day, her memory and legacy will live on for decades to come—thank you Claire—I miss you. The following have also "served bravely in the field of duty"—putting up with my verbose e-mails and constant debates about the economy and markets: Barbara Weisen, Susan Monosson, Wendy Wiesel, Sam Reiner, Dr. & Mrs. Paul Brandoff, Bob Singer, Ronald J. Morey, Jed Morey, Howard Maier, John Catsimatidis, Danny Frank, Paul Watson, Jules Weiss, Peter and Susan Furth, Dr. Harvey Stern, Dr. and Mrs. Jack Giannola,

Dr. & Mrs. Greg Fiasconaro, Stuart Henry, Stan Henry, Dara Schlesinger, Robert Larocca, Peter and Barbara Serenita, Roy and Kim Collins, Toby Caldwell, Danielle Fehling, Ron & Kathie Eckert, Michael McManus, Dr. and Mrs. Wechterman, and Terry Plavnick.

I would also like to thank my extended family and friends for their continued support and encouragement. Finally, I would like to thank my family—my wife of nearly two decades, and my three children, without whom I am not complete and with whom, by my side, together, we can scale any mountain, overcome any setback, and celebrate every milestone.

—*Peter J. Klein*

I must start my acknowledgments with the most important of all. Peter J. Klein is not only my co-author of this work; he was my first supervisor at my first job in the finance industry. I couldn't have asked for a more inspirational and wise mentor as I was getting started in security analysis myself. I thank him for giving me the opportunity to come along for the ride on this book adventure.

At the Wharton School, I have professors such as Nick Gonedes to thank for giving me the finest business education available in the world today. At Harvard, my eyes were opened to a world of new possibilities. Most notably, Professor Linda Bilmes was and continues to be an amazing source of support, advice, and motivation.

I have been blessed with wonderful colleagues throughout my professional life, but none more so than the Managing Partners of Westport Point Capital, Mary Lou Boutwell and Erin O'Boyle. I thank them not only for enthusiastically supporting this book, but also for patiently supporting me in my growth from real estate novice to published author. Tom Welch and Seth Rosen of Colliers Meredith & Grew also provided me invaluable insight into the complex world of mortgage-backed securities.

Last but certainly not least, my friends and family provide the backbone of all that I do. My parents Nick and Eileen, sister Susan, brother-in-law Ross, Aunt Ethel and Uncle Frank, and Grandma Rachel have supported me throughout my life, and my nephews Timothy and Peter have provided ample diversion from the world of finance. My in-laws Pat and Andrea Hamilton, along with their entire families, have made me feel like one of their own. Finally, I thank my wife, Meredith Hamilton, without whose encouragement my name would not appear on the cover of this book. A theme of this book is that finance is by necessity an imperfect science, but my life is perfectly imperfect with her by my side.

—*Brian R. Iammartino*

Introduction

You are about to begin a journey into the science of investment analysis. Many of you may think that using the word *science* to describe the activities of Wall Street is a misnomer. Luck, chance, or voodoo are probably closer to your explanation of investment activity. We hope to convince you otherwise. As you make this journey, it should become obvious that investment analysis and its related extensions are rigorous enough to be taken as an actual science.

Like other scientific disciplines, investment analysis requires a working knowledge of its basic concepts. Part 1, "Tools of the Trade," explores these concepts, with considerable emphasis on exercises that hone awareness, expertise, and understanding of this once arcane subject. A century ago, the task of investment counseling belonged to men of prudence who, for fear of being wrong, usually invested funds with guaranteed returns and did not rely on scientific discipline. The fear of not being beyond reproach—otherwise known as "reputation fear"—provided enough guidance for these men. Typically the wealthy and elite, they did not see the utility of investment analysis for the simple reason that they did not have to—they were already rich.

Today, investment analysis plays a meaningful role in planning for a comfortable financial future. This book provides the reader with a firm foothold on this important subject (although the basic concepts may prove helpful in many of life's other exercises). Mastery of investment analysis takes much more than a cursory read through this text; it requires years of study and perhaps decades of practical experience. Our hope is to provide today's investor—novice or seasoned—with enough understanding to

1

simulate the workings of Wall Street analysts. An investor, after reading this manual, will have a fundamental store of financial information; will understand the terms, pricing, and research of a financial services provider; and will find the daily financial papers more interesting.

Many investors are well aware of the basics of financial planning through exposure to myriad seminars, books, magazines, and web sites. They need the next level of information. Just think about how many of your friends understand the risk-return trade-off (more risk, more return), asset allocation (spreading assets around into many classes), and the need for long-term investing habits. But how many wish they understood how a company's shares are valued, or how the workings of regression analysis and the typical economic releases in a given month directly affect the value of their investments? Part 1 is designed to provide this essential background.

Part 2, "Fundamental Financial Security Analysis," sets forth the notion that the tools described in Part 1 can be of practical use only if the investor understands how a given company is valued. Thus in this part, we explain the methodology behind the valuation techniques of a company's equity and debt securities:

> With tomes of data available, how should we quantify the value of this company? Which calculations must be executed to ascertain the true value of this company?

Consequently, these valuation techniques build on the lessons of Part 1. Without a firm understanding of the tools analysts use, it is impossible to firmly grasp the true valuation process.

Part 3, "Portfolio Management," is a discussion of the investment management process—the symbiosis of the tools and valuation techniques with the financial planning process. It includes an examination of the laws and regulations that govern this highly regulated industry. To fully grasp these legal constraints, today's serious investor must understand and be able to use the investment management process.

Lastly, as a housekeeping item, the reader should be aware of some literary licenses taken in this text. The pronouns "he" and "she" are used interchangeably throughout; this is done for stylistic simplicity and does not reflect the current percentage breakdown in the investment analysis field. The terms *VFII* (*Very Financially Interested Individual*—pronounced "vif-fee") and *NFII* (*Not Financially Interested Individual*—

pronounced "nif-fee") are introduced early on in this text and refer to the current investment-user market. People who have started to read this book should consider themselves either a VFII or a reformed NFII. The terms *analyst, practitioner*, and *investor* (seasoned or novice) are also interchangeable throughout this work, and in each case the word refers to the user of investment analysis. From professional to novice, all analysts should be in the continual learning phase. The professional analyst specializing in real estate may require a briefing on the workings of the equity market, just as a seasoned investor could be brought up to date on the changing dynamics of macroeconomics releases.

While the ultimate purpose of this book is to educate today's proactive investor in the science of investing, by no means can it serve as a proxy for a complete education in this expansive field. It can, however, provide the investor with a solid foundation of knowledge. Any interested investor (VFII) can request an incessant flow of research reports from either his representative at the issuing firm or the company itself (most companies will release the research reports; however, they require the prior permission of the analyst's firm to do so); but understanding jargon-laden reports usually takes more than a cursory background in the subject.

Investment Report Checklist

As a first step toward a better comprehension of the research reports issued by firms, it is a good idea to study what the professional groups look for in a quality report. See Table I.1.

Industry considerations. Investigate the industry (or, if a diversified company, the principal industries) of the issuer of the security. Considerations should include historical growth and future potential, the nature of worldwide competition, regulatory environments, capital requirements, methods of distribution, and external and internal factors that might change the structure of the industry.

> ✔ *Company's (or issuer's) position in the industry.* Analyze the company's strengths and weaknesses within the industry environment. This analysis should not only be based on discussion with the company's management, but should also include information from competitors and such trade sources as distributors.

TABLE I.1 Security Analysis Checklist

Economy

What are the trends in the economy? Expansionary or contraction? Where does the company fall in the spectrum—cyclical? Or countercyclical?

Are rates accommodative? The credit markets for companies in their industry?

How does the health of the consumer look? Home prices? Unemployment rate? Availability of credit?

Are there inflationary headwinds or does inflation help this company's sales? Can they pass these increased costs along?

The Business

What does the company do? Can you explain their business model to a high school student?

What is their business model?

Is their model repetitive? Annuitized? A franchise with recurring earnings?

What markets are they involved in?

Who are their major customers? Relationships?

Are they focused in one market? Diversified in many markets?

Is the company a leader in their industry?

How do they penetrate these markets? Sales force? Incentives to perform?

Who are their suppliers? Relationships sound?

Competitive forces in the industry? Does the company have a competitive advantage? A "moat" around their business?

Management–Average tenure of current senior management? Leaders in the industry? Engaged? Involved in trade groups and associations?

Management–Shareholders? What percentage of their assets are in the shares of the company?

Capital Structure

How is the "ownership pie" broken up?

Number of shares outstanding? Market cap? Any dilutive forces (i.e., warrants, options) or anti-dilutive measures (i.e., buybacks)?

Debt outstanding? Face value vs. market value? Terms? When does the debt need to be refinanced? Covenant and other creditor agreements?

Hybrids—Preferreds? Convertibles?

Calculate the Total Enterprise Value: equity market cap + debt outstanding—cash & equivalents. Use value as a comparison to private companies in industry.

TABLE I.1 Security Analysis Checklist *(Continued)*

The Financials

The Income Statement: Revenue trends? SG&A trends? Net income trends? Artificially low tax rate? One-time affects?

The quality and consistency of the earnings? Reported earnings versus consensus expectations?

The quarterly earnings conference calls? The tone and message?

Profit margins? Consistent? Versus peer group? Trend with SGA expenses? Does the company need to hire new employees? Pricing trends for talent? What is the inventory management protocol?

Search for Red Flags: Is the audit firm of a substantial size compared to the company? How have the SG&A expenses trended with revenues?

Valuation

The peer group's average valuation metrics: Price to Earnings; to Book Value; to Cash Flow; to Sales

Using the Dividend Discount Method to arrive a Fair Value estimate matrix

Valuation metrics using forward estimates of earnings, and so on

✔ *Income statement and statement of cash flows.* Review statements for a period covering two business cycles and investigate reasons for annual and seasonal changes in volume growth, price changes, operating margins, effective tax rates (including the availability of tax loss carryforwards), capital requirements, and working capital.

✔ *Balance sheet.* Investigate the reasons for historical and prospective changes in the company's financial condition and capital structure, plus the conformance of accounting practices to changes either proposed or implemented by accounting rule-making bodies.

✔ *Dividend record and policy.*

✔ *Accounting policies.* Determine policies and examine the auditor's opinion.

✔ *Management.* Evaluate reputation, experience, and stability. Also evaluate the record and policies toward corporate governance, acquisitions and divestitures, personnel (including labor relations), and governmental relations.

✔ *Facilities/programs.* Review plant networks, competitive effectiveness, capacity, future plans, and capital spending.

✔ *Research/new products.*

✔ *Nature of security.*

✔ *Security price record.*

✔ *Future outlook.* Examine principal determinants of company operating and financial performance, key points of leverage in the
future (e.g., new markets and geographical expansion, market-
share improvement, new products/services, prospects for profit
margin improvement, acquisitions), competitive outlook, major
risks (e.g., competition, erosion of customer base, abbreviated
product life cycles, technological obsolescence, environmental
hazards), and financial goals (for the short and long term) and
the analyst's level of confidence in achieving them.

The checklist should not be viewed as a complete methodology
from which to judge the competency of a research report, but it certainly
lends itself to further investigation.

A proactive investor never stops honing his skills, permitting his in-
tuition a better shot at being right. Perhaps he will search for the characteristics common to the best companies. Identifying this set of traits could
allow the investor to find the next great company and, hopefully, a great
(read: inexpensive) stock. Remember to make this differentiation between
company and stock. A great company may be so outstanding that the
market will bid up its share price to a level that makes the stock an im-
prudent candidate for any true fundamentalist. Value investors seek to
purchase equities whose fundamental value has not yet been discounted
by the market. While the value investor's analysis will be sensitive to the
equations in this text (Dividend Discount Model, DuPont Method of the
Return on Equity Equation, sustainable growth), it will also call on a considerable understanding of qualitative and management analysis.

Borrowing from the tenets of value investors, we have developed a
methodology that gives the investor a starting point for fundamental
equity analysis. The acronym PATIROC summarizes the characteristics
critical to the equity investor:

✔ People
✔ Assets
✔ Technology
✔ International Strategy
✔ Return
✔ Operations
✔ Cost-Effective Management

People

People make a company. A company that inspires its employees and creates a strong, cooperative morale will benefit in the long run. When deciding whether to purchase the equity of a company (stock), an investor should make it part of due diligence to try to learn something about the employees (and the culture of the firm). We don't mean just about top management (CEO, CFO, or investor relations director), for they are often well trained to represent the facts in a somewhat optimistic, overly biased tone. Try to find out about the employees of the company—the middle management and the factory or "line" workers. They represent the true test of the morale of a company:

> How do the frontline employees feel about their company? Do they participate in the company's retirement plans? Go to company functions? Understand the business and, furthermore, are interested in the success of the company?

Several years ago during an equity search, we came across a company that had this positive "People" characteristic. The company was a fast-growing enterprise that rewarded its employees for achievements above stated goals with stock options. Some employees on the factory floor had over $1 million in stock options. These employees were happy, to say the least, and it showed in the way they spoke about their company and its market share, competition, and new ventures. To an investment professional this was like stepping into nirvana, except that when we asked the human resources director about the prospect of doing investment seminars, he responded, "Our employees would be happy to teach your clients about investments, but wouldn't that be kind of strange, since they're your clients?" After catching our breath, we realized that he was dead serious and that we should seek other potential educational seminar opportunities.

Another element of this characteristic is the function of ownership; that is, who are the shareholders, the equity partners, of the company? We want to enjoy the company of smart investors (those professionals with an outstanding record of performance) and most importantly, of management. Insider ownership is compiled and published on a periodic basis and could give the investor valuable insights about the intentions of senior management.

Is this management long-term in their expectations or are they seeking the quick buck? How much of total compensation is made up of stock options? What is the value of management's share position? Have they purchased more shares during the recent price decline?

While answers to such questions can be informative to the investor, there is a caveat—because of the increasing use of stock options, many of today's senior management may choose to sell (or "exercise" in the parlance of options) their shares merely as a means of diversification rather than as a portent of an imminent price decline.

Assets

A strong balance sheet is a wonderful characteristic for a company in search of fame and fortune in the annals of great stocks. Assets take many different forms, the most obvious and arguably the easiest to spend being cash or cash equivalents (short-term money market instruments). But when utilized properly, certain noncurrent assets (typically assets that cannot be translated into cash within one operating cycle) can be top performers for a given company. Take, for example, the new factory with the very best in high-tech machinery, or the 30,000 acres of land in the Pacific Northwest that happens to be within one hour's drive from the Microsoft World Headquarters. While these assets are not easily converted into cash, they are certainly assets. Furthermore, the land can be carried at cost (not current market value) on the company's balance sheet. The well-trained "asset hound" seeks to break down a company's balance sheet in search of either the underutilized asset or the undiscovered or unrecognized (by accounting tenets) asset. In many situations, as value investors come to realize, the sum of the parts equals more than the whole.

Technology

Effective application of the newest technical advances makes a business more efficient. Inefficient use of or lack of technology can consequently doom an enterprise to underperformance. A business in the twenty-first century cannot operate in the same fashion as it did 15 years ago—when, for example, was the last time you purchased a good that was not scanned in some way? This often-pervasive act of electronic accounting has a significant dividend to the merchant—inventory control. These cash registers (a term that probably will soon be as antiquated as buggy whip is today) are often plugged into a database that can analyze each store's sales, margins, discounts, returns and, most importantly, need for reordering. Some economists postulate that this information-driven inventory control mechanism (technology dividend) contributes to the current period of continued low inflation.

Dedication to research and development, within a company's given area of focus, belongs in this category. Often the savviest investors seek those companies that have consistently posted high R&D expense ratios (as a percentage of revenues). This type of research support differentiates the serious player from those companies (or managements) that are in just for the quick buck. While it may be a non-income-producing expense today, this dedication often pays off. For example, a biotechnology company may have committed millions of dollars over the past four years to a particular new drug discovery technique. This technique, based on genetic research, then yields a major breakthrough that provides the company a significant joint-venture relationship with a major pharmaceutical company.

International Strategy

Only the company that can successfully implement an international strategy can fully compete in the new global community. The expanded marketplace (read: global community) for a company's goods and services, subjects a company to different currency flows as well as increased competition. Economists have also pointed to this increased market as a contributing factor to the low inflation recently enjoyed by the restructured U.S. corporation. How can a large U.S.-based producer of paper raise its prices aggressively when several internationally based companies stand ready to gobble up market share? The proactive treasurer (and entire financial management team) in a globally sensitive company needs to be aware of the new playing field to maintain effectiveness.

Return

This is the lifeblood of a well-run company; without it, sooner or later, the company will die. Equity investors invest their capital in shares of companies that they expect to post a worthwhile return. This return, or its expectation, provides the groundwork for the share value. In some cases, investors will use a price-to-earnings ratio or perhaps, as described in Chapter 5, a dividend discount method to arrive at a fair value for the company's shares. As discussed in Chapter 1, the investor needs to pay careful attention to the manipulations of net income that affect the ultimate value of the shares.

Operations

This characteristic reveals the inner workings of the company. How does this business operate? What is the industry like? Competitors? In this category, the investor seeks to identify the company as a business, pure and simple. The investor attempts to divorce himself from the emotions of stock investing and focus on the value of the business, per se. Investors should seek companies with a franchise value, that is, a product or service that is duplicated in a multitude of markets. Companies that come to mind in this category are McDonald's, PepsiCo, Coca-Cola, and Wells Fargo Bank. In addition to having a franchise value, the company should also be an adept acquirer:

> What happens if the company's market share peaks? What will drive forward the company's top line and market share expansion?

Acquisitions can be an important part in this equation. The investor should seek companies that have a strong competitive advantage in the acquisition exercise:

> Does management endorse expansion through acquisitions? Are they patient enough to wait for the right price? Do they have the assets (high cash levels, low debt levels) to support such a campaign?

Cost-Effective Management

Perhaps a more euphemistically sensitive title would be "lean" (but then the acronym wouldn't be as catchy). In any sense, the more frugal a company is with its expenses, the more likely that it is a tightly run ship. And companies run this way typically have greater staying power in a bad economy or market (for their products). All too often, small companies raise capital through the equity market only to spend millions on a "world headquarters"—a 30,000-square-foot architecturally imposing structure, landscaped on a 10-acre campus sporting flags from every nation, expensively appointed in imported carpets and mahogany furniture. In no way are we suggesting that a growing company should avoid spending money to improve its working environment or competitiveness within its market. But there is a limit to what can be classified as an expense—or simply expensive. An expense is an expending of capital with a probability of a return to justify that expense; conducting business in an expensive way is often proof that a company is out of control. If you were the owner of a small hardware store in town and a candidate for a clerk position walked in and demanded $15 per hour, hiring this applicant would be expensive (unless the person possessed some extrasensory abilities to attract a strong increase in hardware buyers in the town). On the other hand, if you decided to hire three clerks at $5 per hour each, to work the floor simultaneously in order to achieve a "full-service" hardware store strategy (to differentiate from the warehouse strategy of the large chains), then this expense can be justified (as an attempt to increase market share through a differentiation strategy).

While these "PATIROC" characteristics are not the only traits that define a good company, they certainly give the investor the right direction. With these screens in place, the investor has the further responsibility to be skeptical of price. Don't overpay for a great company. Should the music ever stop, even for a quarter or two, the price action in the stock would be unforgiving. Look for great companies with specific characteristics, and then apply a good dose of skepticism to the price of the shares. Investing in a great company with an inflated price tag does not make much fundamental sense. We, as prudent equity investors, must have a well-defined exit strategy that focuses on changes that can affect the company's ongoing operations or stated value. Such changes include the departure of senior or founding management, industry fragmentation, new product or company entrants, and—most pervasive—the increased valuation of the company's share price. While all investors hope for an increase in the share price of the underlying equity, one needs to be acutely aware of the implications toward value:

> Is this increased valuation warranted or is it due to external market forces (too much capital chasing too few good investments)? Has the company's management endorsed, by increasing their own positions, this increased share price? Is this price appreciation industry-wide? Does it speak to euphoria or is it firmly footed in sensible valuation?

To achieve success, equity investors must often ask themselves these questions, always second-guessing their research to uncover any flaws. Maybe that is why it can be such a gut-wrenching but rewarding exercise.

Finally, throughout this journey, please remember that investment analysis is not a game but rather a venerable discipline firmly entrenched in many scientific disciplines. As a means of support and proper manners, however, we still offer all readers good luck.

Part

1

Tools of the Trade

Part 1 requires the working knowledge of certain important disciplines that are firmly footed in the mathematical and economic sciences. Any financial analyst needs to study these disciplines—work with them time and time again—before being ready to progress farther into the financial analysis maze. As with many other professional pursuits, most of the early work (grunt work, "paying your dues," "coming up the ladder") builds a foundation on which the higher skills depend. They are the building blocks that the investor will use countless times in the construction of a portfolio.

The tools of financial analysis are as critical to investment success as surgical instruments are to a brain surgeon. With a working knowledge of these tools, the financial analyst, whether a beginner or a seasoned investor, will have the skills to recognize a timely investment opportunity.

The four tools of financial analysis are:

1. Accounting
2. Economics
3. The mathematics of finance
4. Quantitative analysis using basic statistics and regression analysis

In Chapter 1 we discuss the all-important science of accounting, or as we call it—"the scriptures of business." Accounting is the written language of business—the figures that bring it all together and the universal language an analyst uses to understand the business. A working knowledge of accounting enables the investor to dissect the company's financial statements to better understand the specifics within a business as well as searching for any inconsistencies or red flags. In this case, the investor acts as a detective, searching through data from sources initiated by several types of media, to identify information that permits an analysis and subsequent valuation.

Additionally, careful examination of financial statements can lead to a better understanding of management's policies and style:

> Does management have a conservative or liberal bias with regard to accounting policies? By which method are non-current assets depreciated? What is the "quality" of the earnings? How are the revenues determined? What methods are employed?

Answering such questions can lead to a more comprehensive valuation of any company.

Chapter 2, "Economics," focuses on the items, such as government indicators and the important parity conditions that exist in international economics. Studying these areas is essential for attaining a more complete picture of how economic events affect the valuation of financial instruments:

> When are the major economic indicators released and what do they tell us about the economy? Does the economic business cycle permit an advantage in timing of the stock market? What role does the Federal Reserve play in the conditioning of our financial markets? How have the theories of economic science differed in the past 100 years?

Chapter 3, "Investment Mathematics," deals with the underpinnings of the entire study of investment finance—the mathematics behind the future value of money. After a discussion of the different formulas used to calculate this all-important mathematical concept, several problems are presented that permit the practitioner a repetitive learning format. This "problem set" format lends itself to much of this chapter, for *investment mathematics*, simple enough in theory, requires the practical understanding that comes with repetitive problem solving (e.g., What is the future value of $1,000 in 6 years at a compounded rate of 6 percent per year? What is the internal rate of return, or valuation, of a specific investment project?).

Chapter 4, "Quantitative Analysis," is the final chapter in Part 1. The quantitative approach to investment analysis is critical when the investor is making a hypothesis about the relationship between independent variables and a particular firm's earnings. This chapter also discusses the differences between simple and compounded annual returns so to better evaluate the returns quoted in the financial press and within the industry. Again, the problem set format is used to further reinforce the practical applications of this theory (in addition, the appendix in Chapter 4 covers regression analysis).

Okay, so let's buckle up our tool belt and begin this journey into the world of Security Analysis.

Chapter 1

Accounting

In this chapter, you will learn the following aspects of accounting:

- ✔ The big three: the balance sheet, the income statement, and the cash flow statement.
- ✔ The basics of managerial accounting.

The practice of accounting is the tabulating and bookkeeping of the capital resources (in currency terms) of a particular firm. The actual entries listed on the accounting statements do not tell us anything concrete about the firm's business activities, but reflect how accountants record these activities. That is not to say that accounting statements are without value; they are among the most important pieces in the valuation puzzle, but without careful study, they do not reveal any information of consequence. This inadequacy of accounting data lies within the procedures themselves; in most cases, an investor needs to be proficient in this art to gain any insight into the future prospects of the concern in question.

The Big Three

The financial statements of a business enterprise are essentially their scribes—the books, as we affectionately call them. These "books" document—in the universal language of numbers—the ins and outs of the flow of capital within a business enterprise. The books come in three chapters, if you will: the balance sheet of assets and liabilities, the income statement of revenues and costs, and the cash flow statement which reconciles the inflows and outflows of cash. These three statements are interlinked, as we will soon see, and their interaction—and the understanding of the implications between each statement—is a critical part of the analyst's core competency. In the sections that follow we discuss each statement in detail.

The Balance Sheet

The balance sheet serves as a snapshot of the current net worth of a particular firm at a given moment in time. It illustrates, in some detail, the asset holdings (fixed and current) as well as the liabilities, in such fashion that the offsetting amounts equal the net worth of the company (equity). In its simplest form, the Balance Sheet offsets the enterprise's assets (the value of things they own) with the liabilities (the value of things they owe), which results in the equity (the net worth) of the enterprise. As we will see, the key in this statement is how these assets and liabilities are valued—this will give the analyst and investor keys to unlocking value opportunities or red flags of caution. When examining the balance sheet be mindful of the inputs—in other words, how these values came to be—for, as in many business pursuits, the devil is in the details. These details are compiled in the often forgotten "fine print" of the footnote section of the accounting documents. It is here, in these footnotes, that the perceptive analyst ("detective") can uncover opportunities and important issues. The following definitions provide an understanding of this financial statement's individual components. (See Table 1.1 for a sample of this statement.)

Assets

The first major section of the balance sheet lists assets, including the following:

Current Assets   This consolidation entry includes assets that can be converted into cash within one year or normal operating cycle. The following entries are components of current assets:

TABLE 1.1   ABC Products—Balance Sheet 12/31/08

Current Assets		Current Liabilities	
Cash	$156,663	Accounts Payable	$388,834
Portfolio of Marketable Securities	$100,000	Income Tax Payable	$13,394
		Short-Term Notes Payable	$425,000
Accounts Receivable	$578,745	Accrued Expenses	$188,539
Inventory	$978,094	**Total Current Liabilities**	**$1,015,767**
Prepaid Expenses	$117,176	**Long-Term Notes Payable**	**$550,000**
Total Current Assets	**$1,930,678**		
Property, Plant, and Equipment	$0	**Stockholders Equity**	
		Capital Stock	$725,000
Land, Building, Machines	$0	Retained Earnings	$1,174,230
			$1,899,230
Equipment and Furniture	$1,986,459	**Total Liabilities and Equity**	**$3,464,997**
Accumulated Depreciation	−$452,140		
Other Assets	$0		
Total Assets	**$3,464,997**		

☑ *Cash.* Bank deposit balances, any petty cash funds, and cash equivalents (money markets, U.S. Treasury Bills).

☑ *Accounts receivable.* The amount due from customers that has not yet been collected. Customers are typically given 30, 60, or 90 days in which to pay. Some customers fail to pay completely (companies will set up an account known as "reserve for doubtful accounts"), and for this reason the accounts receivable entry represents the amount expected to be received ("accounts receivable less allowance for doubtful accounts").

☑ *Inventory.* Composed of three parts: (1) raw materials used in products, (2) partially finished goods, and (3) finished goods. The generally accepted method of valuation of inventory is the lower of cost or market (LCM). This provides a conservative estimate for this occasionally volatile item (see Aside on page 30: LIFO versus FIFO).

✔ *Prepaid expenses.* Payments made by the company, in advance of the benefits that will be received, by year's end, such as prepaid fire insurance premiums, advertising charges for the upcoming year, or advanced rent payments.

Fixed Assets (Noncurrent Assets)   Assets that cannot be converted into cash within a normal operating cycle. The following are fixed assets:

✔ *Land, property, plant, and equipment.* Those assets not intended for sale, and used time and time again to operate the enterprise. The typical valuation method for fixed assets is cost minus the accumulated depreciation—the amount of depreciation that has been accumulated to this point. This is an important consideration—the fact that certain long-term assets are not marked-to-market (a term that has clearly entered our lexicon in the last year or so)—for it lends itself to some potential uncovering of value. A value investor seeking equities that the market is not correctly valuing, for a host of reasons from misunderstanding the company's business to not correctly valuing its assets, can often find opportunities to be marking-to-market these long-term assets.

Liabilities

The next major portion of the balance sheet lists liabilities, including the following:

Current Liabilities   This entry includes all debts that fall due within 12 months (or one operating cycle). By matching the current assets with the current liabilities, the investor can get a good idea of how payments will be made on current liabilities:

✔ *Accounts payable.* Represents the amount the company owes to business creditors from whom it has purchased goods or services on account. This is often referred to as "Trade-Related Debt."

✔ *Accrued expenses.* The amounts owed and not yet recorded on the books that are unpaid at the date of the balance sheet.

✔ *Income tax payable.* The debt due to the Internal Revenue Service (IRS) or other taxing authorities but not yet paid. These are, by definition, accrued expenses, but because they are tax related, they carry with them a certain importance to the analysis of the firm.

Long-Term Debt   These are debts due beyond one year (or one operating cycle).

Stockholders' Equity

The last major section of the balance sheet is the stockholders' equity section, which includes the following:

Stockholders' Equity   The total equity interest that all shareholders have in the company. Stockholders' equity, like any other equity, is the net worth remaining after subtracting all liabilities from all assets. The true measure of the firm's reputation as an outstanding company resides in its ability to grow this equity amount. The book value of a firm is calculated as the stockholders' equity—the assets minus the liabilities.

Retained Earnings   The amount of earnings, above the dividend payout, accumulated by the firm. Although retaining earnings may be an appropriate strategy at a given point in a firm's life cycle, it can also be an invitation to an activist investor seeking a cash cow investment opportunity. Furthermore, a company retaining too much of its earnings can open questions about why these cash flows haven't been reinvested in high net present value (NPV) projects so the company can continue to grow. (Is this firm running out of good opportunities?)

The Income Statement

Whereas the balance sheet is the record of net worth for the firm, the income statement illustrates the firm's operating record. In this statement, the firm's income and expenses are reconciled to arrive at a value of net income for the period in question. Very often, the analysis of equities focuses on this net income value (known as earnings). The information gleaned from one particular year is not as critical to the analysis of a particular firm as the data for several years or, better yet, the projected (future) earnings information. It is this forecasting exercise that can make or break an investment decision, regardless of the security in the capital structure. An analyst used a myriad of inputs (macroeconomic data as well as company-specific expectations) to ascertain a spectrum of likely earnings in future years. The analyst who can consistently forecast a firm's earnings most accurately will earn heavy kudos (not to mention an increase in institutional trading revenues for his firm's trading desks).

To put the corporate accounting statements in perspective: The income statement is similar to your personal tax filing for a given year, reconciling income (W-2, capital gain and dividend earnings, etc.) versus expenses (mortgage expense, business expenses, etc.). The balance sheet, on the other hand, is similar to your personal net worth statement that you might organize for an estate planning document or mortgage application.

The following definitions should aid in understanding this financial statement (see Table 1.2):

- ✔ *Revenue.* The amount received by the company for rendering its services or selling its goods. The total revenue is calculated by simply multiplying the number of goods sold by the price per unit (quantity sold × price per unit). Revenue always initiates the income statement because, by definition, it is the starting point of operating activities. Net total revenue takes into account any returned goods and allowances for reduction of prices.

- ✔ *Cost of goods sold* (COGS). The primary cost expense in most manufacturing companies—all the costs incurred in the factory to convert raw materials into finished product. The cost-of-goods expense also includes direct labor and manufacturing overhead associated with the production of finished goods. The *fixed cost* is the amount that will not typically increase with increases in output of the finished product; it includes expenses in operating an enterprise (e.g., rent, electricity, supplies, maintenance, repairs), often called "burden," or "overhead." A *variable cost* can be directly traced to the production process and therefore will typically increase as the number of units produced increases (e.g., raw material costs, sales commissions).

TABLE 1.2 ABC Products—Income Statement 12/31/08	
Revenue	$6,019,040
Cost of Goods Sold	($3,912,376)
Gross Profit	$2,106,664
Operating Expenses:	
Sales, General and Admin	($323,288)
Utilities	($200,000)
Salaries	($700,000)
Marketing/Advertising	($300,000)
Total Operating Expenses	**($1,523,288)**
Operating Earnings before Interest, Taxes, Depreciation, and Amortization (EBITDA)	**$583,376**
Depreciation Expense	($112,792)
Operating Earnings	**$470,584**
Interest Expense	($76,650)
Earnings before Income Taxes	**$393,934**
Income Tax Expense	($133,938)
Net Income	**$259,996**

✔ *Gross profit.* The amount of excess of sales over the cost of sales. Gross profit is often represented as a ratio (in percentage form):

$$\frac{\text{Gross profit margin}}{\text{(expressed as a percent)}} = \frac{\text{Gross profit amount}}{\text{Revenues}}$$

The following example illustrates the gross profit margin (see Table 1.2):

Revenues (or sales)	$6,019,040
COGS	3,912,376
Gross profit	$2,106,664

Therefore the gross profit margin is $2,106,664 divided by $6,019,040 or 35 percent.

✔ *Operating expenses.* This line item serves as a heading for the consolidation of the non-direct costs incurred in the operations of a business. Selling, general, and administrative expense is the most typical operating expense for a company. As businesses differ operationally and economically, so will their allocations toward operating expenses. For example, the computer software development company will have a higher commitment toward operating expenses (salaries, bonuses, educational seminars, marketing, etc.) versus a wholesale manufacturing company whose largest costs are typically the raw materials used in the production process. Sales, general, and administrative expenses (SG&A) are important items in the analysis of a company for they illustrate the management's fiscal restraint or resistance to temptation. When a VFII notices the sales of a company increasing but the SG&A growing at a faster rate, a yellow flag of caution is raised. Components of SG&A include salaries, commissions, advertising, promotion, office expenses, travel, and entertainment expenses.

✔ *Operating earnings before depreciation (earnings before interest, taxes, depreciation, and amortization—EBITDA).* Known as a measure of cash flow, for it factors out the non-cash charges included in depreciation and amortization expense. Many analysts, especially those specializing in relatively new, very capital-intense industries rely on this measure as the true earnings of the company.

✔ *Depreciation and amortization expense.* The estimated amount that management expects to use in the future to replace its operating facilities. It can be thought of as an escrow account where the company sets aside a specific (defined by tax policies, equipment's salvage value, and estimated useful life) amount each year to be used in the future to repurchase the operational necessities (plant and equipment) of the enterprise. Amortization is depreciation, but instead of referring to a tangible asset, it refers to an intangible asset (e.g., goodwill, patents).

✔ *Operating earnings.* Earnings attributed to the activities of the company without any impact from the financing of its balance sheet. This earnings figure is used in the calculation of an "enterprise value" or value of the business as if it were a private concern.

✔ *Interest expense.* Amount that equals the company's outstanding debt multiplied by its debt expense (i.e., interest owed to bondholders). Under current corporate tax law, the debt payments made to bond holders are tax deductible: This amount is subtracted from the operating earnings before calculating the taxes.

✔ *Income tax expense.* Tax rate (approximately 36 percent on the corporate level) multiplied by the pretax earnings.

✔ *Net income.* Earnings, plain and simple—the last entry on the income statement, the bottom line. Ironically, it is the opening entry for much of what is known as fundamental analysis—the analysis of a business utilizing quantitative models to determine the earnings and subsequent valuation.

The Cash Flow Statement

The cash flow statement is the third statement in our accounting statements and is considered by many to be one of the most important. Unlike the Income Statement and Balance Sheet, the Cash Flow Statement illustrates the movement of cash rather than incorporating accounting rules and treatments to arrive at values. In the cash flow statement what we are getting is the "best" view of the activities of the company without the vagaries of accounting rules. The bottom line is that the Cash Flow Statement can tell us *"Where did the money come from?"* and *"What was it used for?"*—two very important questions for investors to grasp. It is important to understand that in the cash flow statement we are only interested in cash and cash equivalents (highly liquid fixed income securities with maturities less than three months).

There are two methods used to formulate the cash flow statement—the Direct Method and the Indirect Method (shown in Table 1.3). In the Direct Method we start with Net Cash Received from customers (the actual amount of cash—not sales—that came into the company over the period) and add or subtract from this figure other "sources" or "uses" of cash over the period, to arrive at the value for Operating Cash Flow. The Indirect Method starts with Net Income and makes a series of adjustments to that number to arrive at the value for Operating Cash Flow.

There are three pieces to the Cash Flow Statement—Cash Flow from Operations, Cash Flow from Investing Activities, and Cash Flow from Financing Activities. While the resulting net number from all of the three is used as the figure for the "Net Change in Cash" for the period—it

TABLE 1.3 Cash Flow Statement—ABC Company for the Year Ended 20XX: Indirect Method	
Cash Flow from Operations	
Net Income	$ 300
Additions (Sources of Cash)	
Depreciation	$ 200
Increase in Accounts Payable	$ 40
Increase in Accrued Income Taxes	$ 10
Subtractions (Uses of Cash)	
Increase in Accounts Receivable	$ (150)
Increase in Inventory	$ (50)
Net Cash Flow from Operations	$ 350
Cash Flows from Investing Activities	
Equipment	$ (400)
Cash Flows from Financing Activities	
Activities Notes Payable	$ 30
Net Change in Cash	$ (20)

is the Cash Flow from Operations that many analysts focus on as a clue to evaluating the management's abilities and the overall strength of the company.

Cash Flow from Operations

Cash Flow from Operations is any cash transaction related to the company's ongoing business—that is, the business activities that are responsible for most of the profits. Operating activities usually involve producing and delivering goods and providing services. Cash flow from operations is the healthiest means of generating cash. Over time, Cash Flow from Operations will show the extent to which day-to-day operating activities have generated more cash than has been used.

Direct Method

While not the most widely used method to calculate cash flow, the Direct Method must be also done if the Indirect Method is chosen. What we are doing in this method is seeking a guideline to the flow of cash in and out of the company. So we need to study each piece of the company in order to ascertain this flow of cash. The basic equation here is:

Cash received in the operation of the business (that is, from sales of goods and services) MINUS the cash used to operate the business (that is, the costs of the goods and services) EQUALS Operating Cash Flow (direct methodology). The following is a good template:

Cash Flow From Operations:

(+) Cash received from customers

(+) Other operating cash receipts (if any; i.e. dividends)

(−) Cash paid to suppliers (including suppliers of inventory, insurance, advertising, etc.)

(−) Cash paid to employees

(−) Interest paid

(−) Income taxes paid

(−) Other operating payments, if any

(=) Total net cash provided (used) by operating activities

In Table Format:

Sources of cash (additions):

Cash received from customers

Dividends received

Cash provided by operations

Uses of cash (subtractions):

Cash paid for inventory

Cash paid for insurance

Cash paid for selling expenses

Interest paid

Taxes paid

Net Cash from operations

So what we are doing in this Direct Method of Cash Flow from Operations is to seek the actual flow of cash in each piece of the business that either generates or uses cash. One option that might make the calculation of cash received from customers easier is to estimate it based on changes in some balance sheet accounts: Take accounts receivable at the beginning of the year, add to it sales for the period, and then subtract accounts receivable at the end of the year to compute how much in cash was collected. This interaction between accounting statements is a definitive advantage to the VFII who is seeking data that others may not have the time or expertise to uncover.

Indirect Method

Here we start with the Net Income figure (from the Income Statement) and we go through pieces of the enterprise to ascertain if the change (from period to period) led to an addition to cash (Source) or a decrease of cash (Use). Part of this exercise is counter-intuitive—for example, an increase in deferred taxes is a Source (or addition) of cash because we are deferring the payment of cash, while an increase in inventories is a Use (or subtraction) of cash because we are buying more goods with cash.

The following list is the basis to these entries:

Net income
Adjustments:

Depreciation and amortization	SOURCE
Deferred taxes	SOURCE
Decrease in accounts receivable	SOURCE
Increase in inventories	USE
Increase in accounts payable	SOURCE
Increase in accrued interest receivable	USE
Increase in accrued interest payable	SOURCE
Gain on sale of property	USE

Net cash flow from operating activities

In the Indirect Method we sort of jump a bunch of smaller steps (in the Direct Method) by starting with Net Income and then making the necessary adjustments to arrive at Cash Flow.

Once the Operating Cash Flow is computed we need to do a similar procedure to the Investing and Financing parts of the Cash Flow Statement.

Net Cash Flow from Investing Activities

In this part of the cash flow statement we focus on those changes to the cash position of the company having to do with investing activities. Examples of investing activities are:

- Purchase or sale of an asset (assets can be land, building, equipment, or marketable securities)
- Loans made to suppliers or customers

The purchase of an asset is a use of cash, whereas a sale of an asset is a source of cash. Similarly, loans made to others is a source of cash. So what we do in this section is look at the balance sheet changes for items like land, building, equipment, and securities. By looking at these data points we can determine the changes in Cash Flow from Investing Activities.

Cash Flow from Financing Activities

In this section we are focused on the changes in cash from activities related to the financing of business. So changes in debt, loans, or dividends are accounted for in cash from financing. Changes in cash from financing are a source of cash when capital is raised, and they're a use of cash when dividends are paid. Thus, if a company issues a bond to the public, the company receives cash financing (source); however, when interest is paid to bondholders, the company is reducing its cash (a use of cash). Here again we look at the balance sheet and income statement data to determine the changes in these specific areas.

A company can use a cash flow statement to predict future cash flow, which helps with matters in budgeting. For investors, the cash flow reflects a company's financial health: basically, the more cash available for business operations, the better. However, this is not a hard and fast rule. Sometimes a negative cash flow results from a company's growth strategy in the form of expanding its operations.

By adjusting earnings, revenues, assets, and liabilities, the investor can get a very clear picture of what some people consider the most important aspect of a company: how much cash it generates and, particularly, how much of that cash stems from core operations.

Having defined the basic components of the accounting statements, we can begin to analyze these components. Managerial accounting simply refers to using and analyzing accounting data to maximize the resources of the company. Decisions about the method chosen to depreciate an asset (straight-line or accelerated) could be crucial to the profitability of a company. The decisions surrounding the evaluation of a company's fixed cost structure (the allocation of costs that do not change with the level of output, e.g., rental cost) versus its variable cost structure (expenses that vary with the amount of output generated, e.g., raw materials, selling expenses) could also be crucial to future planning.

LIFO versus FIFO

Last in-first out (LIFO) and *first in-first out* (FIFO) are methods by which inventory is valued on a company's balance sheet. The typical company is continually purchasing new goods and selling existing goods, both of which come from the inventory account. The method used to determine the value of the inventory account is as follows:

Beginning period inventory value + Value of new purchases − Inventory used in COGS = Ending period inventory value

Whether the LIFO or FIFO method is used in inventory valuation determines whether the amount expensed as cost of goods sold (COGS) comes from new purchases (LIFO) or existing inventory (beginning period) as in FIFO.

The following guidelines shed some light on this area.

LIFO

Undervalues inventory (given increasing prices) on balance sheet because the more expensive items are expensed as COGS rather then being kept on the balance sheet as inventory—hence, last in-first out. This method became more widely used during the inflationary 1970s, when companies attempted to match their current operations with current costs so as not to incur artificially high profits (with high profits come very real high taxes).

FIFO

Correctly values inventory on the balance sheet (in inflationary environment) due to an expensing (as COGS) of the previously purchased (at lower prices) goods, therefore providing an inequitable match of revenues with COGS, resulting in an overstatement of earnings and subsequent tax expense.

PROBLEM SET: UNDERSTANDING ACCOUNTING
AND THE STATEMENTS

Question 1

The Brittany Company, which manufactures robes, has enough idle capacity available to accept a special order of 10,000 robes at $8 per robe. An expected income statement for the year without this special order is as follows:

	Per Unit		Total
Sales	$12.50		$1,250,000
Manufacturing costs:			
Variable	$6.25	$625,000	
Fixed	1.75	175,000	
Total manufacturing costs	8.00		800,000
Gross profit	**$ 4.50**		**$ 450,000**
Selling expenses:			
Variable	$1.80	$180,000	
Fixed	1.45	145,000	
Total selling expenses	3.25		325,000
Operating income	**$ 1.25**		**$ 125,000**

Assuming no additional selling expenses, what would be the effect on operating income if the company accepted the special order?

Answer

The three important facts in this problem are:

1. The idle capacity situation that currently exists within the company; this relates to a fixed cost structure that is able to take on more capacity without increasing its (fixed) costs.
2. The rather large size of the order that is being considered.
3. The assumption that no further selling (variable) costs would be incurred in this order.

The following computation breaks down the accounting data to better illustrate the problem:

The Brittany Company			
	Contribution Approach	Effects of Special Order	With Special Order
Sales	$1,250,000	$ 80,000	$1,330,000
Variable costs	800,000	62,500	885,000
Contribution	$ 450,000	$ 17,500	$ 444,500
Fixed costs	325,000	0	320,000
Net	$ 125,000	$ 17,500	$ 142,500

The preceding calculations indicate that it would be advantageous (to the tune of $17,500 in additional profits) to accept this special order.

The other (quick and intuitive) method is to examine the per unit costs:

- ✔ Revenues from special order are $8 per unit.

- ✔ Variable costs per unit are $6.25; assume that due to idle capacity there are no additional fixed costs.

- ✔ Net profit is therefore $1.75 per unit, or $17,500 for 10,000 units.

Question 2

From a particular joint process, The UTA Company produces three products—X, Y, and Z. Each product may be sold at the point of split-off or processed further. Additional processing requires no special facilities, and production costs of further processing are entirely variable and traceable to the products involved. In 2007, all three products were processed beyond split-off. Joint production costs for the year were $60,000. Sales and costs needed to evaluate UTA's 2007 production policy follow:

			If Processed Further	
Product	Units Produced	Sales at Split-Off	Sales	Additional Costs
X	6,000	$25,000	$42,000	$9,000
Y	4,000	41,000	45,000	7,000
Z	2,000	24,000	32,000	8,000

Joint costs are allocated to the products in proportion to the relative physical volume of output.

To maximize profits, UTA should subject which products to additional processing?

Answer

We need to calculate the incremental increase in revenues that the further production would bring, as well as the subsequent net income.

X: $42,000 (end revs) − $25,000 (split-off revs) = $17,000 (incremental increase)

$17,000 (additional revs) − $9,000 (additional costs) = $8,000; therefore we should accept additional output.

Y: $45,000 − $41,000 = $4,000

$4,000 − $7,000 = ($3,000); this is a negative value (loss); therefore reject additional output.

Z: $32,000 − $24,000 = $8,000

$8,000 − $8,000 = $0; although not a loss, this represents a break-even amount and is therefore also rejected for additional output.

Question 3

The following information is given for the Lone Hill Company:

Initial cost of proposed new equipment	$130,000
Predicted useful life	10 years
Predicted salvage value (end of life)	$10,000
Predicted savings per year in operating expenses	$24,000

Ignoring income tax effects, what is the depreciation expense per year by straight-line method?

Answer

This example involves evaluating the straight-line depreciation method, one of the most common methods in accounting. In the straight-line method, the calculation is as follows:

$$\text{Depreciation expense per year} = \frac{(\text{Initial cost} - \text{Salvage value})}{(\text{Useful life})}$$

Apply this method to the data in the problem:

$$\text{Depreciation expense per year} = \frac{(\text{Initial cost} - \text{Salvage value})}{(\text{Useful life})}$$

$$\frac{(\$130,000 - 10,000)}{(10 \text{ years})} = \$12,000 \text{ per year depreciation expense}$$

Question 4

Developing a Cash Flow Statement. See Table 1.3 and the Cash Flow Statement for ABC Products Company.

Clearly there is much work to be done here—and you are just the budding analyst to do it! Please utilize the information in the ABC Products Balance Sheet (Table 1.1) and Income Statement (Table 1.2) as well as the data following to complete the statement (shown in Table 1.4).

Datapoint 1: Accounts Payable on 12/31/07 was $488,834

Datapoint 2: Accounts Receivable on 12/31/07 was $378,745

Datapoint 3: Inventory was valued at 12/31/07 at $950,000

Datapoint 4: On 12/31/07 "Building" value was $200,000

Datapoint 5: Portfolio of Marketable Securities was valued at $0 on 12/31/07

Datapoint 6: Long Term Notes Payable on 12/31/07 was $750,000

Datapoint 7: In 2008, ABC Products is paying a dividend using a dividend payout rate of 15 percent

Answer

TABLE 1.4 ABC Products—Statement of Cash Flows 12/31/08		
New Income	$259,996	From Income Statement
Depreciation and Amortization	$112,996	Source of cash; from IS
Decrease in Accounts Payable	($100,000)	Use of cash, from BS
Increase in Accounts Receivable	($200,000)	Use of cash, from BS
Increase in Inventories	($28,094)	Use of cash, from BS
Net Cash Flow from Operations	$44,898	
Changes in Cash Flow from Investing Activities		
Sale of a Building	$200,000	Source of cash, from BS
Investment into a Portfolio of Marketable Securities	($100,000)	Use of Cash, from BS
Changes in Cash Flow from Financing Activities		
Retirement of Debt Outstanding	($200,000)	Use of cash, from BS
Dividends Paid	($38,999)	Use of cash, from IS (NI × Pay %)
Net Cash Flow	($94,101)	

Chapter

Economics

I n this chapter, you will learn the following:

✔ The international parity theorems that serve as the underpinnings for financial currency and international trade valuations.

✔ How to measure the health of the economy and understand the U.S. government's monthly economic releases.

✔ How the Federal Reserve and the U.S. banking system work.

✔ The business cycle and the implications to investment timing.

✔ The classical theories of economics—from Monetarism to Keynesian.

Economics can be a paradoxical science; whatever you would normally think to be a correct and logical relationship turns out to be the complete opposite. The majority of nonfinancially interested individuals (NFIIs) would regard a strong growth economy as the best possible scenario for an increasing valuation of financial assets. However, this scenario could actually portend greater inflation (the nemesis of financial assets) and higher interest rates (to combat these higher rates, see "Purchasing Power Parity" later in this chapter), and lower valuations for financial assets because the cash flows generated within will be discounted at higher rates, resulting in lower present values (see Chapter 3).

Another NFII may associate a strong U.S. dollar with increasing interest rates because "higher interest rates generate a greater demand for the domestic currency." But one theoretical application of international parity conditions states that as domestic interest rates increase (vis-à-vis foreign interest rates), the value of the domestic currency (vis-à-vis the foreign currency) actually should weaken to allow parity (at which no arbitrage or "free-profit" opportunities exist) between both nations.

Opportunities also exist whereby a well-positioned (within the Wall Street community) VFII can profit through rare mispricing or inefficiencies that exist, albeit for only a brief moment, between foreign currencies and interest rates. This type of arbitrage, defined as the ability to purchase a certain asset on one market and then sell the very same asset on another market at a higher price without any risk, is known as interest rate arbitrage. However, like any inefficiency in the market, the opportunity quickly disappears as the buying action of profit-hungry investors forces the inefficiency back into parity.

Also, one needs to understand the underlying tenets of the economic sciences—the give and take of incentives. At its core, economics is the understanding of incentives between two parties or two nations. On a macro level we can speak about the differences between nations whose currencies are linked (or should be) by parity conditions, but due to changes in interest rates may not be through a certain period. On the micro level we can speak about two firms—where one is acting as a supplier of goods to another. The buyer may choose to seek a lower cost from the supplier, given decreased costs (shipping expenses mitigated if he joins with others in his industry) from suppliers abroad. As we move through this chapter we need to keep in mind these issues of incentives and ask ourselves *"What is that firm's incentive to do that—What do they get out of it?"* and from there we can work through the motivations to arrive at a specific glide path of likely outcomes.

Determining the Health of the Economy

At this point, we face one of the more daunting tasks of any investor—surveying the health of the current economy. This text covers macroeconomics only on a cursory basis because the myriad economists, investment strategists, and others of this guru sect force efficiency (or information flow) in the marketplace. The volumes of research orchestrated by these men and women drive the investing public's info flow into a state of efficiency. With all this information at their fingertips, how could investors of sound mind and reasonable resources make mistakes?

In the ivory towers of Wall Street, the sources of this economic research have a difficult time determining the health of the economy. A report by Stephen McNees (see Bibliography) states that there is a wide disparity between the forecasts of these professionals and the actual outcomes. Although these forecast errors are often adjusted through the revision process, there seems to be no improvement in forecasting accuracy over time. Furthermore, for certain financial variables (e.g., interest rates, stock prices), naive models (simple statistical models) are typically no better than the professional forecasts. So what is an investor to do? If trained economists can't judge the health of the economy with consistent accuracy, what is the likelihood that today's typical investor can?

Well, candidly, he cannot. But what the investor can do is understand the underlying tenets of macroeconomic relationships and therefore learn to judge the value of financial assets under certain scenarios. For example, the investor who notices a trend of decreasing new home sales can surmise that the revenues (and probably, as a consequence, the share price) of companies in the building products and mortgage industries should decrease. To further fine-tune his hypothesis, this VFII could employ some simple regression analysis (see the appendix in Chapter 4) to calculate the correlation (if any actually exists) between a decrease in this macroeconomic variable and the earnings of the companies that fuel this business. However, the flag of caution is raised, for it may not be as simple as just described. Perhaps there is a lag between the decrease in new home sales and the effects on the suppliers to that industry. Or this macroeconomic trend may be an aberration. How "good" is the release? Is it two months old? Is this indicator subject to revision, and if so, what has been the trend in this regard?

This chapter summarizes the major economic releases. Like the information throughout this book, this summary can serve as a factsheet or guideline. An investor today need not understand all the intricacies involved with economic indicators but rather must grasp the effect on financial assets when these releases are made public.

Consider this example. An investor has decided to position $100,000 into zero coupon treasuries maturing in 25 years (February 15, 2034) for his pension account. The cost of each bond is approximately

$375.11 ($1,000 face value at maturity) and therefore has a stated yield to maturity of 4 percent (ignoring any fees, commissions, or markups).

Price	Yield to Maturity
$375.11	4%

The following chain of events occurs:

1. Friday at 8:30 A.M. (EST), the Department of Labor reports a significant and unexpected (and this is the key—for if it was expected, then the bond market would have already adjusted) decrease in the number of unemployed (or increase in the non-farm payrolls). This is a negative for the bond market because stronger growth (the more people employed the more they can spend) usually leads to higher inflation. Inflation is the nemesis of the fixed income market, for it depreciates the buying power of a fixed rate of return.

Unemployment Rate	Inflation
Decreases	Increases

2. Interest-rate-sensitive securities begin to decline in price immediately (increase in yield).

Inflation	Bond Price	Bond Yield
Increases	Decreases	Increases

3. As seen above, Treasury bond prices decrease sharply, and therefore yields on treasuries are now 4.12 percent.

Treasury Bond Prices	Treasury Bond Yields
Decreases	Increases

4. The price of the zero coupon bond is now $364.45 (offered price or buy price) per bond, with a yield to maturity of 4.12 percent.

The trade would now cost only $36,445 versus $37,511, for a savings of $1,066, or about 3 percent of the investment. Not much of a difference, especially in the long run, but when multiplied by several other similar occasions or a more significant investment (if the pensioner was to purchase a $500,000 face amount—$182,225 versus $187,555—the savings would have been $5,330), it is evidence as to why a VFII may consistently outperform his uninterested counterpart.

I am not advocating timing of the bond market (or any other market for that matter); but careful attention to such a glaring potential loss (or gain) from economic data can add a percentage point or two to an investor's total return. Today's investor should be fully aware of the risks (and rewards) of a particular investment opportunity: Don't just take your financial services provider's (FSP) advice, no matter how professional his judgment may be, but rather question it, be proactive, and debate the issue at hand. Ultimately, this FSP's advice should be more than adequate. However, his support of the idea really determines his worth. Does he have a true conviction (and here is the crucial part) based on some definable and accurate analysis, or is he just selling you something? Is this FSP truly committed to the science of his profession, or is he simply towing the firm's line and reciting the "morning research call"? Fortunately, I have the pleasure and good graces to work in an environment that promotes the professional development of colleagues who value the science of the investment management process.

This attention to detail permits the VFII to consistently outperform even the luckiest NFII year after year. The underlying premise of this book is to help the average investor become a more astute investor who understands the relationships between financial assets and the economy; an investor who is able to read and understand the *Wall Street Journal*, the *Economist*, and a brokerage firm's research report with ease and enjoyment. An investor who develops a "think-tank-like" relationship with his FSP—in which ideas are shared on a more evenly aligned playing field. I am sure that many FSPs will admit that many of their best investment ideas have come from discussions with clients. Occasionally a client would recognize certain trends in his own industry that may have implications for a particular company or another industry. Or perhaps a client would become a big fan of a particular new product (or service) and then, with the help of the professional, investigate the company's investment merits. This, in my estimation, is the foundation of the New Age of investment management—the sharing and free exchange of information and ideas between investors and professionals for the achievement of a common goal—profits. Clearly, the implications of this joint-venture can be extraordinary.

Government Releases and Indicators

The economic information released by the government periodically, collectively known as indicators, supposedly indicates the health of the economy. My skepticism is a by-product of the very nature of these releases (usually representative of a lag of 1 to 2 months), and the empirical evidence that supports the notion that even with all this information at their computer-tapping fingertips, economists have a pretty difficult time being consistently accurate with their macroeconomic views.

Although the current process of economic releases is better than in most developed countries, small inconsistencies remain, including the revision procedure and the measurement protocol for many of the more important releases. However, there is a continual effort for improvement in this critically important area, for in the United States, the market (and its participants) demands the most accurate information possible from the suppliers of this data.

What Is Inflation?

You probably can think of a description or even a definition of inflation—it is what you feel when you go to the checkout counter at the supermarket. When I find myself enduring this experience, the numbers just fly by in some type of exponential haze. I usually ask the checkout operator, armed with the newest in bar technology, to slow down (and I am often in a rush) because I think there is a problem with the machine. How could these prices be so high, if the CPI just came out last week and registered a decline in the core rate of inflation? The price on that cereal box must be a mistake! How much per pound for those mangoes?

Empirically, the inflation effects on interest rates, known as the "real" rate, are simply the product of the nominal interest rate and the inflation rate, seen as:

Nominal interest rate = Real interest rate × Inflation rate

This equation is embedded in the theory known as the International Fisher Parity Condition.

If the rate of inflation is 4 percent and the nominal rate is 6 percent, what is the real interest rate?

What Is Inflation? *(Continued)*

We could use some algebra to get:

6% = 4%x, which equals 1.5%

Or we could apply the approximated linear relation:

Nominal rate = Real rate + Inflation

We get a lower number when actually calculating the multiplication instead of the arithmetic because multiplication affects numbers faster and more significantly than arithmetic. The simple reason for this is that elusive tenet of finance known as compounding.

Two economic views differ significantly on the subject of real interest rates:

1. Fluctuations of interest rates are caused by revisions in inflationary expectations, since real rates are very stable over time. As explained by Alan Shapiro (1992), "If the required real return is 3 percent and expected inflation is 10 percent, then the nominal interest rate would be 13.3 percent. The logic behind this result is that $1 next year will have the purchasing power of $.90 in terms of today's dollars. Thus, the borrower must pay the lender $1.13 to compensate for the erosion in the purchasing power of the $1.03 in the principal and interest payments, in addition to the $.03 necessary to provide a 3 percent real return" (*Multinational Financial Management*, 4th ed.).

2. Keynesians provide a different view: Monetary shocks leave short-term inflation unaffected because of "sticky" goods prices (prices take time to adjust to inflationary pressures), whereas real rates react immediately to liquidity conditions. For example, if a sudden contraction in money supply growth leads to an immediate increase of nominal interest rates, then the real interest rate will increase because money becomes rare while short-term inflation expectations are unchanged.

How should the investor use the multitude of economic data that is reported each day? Which reports are important and which are not? What effect does an economic report have on a given portfolio? The effect depends on the type of portfolio (equity or debt) and the magnitude and direction of the economic release. The simple rule of thumb is this: As the economy expands, pressure exists on the Federal Reserve to increase short-term interest rates to mitigate any potential inflationary effects.

As interest rates increase, the present value of future earnings decreases and thereby the value of financial assets, which are based on the present value of future cash flows, also decreases. So, in a nutshell, as the economic reports "hit the tape" the investor must decipher whether the report is above or below consensus estimates (an average of the Wall Street community's economists forecasts) and furthermore whether this portends an expanding or contracting economy.

One way to think of this mechanism is by relating the economy to a car engine—the more gas the driver gives (by stepping on the accelerator), the more the engine will rev, and if the engine revs up too fast for too long, it will overheat. With the economy, liquidity (or capital) is the fuel, interest rates act as an accelerator to the economy (lower rates accelerate economic activity, higher rates slow activity), and inflation is the symptom of an overheating economy. So the question for the investor monitoring the economy should be whether the economic release signals increased or decreased economic activity and whether a trend up or down can be determined over several releases.

The investor should also pay attention to the specific industry being studied to determine its current economic picture. The economy does not move in lockstep but is segmented, and consequently certain sectors will grow at different rates and times than others. For example, the housing market could be in a growth pattern, evidenced by the upward trend of new home sales and housing starts/building permits, but the manufacturing sector could be registering a slowdown, evidenced by a downward trending Institute for Supply Management (formerly the National Association of Purchasing Managers) report. While the investor holding shares in home-building companies would expect a positive outlook for the earnings of these companies, the impact of this (manufacturing sector) growth could affect an increase in interest rates and thereby reduce the demand for new homes (due to increased mortgage rates). This two-tiered guessing game keeps Wall Street's cadre of economists, analysts, and strategists busy each weekend. In its basic form, stock prices move up or down depending on two factors—earnings and interest rates; as explained in Chapter 5, the current value of an equity is the present value (using a discount rate) of future cash flows (earnings).

In evaluating the economy as a whole, how does an investor know which indicator should be analyzed to base his decision of interest rate forecasts? Which indicators are more sensitive to the inflationary threats in the economy? Enter the Federal Reserve; a group of top economists, practitioners, and academics who attempt to determine the temperature of the economic engine.

> Perhaps an increase in housing data is due to some seasonal affect, or perhaps it is just consequence of an enduring period of low interest rates and high personal savings. Maybe, at this current juncture, the increase in housing data is being met with sufficient supply, and therefore price pressures are not much of a concern.

How the Federal Reserve Works

If the Fed wants to stimulate the economy:

- ✔ *Decrease in federal funds rate.* This is the rate set by the Fed for overnight loans between member banks, so they can meet their reserve requirements. These loans are typically made to smaller, regional banks by larger, commercial banks.

- ✔ *Decrease in discount rate.* This mechanism is rarely used and that is perhaps why it receives such fanfare when it is used. The discount rate is the rate charged to member banks for loans directly from the Fed.

- ✔ *Federal Open Market Committee (FOMC) activities:* If the Fed requires its member banks to hold more capital in reserve, that action provides more capital for the bank to lend out to customers thereby stimulating the economy and lowering the cost of capital (interest rates). The mechanism used in this procedure is the Fed's buying of U.S. Treasury securities from the member banks, thereby increasing the member bank's reserves.

If the Fed wants to restrict economic activity:

- ✔ *Increase in the federal funds rate.* As with anything, if you desire to decrease demand of any good—in this case capital—you need only to increase its price—in this case interest rates. An increase in the federal funds rate would make banks more prudent with their reserves so that they would not have to borrow at the higher rates. A bank would be less likely to make a borderline credit quality loan, because if the bank fell short on reserves and had to borrow,

How the Federal Reserve Works *(Continued)*

the costs of this borrowing would have a negative impact on its profits.

- ✔ *Increase in the discount rate.* Like the preceding, an increase in the discount rate would also have a contradictory effect on the banks' profit margins and therefore would be expected to slow down lending activity. Once again, if businesses are unable to obtain capital inexpensively, they may choose to postpone their plans for expansion, new equipment, or new employees. This type of action has its impact throughout the economy.

- ✔ *FOMC activities:* Here, the Fed sells U.S. Treasury securities to the member banks (which are required to buy a predetermined amount) thereby reducing the capital that the banks have on deposit and, consequently, available to lend.

- ✔ *Quantitative Easing*—while this term has found its way into our economic lexicon over the last year or so, its mechanics have always been part of the Fed's toolkit. Here, unlike "jawboning" where the Fed simply talks their strategy in hopes of impacting the market, QE actually is using the Fed's balance sheet to purchase assets in the open market. Typically, because interest rates and the slope of the yield curve are the overriding main mandate (together with inflation control) the Fed will choose to focus their purchases on the long end of the Treasury curve. As you can see, more buying of long-term bonds will increase the price and consequently decrease its yield, and will therefore have a larger impact on other securities "linked" to these long-term bonds (i.e., mortgage rates and consumer loans).

The preceding musings are, I expect, the type of discourse that is often analyzed by Federal Reserve governors and their staffs. An investor should be aware of the Fed's current concern and the indicators that relate to this concern. Several years ago, the "release-of-concern" was the deficit data, and prior to that the trade-gap data, and 10 years ago it was the inflation expectations that were building in the economy. The point here is important—the Fed is as fickle as the economy and therefore an investor needs to be aware of the current "indicator-du-jour" to understand how the impact of a certain release will affect the market. It is important to differentiate the investor's concern with economic releases with regard to the effect on the market and on an investment portfolio. A word of caution to the investor who is under the impression that an understanding of economic indicators is the key to the temple of investment outperformance: Economic releases are volatile and fickle. An investor cannot fully rely on one data set to make a decision, but must assemble a bevy of releases (over time) to make an effective analysis of expected future conditions. That is not to say that the market itself will be so tempered in its reaction to the latest economic release—the traders, who make their living on volatility and volume, will ensure that any reaction is anything but boring.

In addition to the fickleness of the market and uncertainty about the importance of economic releases, the media romanticize each tiny movement as an earth-shattering development. This is not to say that the increased awareness of financial information, due to the different media sources (cable television, Internet sites, and dedicated financial radio stations), is a negative. Just the contrary; it probably accounts for more of the increase in individual investor participation than any other single source. However, my concerns lay with the media's overemphasis on the economic report of the day, challenging the investor to make decisions based on this volatile information flow. While this information is pertinent to traders and speculators of the fast-money ilk, it may not be material to the investor who has a further investment horizon. However, the investor should not ignore this data, for when analyzed over some period, it can provide insights to the economy on a whole as well as specific industry sectors.

Keeping with the function of this book, we have provided details of only the most important economic releases. For simplicity and ease of use, 41 different economic indicators typically monitored by Wall Street investment firms are organized into 13 different categories:

1. *Employment and Unemployment*
   Change in payroll employment
   Unemployment rate, civilian

2. *Income and Production*
   Gross domestic product
   Personal income
   Index of industrial production
   Rate of capacity utilization

3. *Consumption*
   Retail sales
   Retail chain store sales index
   Personal consumption expenditures

4. *Housing*
   Housing starts
   Building permits
   Existing home sales
   New homes sold and for sale

5. *Autos*
   Retail unit sales of new passenger cars

6. *Credit*
   Consumer installment credit

7. *Deficit*
   Federal budget

8. *Trade*
   International trade balance

9. *Confidence Measures*
   Conference Board Business Executives Expectations
   Conference Board consumer confidence index

10. *Composites*
    Leading indicator composite
    Institute for Supply Management Index

11. *Financial Indicators*
    Dallas Fed exchange rate indexes
    Federal Reserve Board trade-weighted exchange rate
    M1 (M1 includes funds that are readily accessible for spending)
    M2 (includes M1 plus savings accounts and some CDs)
    3-month Treasury bill rate
    30-year Treasury bond yield
    S&P 500 stock price index

12. *Prices, Costs, and Productivity*
    Consumer price index (CPI)
    CPI ex food and energy
    Producer price index (PPI), finished goods
    PPI ex food and energy
    Agricultural price index (API)

West Texas Intermediate crude oil, spot price
Productivity, nonfarm business
Unit labor cost, nonfarm business
GDP deflator

13. *Business Sector*
Advance report on durable goods
Manufacturing
Manufacturing and trade
Corporate profits in current dollars

Table 2.1 illustrates a typical month's most important economic releases in calendar format. The following are the most important (to the financial markets) indicators.

Automobile Sales

U.S. automobile manufacturers release data on car and light truck sales three times a month: the first 10 days, the middle 10 days, and the final 10 days (although this last release can range between 8 or 9 days in February to 11 days in the 31-day months). This release is measured as an annual rate representing the retail unit sales (millions) of new passenger cars. Domestic and foreign are each stated separately.

Manufacturer's Shipments, Inventories, and New Orders for Consumer Goods

This is the volume of new orders, in addition to the amount in inventories and shipments received by manufacturers of consumer goods. This indicator is representative of the business sector of the economy. It is measured as a monthly rate in percentage terms and serves the 30-day period ending two months earlier (i.e., first week in July report is for May period). The lag of this indicator is its major weakness; furthermore, it is released about two weeks after that month's *Index of Industrial Production.*

Institute for Supply Management Report

The Institute for Supply Management (ISM) has more than 40,000 members in the United States and Puerto Rico. This report has been issued by ISM (formerly the National Association of Purchasing Managers,

Week	Indicator	What It Means
Week 1	ISM Manufacturing Report for previous month	Formerly known as the National Association of Purchasing Managers report—the ISM report is a national survey of purchasing managers that cover new orders, employment, inventories, and backlogs in the manufacturing sector.
	ISM Nonmanufacturing Report for previous month	Same as the above except this covers the non-manufacturing sector. This is a newcomer release and not as of yet closely followed. It is often referred to as the ISM Service Index and is the survey result of 370 companies. Like its sister report (above) the ISM surveys are not specific numbers but rather a thumbs up or down reading—which once calculated using weighting by the ISM, yields the actual percentage reading— a figure above 50 percent suggests expansion and below 50 percent is contraction.
	Construction Spending for two months prior	The construction spending report is comprised of residential, nonresidential, and public expenditures on new construction. Construction spending represents a large percentage of GDP and the figures are volatile and subject to large revisions.
	Factory Orders for two months prior	Represents the dollar level of new orders of both durable and nondurable goods. This report is more detailed than the durable goods report but its details are for the data of two months prior.
	EIA Natural Gas Inventory–Weekly Report	The energy information administration is the source for energy data for the U.S. government. A weekly survey of natural gas storage operators that yields the inventory estimates nationwide.
	EIA Petroleum Status Report–Weekly Report	The energy information administration is the source for energy data for the U.S. government. A weekly survey of oil storage operators that yields the inventory estimates nationwide.
	Pending Home Sales Index for two months prior	The National Association of Realtors developed the pending home sales index as a leading indicator of housing activity—for existing home sales, not new home sales. A pending sale is one where a contract is signed but not yet closed.

TABLE 2.1   Economic Releases Calendar

Week	Indicator	What It Means
	TABLE 2.1 Economic Releases Calendar *(Continued)*	
	Chain Store Sales Report for the previous month	Monthly sales volumes from individual department, chain, discount, and apparel stores are usually reported on the first or second Thursday of each month. Chain store sales correspond with roughly 10 percent of retail sales.
	Weekly Jobless Claims	A weekly compilation to show the number of individuals who filed for unemployment insurance for the first time. A 4-week moving average is also reported which is meant to smooth out weekly volatility.
	Consumer Credit Report for two months prior	The dollar value of consumer installment credit outstanding. The debt-to-income ratio is also an important corollary to this release—it shows how indebted consumers are relative to their incomes—a rising line would suggest that consumers are taking on more debt relative to their incomes.
Week 1	Weekly Money Supply Figures	The money supply figures—M1, M2, and M3—which detail different types of money (checking accounts, money market, savings accounts, etc.) in the system and the growth of that supply are important measures to understand the amount of "lubrication" in the monetary system. An increasing money supply will usually lead to inflationary pressures.
	Unemployment Report for previous month	The non-farm payroll report is reported on the first Friday in a new month for data of the previous month. It is a set of labor market indicators—the unemployment rate measures the number of unemployed as a percentage of the labor force and the non-farm payroll employment counts the number of paid employees, part-time or full-time, working in the nation's business and governement establishments. Also reported is the number of hours worked in an average workweek and the average hourly earnings.
	Wholesale Trade for two months prior	Measures the dollar value of sales made and inventories held by wholesalers in the merchant trades.

(continued)

TABLE 2.1   Economic Releases Calendar *(Continued)*

Week	Indicator	What It Means
Week 2 & 3	International Trade Report for two months prior	Measures the difference between imports and exports (net trade) of both tangible goods and services. Imports may act as a drag on domestic growth, add to inflationary pressures, and may also increase competitive pressures on domestic producers. Export growth is a boost to domestic production.
	Retail Sales for prior month	Provides an early indication of sales of retail and food service companies with one or more establishments that sell merchandise and associated services to final consumers. Since 1953, service companies have made a voluntary effort to respond to the written survey within five days from the end of the previous month.
	Producer Price Index (PPI) for the previous month	Measures the average change over time in the selling prices received by domestic producers for their output. The prices included in the PPI are from the first commercial transaction for many products and some services. The PPI is the first measure we get in a given month for inflation.
	Consumer Price Index (CPI) for the previous month	Produces monthly data on changes in the prices paid by urban consumers for a representative basket of goods and services. While being the broadest measure of consumer inflationary pressures in the economy, the CPI has come under much criticism given the components in its "basket"— specifically the costs of renting or housing.
	Industrial Production Report for the previous month	The Federal Reserve's monthly index of industrial production and the related capacity indexes and capacity utilization rates cover manufacturing, mining, and electric and gas utilities. The industrial sector, together with construction, accounts for the bulk of the variation in national output over the course of the business cycle.
	Housing Starts for the previous month	Issued by the U.S. Census Bureau jointly with the U.S. Department of Housing and Urban Development (HUD). The data is derived from surveys of homebuilders nationwide. As part of the release the following stats are given: housing starts, building permits, and housing completions. A housing start is defined as beginning the foundation of the home itself. Building permits are counted as of when they are granted.

TABLE 2.1   Economic Releases Calendar *(Continued)*

Week	Indicator	What It Means
Week 4	Leading Economic Indicators	The leading economic index is based on the Conference Board estimates, which are manufacturers' new orders for consumer goods and materials, manufacturers' new orders for nondefense capital goods, and the personal consumption expenditure used to deflate the money supply.
	S&P Case Shiller Home Price Index for two months prior	Measures the residential housing market, tracking changes in the value of the residential real estate market in 20 metropolitan regions across the United States. These indices use the repeat sales pricing technique (where a re-sold home is used to factor price change in a given market) to measure housing markets.
	Consumer Confidence for current month	5,000 consumers are surveyed about their sentiments on current economic activity.
	Durable Goods Report	Durable goods orders reflect the new orders placed with domestic manufacturers for immediate and future delivery of factory hard goods.
	New Home sales	New home sales measure the number of newly constructed homes with a committed sale during the month.
	GDP Report for previous quarter (initial, revised, final)	Measures of national income and output for a given country's economy. It is the total value of all final goods and services produced in a particular economy; the dollar value of all goods and services produced within a country's borders in a given year. The most common approach to measuring and quantifying GDP is the expenditure method: GDP = consumption + gross investment + government spending + (exports − imports).
Quarterly/Periodically	Beige Book–reported 2 weeks before the FOMC meeting	This report is published eight times per year where each Federal Reserve Bank gathers anecdotal information on current economic conditions in its District through reports from Bank and Branch directors and interviews with key business contacts, economists, market experts, and other sources. The Beige Book summarizes this information by District and sector.

(continued)

Week	Indicator	What It Means
	TABLE 2.1 Economic Releases Calendar *(Continued)*	
Quarterly/Periodically	FOMC Meetings	Consists of 7 Governors of the Federal Reserve Board and 5 of the 12 nationwide system of Federal Reserve Bank presidents. The NY Fed president is always on the FOMC and the other four seats for the district presidents are rotated yearly. The FOMC has meetings eight times a year to decide the level of interest rates (the Federal Funds rate and the Discount rate) and overall monetary policy for the nation.
	FOMC Meeting Minutes	Reported 3 weeks after the meeting—indicates the amount, if any, dissention among the Federal Reserve governors and the District presidents voting for interest rate policy.
	Corporate Earnings & Pre-earnings "confession" period	While not an economic indicator, the release of corporate earnings each quarter priovides valuable insights to the future (due to all-important management guidance for the forward periods) while detailing potential strains or bottlenecks in the wider economy.

NAPM) since 1931 (except during World War II). This survey is our first complete assessment of manufacturing, a sector that is strongly correlated to the total ("industrial") economy but arguably less so to the services economy that we have evolved into as of the last 3 decades. The major positive that a VFII gets from studying the ISM's PMI report is an early look at economic activity, for this release is a leading indicator rather than a lagging one. Furthermore, it has been shown through studies that there still exists a high correlation between the overall economic activity and the manufacturing sector.

Over 300 industrial purchasing executives serving 21 industries in 50 states are represented on the Membership of the Business Survey Committee. The Committee is diversified by Standard Industrial Classification (SIC) category, based on each industry's contribution to gross domestic product (GDP). These executives must respond to the following areas:

- Inventories
- Vendor performance/supplier deliveries

✔ Employment

✔ New orders, backlog of orders, new export orders

✔ Imports

✔ Production

✔ Prices paid index

The ISM's Purchasing Manager's Index (PMI) is measured through a questionnaire that purchasing executives respond to by indicating either *Up, Down, or Unchanged* for each area in the preceding list. The report is calibrated in percentage terms: Above 44.5 percent typically indicates an expanding manufacturing sector, and below 44.5 percent a contracting sector. The resulting single index number is then seasonally adjusted to allow for the effects of repetitive intra-year variations resulting primarily from normal differences in weather conditions, institutional arrangements, and differences attributable to holidays. All seasonal adjustment factors are supplied by the U.S. Department of Commerce and are subject annually to relatively minor changes when conditions warrant them.

The Employment Situation

This economic release covers the change in nonfarm payroll employment. In addition, the *unemployment rate* is stated (annual percentage rate of civilians who have filed for unemployment compensation) as well as the *Employment Cost Index* (average hourly earnings). This crucial report is broken down into two separate surveys: an establishment survey and a household survey. The establishment (industry) survey looks at the payroll employment (hours, wages, and overtime) of the following industries: goods producing, manufacturing, construction, mining, service producing, transportation, public utilities, wholesale trade, finance, insurance, and real estate.

The household survey, on the other hand, dutifully queries 59,500 households (although I know no one who has ever received such a call) through the efforts of 1,500 trained Census Bureau employees, on the status of employment. The first question—"Do you have a job?"—is used as an estimate of the labor force figure (or in other words, the base against which the unemployment rate is measured). The status of job seeking is determined by asking, "Are you looking for a job?" The answer to this question is used to establish the unemployment rate.

The *employment situation indicator* is measured in thousands of newly employed; the total amount and the manufacturing-only amount are both stated. It is released by the Labor Department at 8:30 A.M. (EST), on the first Friday of each month and covers the previous month.

On each Thursday at 8:30 A.M. (EST), the Department of Labor reports the number of new unemployment claims for the previous week. The "rolling nature" of this report allows the unemployment situation for the month to be estimated very accurately, and any aberrations to this widely expected reading on employment might disturb the markets. As stated earlier, it is not the release that can be disturbing, but rather the amount of change compared with the consensus forecast. And forecasts for employment situation releases are anticipated to be more accurate than other releases.

The Index of Leading Economic Indicators

In the first week of each month (actually the last business day of the previous month) the Conference Board (a not-for-profit economic research concern with more than 2,700 corporate and other members in 60 nations) releases the Index of Leading Economic Indicators (LEI). Up until early 1996, the U.S. Department of Commerce had taken the responsibility for reporting this important composite indicator; since then the mantle has been taken up by the Conference Board. The underlying premise of this release is its strong correlation with the future direction of the economy. The design of the LEI allows it to serve as a barometer of the future direction of the economy. The LEI is actually a composite of 11 distinct indicators, each of which is separately reported throughout the month. In this way, government economists hope to create one indicator that forecasts the future direction of the economy with a good amount of accuracy.

Has it worked? The jury is still out, but this index has been reliable in predicting downturns in the economy 8 to 18 months in advance; however, it has also rung a false alarm about once each cycle. In the Fall 1984 period, the LEI suggested a weaker than expected rate of growth in 1985, despite professional forecasts of a strong economic expansion. As it turned out, the LEI beat the forecasters for 1985—a year of subpar growth.

Most of the components that make up the LEI are what you would expect from a release that tries to forecast the future:

- ✔ *Contracts and orders for plant and equipment.* As orders for new equipment increase, the future would appear bright. A typical owner of a manufacturing plant is certainly not going to buy new equipment unless he expects a strong level of growth well into the future. This same premise can be extrapolated, in a more basic sense, to your own situation: Would you feel comfortable putting an extension onto your home when your business is not growing? Or when there have been layoffs in your division at the office?

- ✔ *Permits issued for new housing, formation of new businesses, and manufacturer's new orders.* When the number of permits issued for new housing is on the decline for several consecutive months, an investor could make the supposition that either we are approaching a recession or, more likely, are already in one. The housing sector has a great impact on the total economy, from interest rates to related industries (furniture, landscaping, remodeling, etc.), due to its relative high correlation with the consumer, whose purchasing habits typically account for more than 66 percent of GDP. The formation of new businesses acts like a proxy measure of the level of optimism about the future and the willingness of investors and businesses to invest and spend. As more businesses come into the economy, not only does the level of the economy grow but the comfort level of many investors also grows. This will snowball into greater consumption and investment.

The basic principle of the LEI is that changes in the business cycle can be a guide to the future direction of the economy, and its forward-looking nature guarantees close attention from Wall Street. The LEI is measured on a monthly rate in percentage terms for the time period of the previous month (i.e., in late July the report comes out for June); this remains one of its major criticisms.

The LEI is a composite of 10 different indicators:

1. *Average workweek of production workers in manufacturing.* Due to the uncertainty associated with timing of the business cycle

(the economic outlook in the early stages of a recovery or in the early stages of a recession), employers are more likely to adjust the hours of existing workers before hiring new workers during a recovery or laying off workers during a recession. Therefore, this average workweek is an important look into the head of the production manager in charge of hiring and firing.

2. *Average initial weekly claims for state unemployment insurance.* Like the preceding indicator, this indicator, which shows the increases and decreases in unemployment (released on Thursday mornings), reflects the business expectations of the demand for labor.

3. *Manufacturer's new orders for consumer goods and materials, adjusted for inflation.* Business commitments for new resources and materials are an indication of future economic activity as well as demand for the labor needed to produce the final goods.

4. *Vendor performance (companies receiving slower deliveries from suppliers).* This is an interesting approach to determining the strength (on a forward basis) of the economy—the speed by which vendors deliver orders is an inverse relationship with the strength of the economy (i.e., the economy is strong when delivery time is slow). The reasoning may not be clear at first—slower delivery times indicate a large amount of back orders, representing a stronger economy.

5. *Contracts and orders for plants and equipment, adjusted for inflation.* As mentioned, the increased amount of contracts or orders reflects a stronger economy.

6. *Building permits for new private housing units.* Also as mentioned, the increased level of permits for new construction has a direct, positive relationship to a stronger economy.

7. *The interest rate spread between the 10 year Treasury bond and the Fed Funds Rate.* Essentially, this stat provides a view of the yield curve, which in turn has a strong forecasting record with respect to expecting recessions (see below).

8. *Stock prices, 500 common stocks.* Stock prices, in the words of Federal Reserve Chairman Alan Greenspan (December 1996) could indicate a level of "irrational exuberance" among avarice-minded investors. However, the fact that stock price

levels reflect investor expectations of economic growth is firmly grounded in research and empirical evidence. High stock prices make it easier for businesses to raise funds for plant and equipment by selling new stock on the public market. Conversely, low stock prices increase the likelihood that firms will expand by using debt rather than equity financing. In addition, the typical household generally feels wealthier as its equity investments are rising rather than falling. The dramatic increase in the percentage of equity investments in the typical household's total net worth calculation is becoming more of an acute concern.

9. *Money supply (M2), adjusted for inflation.* This indicator speaks to the amount of liquidity in the economy. As the amount of financial liquid assets increases, the purchasing power available to business and household transactions (materials, capital goods, labor resources, "big-ticket" consumer items) increases. Money supply could either mean savings and checking account balances (M1), or M1 plus money market balances, otherwise known as M2—a more complete measure of total liquidity.

10. *Index of consumer expectations.* Two organizations report a measure of consumer confidence—University of Michigan's Survey Research Center (index of consumer confidence) and the Conference Board ("consumer confidence index"). As expected, these indicators report on the turning points of the business cycle before they are recognized in the economy. As with many leading indicators, one is cautioned to their basic nature; that is, these indicators are more sensitive to the future trends in an economy than to specific forecasts.

In 1996, the Conference Board eliminated two indicators (change in unfilled orders, durable goods industry and change in sensitive material prices) from the leading indicator index due to their poor forecasting power in the past decade. Furthermore, the Conference Board added to the LEI an indicator representing a yield-curve component (a spread-based indicator quantifying the difference between the 10-year Treasury note rate with either the 3-month or 1-year bill rate). A recently published report by two economists at the Federal Reserve Bank of New York credits the yield curve with strong predictive powers of upcoming economic downturns (about four quarters before a recession's onset). For example, if the 10-year rate is 121 basis points (1.21 percent) higher than the 3-month rate, the chances of a recession are only 5 percent. Conversely, if the short-term rate is 240 basis points higher than the 10-year rate, the chance of *not* having a recession is only 5 percent. This Federal Reserve study is firmly entrenched in the expectations hypothesis of interest rates, which states a correlation between long-term rates and current investor expectations for inflation: A normal-shaped yield curve (higher long-term rates than short-term rates) illustrates that investors expect inflation in the future and thereby fixed-income investors require a higher rate to go out longer on the curve, whereas an inverted yield curve (short-term rates higher than long-term rates) illustrates little fear of future inflation and therefore a recession is looming.

It is important to examine the basic tenets surrounding the formation of the leading economic indicators, as well as the related coincident and lagging indicators. Although the LEI is most commonly used in investment finance (for its forward-looking design), the coincident and lagging indicators can also provide important levels of study for industry analysis. The leading, coincident, and lagging indices of economic activity are based on the concept that each phase of the business cycle (see Figure 2.1) contains the seeds of the following phase. This system, adapted from the early twentieth-century business cycle concepts of Wesley Mitchell, assesses the strengths and weaknesses in the economy for clues toward the future growth rates as well as cyclical turning points (shift from recession to expansion).

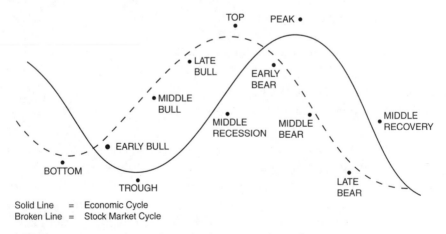

FIGURE 2.1 Business cycle and relative stock performance.

The three classifications—leading, coincident, and lagging (LCL)—refer to the turning points in the business cycle:

1. The *leading index* attempts to pinpoint the time when the economy begins to shift from a contracting phase (recession) to an upward bias or recovery.
2. The *coincident index* mimics the cyclically of the overall economy and tends to coincide with recessions and expansions.
3. The *lagging index* turns down after the beginning of the recession and turns up after the beginning of the expansion.

The underlying tenet of LCL format is the notion that the entire economy revolves around the future expectations of profits in corporate America. That is to say, as business executives believe the sales and profits of their company are on the rise they will begin to institute a more aggressive production campaign, coupling that with a stronger purchasing and investment commitment. This increased activity will eventually lead to a peak in the economic cycle to be followed by a slower, more contracting phase of the economy (see box, "Business Cycle and Investments"). The LCL provides a method to pinpoint these turning points and allows management to plan important investment strategy policies.

Business Cycle and Investments

The *trough* pinpoints the part of the business cycle where corporate sales and investment reach depressed levels with considerable excess in plant capacity. As sales increase, profit expectations begin to creep higher and business managers begin to plan for increased production, increasing working hours, and gradually rehiring previously laid-off labor.

At the *middle recession* phase of the cycle, businesses become uneasy (perhaps due to the higher costs of capital) and begin to pull back on their reins by reducing orders for equipment, cutting back on inventories, and laying off workers. Incomes begin to be reduced (due to the layoffs) and consequently consumers become wary (decrease in spending).

> ## Business Cycle and Investments *(Continued)*
>
> At the *peak*, workers, machines, and materials are beginning to be utilized at capacity and this strong demand exerts increased price and wage pressures (Can you smell a hint of inflation?). Businesses begin to increase their debt loads to finance the expanding levels of inventory and fixed asset commitment. This increased demand for borrowing leads to higher interest rates, which indicates the peak of the economic cycle.
>
> At the *middle recovery* point in the cycle, employee incomes begin to rise, which stimulates personal consumption expenditures (consumer confidence increasing), thereby leading managers to initiate expansion (modernization) of production facilities. These corporate expenditures on capital goods require added jobs and subsequently higher income and consumption levels.
>
> At the end of the recession (beginning of the recovery), credit terms begin to ease and housing construction tends to increase. This leads to increased consumer confidence (in addition to spending), as most determine that the worst (of the economic cycle) is coming to an end.

Personal Income and Expenditures

Personal consumer expenditures are stated in this report, as is the calculation of real disposable income and the personal savings rate. The personal consumption expenditures category is the largest segment of the gross domestic product (GDP), accounting for nearly 66 percent. For this reason, a strong level of consumer spending is often viewed as favorable for the economy as a whole; in addition, the consumer spending statistic is divided into two segments—durable and nondurable goods. Durable goods are those that last longer, are larger and often more expensive, and are more sensitive to changes in the business cycle. The typical consumer would think longer before purchasing a durable good (automobile, furniture, appliances, etc.) than a nondurable good (easily replaceable items, such as food, clothing, sundries).

The personal consumption expenditure is measured as a monthly rate (change from previous report) and is reported in percentage terms. This indicator covers the time period for the prior month and is released at 10 A.M. Eastern time.

U.S. International Trade in Goods and Services—Merchandise Trade Balance

This represents the dollar value difference between U.S. exports and imports on a seasonally adjusted basis. Trend analysis plays an important function in this indicator, for it points to either an expansion or contraction of the trade deficit. Implications are more pronounced in the currency markets: The dollar will be bolstered with a declining deficit because it reflects a more economically sound government trade policy, and therefore the currency becomes more attractive to foreigners. The merchandise trade balance is measured in billions of U.S. dollars on a seasonally adjusted basis. Reflecting the time period of two months prior to its release, this indicator is often viewed as somewhat lagging.

The Producer Price Index

The producer price index (PPI) measures prices at the wholesale level only (formerly called the wholesale price index). The PPI is a leading indicator of inflationary trends in the economy, for it measures the price changes that have not yet moved through the economy. Price increases on the wholesale level take time, often as much as several quarters, to move to the consumer level.

This makes intuitive sense, as the following four-step scenario shows:

1. You are a manufacturer producing widgets in a highly competitive industry.

2. You begin to notice price increases in your raw materials.

3. Deciding to lock in these prices before they rise any further, you purchase more of the raw material than normal.

4. The new widgets are more expensive than those previously in inventory, lowering your profit margins. If it wasn't for the highly competitive nature of the widget industry you would raise your prices, but you fear retaliation by competitors who may have seen the price increases coming before you did and stocked up at lower prices. If you raised your widget price you could leave yourself open to a severe decline in market share. You must wait until the industry, on a whole, increases price (see discussion of consumer price index).

The Labor Department reports the PPI approximately two days before the consumer price index and indicates the average percentage change from the previous period (month prior).

Consumer Price Index

The consumer price index (CPI) is a measure of inflation that is often most directly attributable to the individual investor—the percentage change in the rate of inflation that directly affects your pocket over time. To obtain a more definitive explanation of the inflationary trends within the economy, the Department of Labor compiles a sample basket of goods representing the typical consumer's purchasing habits. The consumer price index measures the monthly changes associated with this basket. This report is published in the month following the measurement (in June the CPI for May is reported). It is presented as the percentage change over the prior month. However, the percentage change from the same month the year earlier is much more sensitive, for it factors out the monthly statistical deviations ("noise").

Often we are told that the CPI (also reported in PPI) may have increased by 0.02 percent for the month, but the core rate of inflation, which factors out the volatile food and energy sectors, was down 0.01 percent. This testifies not only to the volatility within those sectors (for the government would not have had—nor would the markets have demanded—to break them out separately if they weren't so volatile), but also to the sensitivity of the U.S. markets to their old nemesis (recall the Misery Index). It is interesting to witness how the economic system becomes sensitized by the market and the demands of the investors (suppliers of the capital).

A formidable effort has been placed on the redefining of the CPI; specifically a recent assessment that suggests the CPI overstates inflation by as much as 1.1 percent. As in most scientific disciplines, however, an argument suggests the opposite—that the CPI actually understates the true rate of inflation. This view is based on the notion that housing (the largest component of the CPI, accounting for approximately 40 percent of the basket of goods and services) is vastly understated.

Gross Domestic Product

The gross domestic product (GDP) or gross domestic income (GDI) is one of the measures of national income and output for a given country's economy. GDP is defined as the total market value of all final goods and services produced within the country in a given period of time (usually a calendar year). It is also considered the sum of a value added at every stage of production (the intermediate stages) of all final goods and services produced within a country in a given period of time, and it is given a money value.

The most common approach to measuring and understanding GDP is the expenditure method:

GDP = consumption + gross investment + government spending
      + (exports − imports), or,

GDP = C + I + G + (X − M).

Gross domestic product is the most extensive measure of macroeconomic activity in the U.S. economy. GDP can be contrasted with gross national product (GNP, or gross national income, GNI), which the United States used in its national accounts until 1992. The difference is that GNP includes net foreign income (the current account) rather than net exports and imports (the balance of trade). Put simply, GNP adds net foreign investment income compared to GDP.

The GDP is reported on a quarterly basis (as an annualized rate) by the Bureau of Economic Analysis (division of the U.S. Department of Commerce) and is subject to revisions throughout the following months and even into the next couple of years. As a matter of fact, a Wall Street adage suggests that if you want to know what the actual GNP was (grew at) this year, talk to me in about three years when the revision process finally posts the amount to the record books.

International Investing

International investing has grown in importance over the past two decades, due in part to the outperformance of the MS EAFE (Morgan Stanley Europe Asia Far East) index (18 percent average annual return) versus the U.S. stock market (9.9 percent average annual total return of S&P index) between 1970 and 1989. But many constraints exist to international investments besides the obvious political risks (the concern of a riot or some other political turmoil would disturb the financial markets) and currency risks (said to be the greatest "driver" of return and, consequently, the greatest risk, for an international investor). These include technical or accounting differences between nations, which make analysis particularly challenging, and the cultural knowledge required to make intuitive suppositions about future trends. Other concerns for the investor who seeks returns outside his home country include psychological barriers (i.e., cultural differences), legal restrictions (i.e., insider trading laws), transaction costs, and discriminatory taxation (i.e., limitations on repatriation of profits).

The massive scope of international investing is quite beyond the lessons in this manual; it is possible, however, to shed some light on this new and chaotic area of investments. The currency market can provide a focus for the discussion of the differences between investments in different nations.

Let's start at a very simple quote of $1 (American) to 1£ (British). The quote (indirect quote format) of the number of foreign currency units per one U.S. dollar is the format used in the case that follows. The inverse of this quote would provide the number of U.S. dollars per unit of foreign currency.

As the dollar increases in value:

1. The exchange rate between the dollar and the pound will increase (e.g., the number of pounds it takes to "buy" one dollar will increase). Starting from our base case scenario (1£ = $1 U.S.), the exchange rate would go to 1.2£ = $1 for a 20 percent increase in the dollar. The reciprocal exchange rate of 1£ = $.8333 (1/1.2) is another way (direct quote format) to write the same exchange rate. If an American were traveling in London during this base case scenario (1£ = $1), he would have to cough up $1 to ride the subway (assuming that the subway costs 1£); upon returning to London during our "dollar appreciation" case scenario, the American would only need $.83 to take the same ride. This demonstrates the benefit of having a strong currency (while visiting a nation whose currency is weakening).

2. The economic incentives increase for domestic importers, because the currency they use to purchase foreign goods increases in value. Meanwhile, the fortunes of domestic-based exporters would be under pressure, as their goods become more expensive for foreigners to purchase. Now here is where it gets interesting—because of the strong domestic currency, a major foreign

exporter (whose currency is weak) to the strong-currency nation has the ability to lower prices (in domestic terms) because on conversion (from domestic currency to foreign currency) this exporter will receive more domestic currency for each of the stronger currencies paid for the product. Remember, the foreign exporter does not care if his currency has depreciated versus another nation, because he will use his currency in his nation and therefore doesn't need to convert it into another currency.

In summary:

Value of Dollar	Exchange Rate (U.S./Foreign Currency)	Foreign Goods Purchased with U.S. Currency	U.S. Goods Purchased with Foreign Currency
Increases	Increases ($ buys more of foreign currency)	Less expensive	More expensive

Another example can clarify this important notion:

1. A Japanese car manufacturer exports cars to the United States, and expects to receive 10,000 yen (¥) for each car sold.
2. The base case scenario is an exchange rate of $1 = 100¥, so the Japanese company expects to price the cars at $100, therefore permitting their 10,000 yen inflow on conversion.
3. But the exchange rate changes (the dollar appreciates versus the yen) and is now 150¥ = $1. Now, the Japanese company can lower their U.S. price (and possibly increase their market share) to $66.66 per car to maintain their 10,000 yen inflow ($66.66 × 150¥ to the $ = 10,000¥).

The flip side of this equation is the impact on domestic inflation; because the foreign exporter lowers his price (because of changes in the currency), the domestic manufacturer (of the same good) must also lower his price to stay competitive.

In these situations, the corporate finance department of multinational corporations will employ hedging strategies to permit risk management with currency fluctuations. By utilizing derivative products such as options, swaps, forward contracts, and futures, a multinational corporation (MNC) can lock in currency exposure today for some future time period.

Now, look at what happens when the dollar decreases in value:

1. The exchange rate—the number of units of foreign currency per $1—also decreases and therefore, the amount of foreign currency needed to purchase $1 decreases (to $1 = .90£).

2. The economic incentives for domestic importers decrease (their currency, used to purchase foreign goods, is decreased in value), while the fortunes of domestic-based exporters increase (their goods are less expensive for foreigners to purchase).

In summary:

Value of Dollar	Exchange Rate (U.S./Foreign Currency)	Foreign Goods Purchased with U.S. $	U.S. Goods Purchased with Foreign Currency
Decreases	Decreases ($ buys more of foreign currency)	More expensive	Less expensive

There may be several different cause-and-effect reasons for a particular currency to appreciate or depreciate vis-à-vis another currency. Methods to forecast exchange rates are firmly embedded in theoretical and restrictive assumptions about how perfect and efficient trading (of goods, services, and capital) between nations is assumed to be. In the real world, however, these assumptions are lifted to reveal many uncertainties about the future growth and impact of inflation, and the effects on the currency markets. An evaluation of these restrictive assumptions yields some intriguing facts:

- Goods cannot be transferred between nations instantly.
- Shipping costs are prohibitively high.
- Import restrictions (tariffs and quotas) affect international trade.
- Cultural differences make consumption standardization between nations very difficult, and usually drastically flawed.

International parity conditions are explored in greater detail in the appendix to this chapter, including the discussion of interest rate arbitrage as well as problem sets to sharpen skills in this area.

Appendix—International Parity Conditions

Two methods are typically relied on to forecast exchange rates:

1. *Balance of payments method.* As in many economic scenarios, supply and demand determines the price of the good being exchanged; in the case of currency, the exchange of financial "goods" between nations determines the price (exchange rate) charged in the market.

2. *Asset market approach.* In this approach, we rely on two parity conditions to provide some guidance to the future exchange rates between nations. The concepts surrounding purchasing power parity (PPP) and interest rate parity (IRP) are critical to understanding currency exchange rate forecasting.

Interest rate differentials and inflation rate differentials remain the most common and practical drivers to currency exchange rate movement, although these parity conditions do not affect the short run for several reasons. Before exploring the parity conditions and their individual nuances, it is necessary to define certain terms:

Spot rate. Rate of exchange between two currencies; refers to immediate delivery.

Forward rate. Rate of exchange between two currencies; the rate is set today but not recognized until a date in the future. The Foreign Exchange Expectations Theory suggests that the forward exchange rate should be the unbiased predictor of the future spot rate.

Interest rate. Rate charged for money; usually quoted as an annual rate.

Inflation rate. Rate of consumer price increase over a specified period.

Purchasing Power Parity

States that spot exchange rates will adjust perfectly to inflation differentials. If prices of goods rise greater in nation one relative to nation two, then nation one's currency must *depreciate* to maintain a similar real price for the goods in both countries.

If it holds (a matter of debate, at least on the practical level), the purchasing power parity (PPP) implies that the real (inflation-adjusted) "cost" of any good is identical for investors in any country. In lay terms, purchasing power parity presumes the cost for a McDonald's burger is equal, no matter in which nation it is being purchased and with which currency.

As any traveler to the Far East would attest, PPP does not hold, at least not in the short run (research by Adler & Dumas suggests that inflation differentials contribute less than 5 percent of the short-term volatility in exchange rates). Although the empirical evidence suggests that PPP is useful in forecasting exchange rate movements over a longer-term period, according to Bruno Solnik (1991), "Usually it has taken more than several years for the deviation from PPP to be corrected in the foreign exchange market."

Why doesn't this parity condition hold in the short run? Consider the following factors:

- ✔ *Cultural differences.* Different cultures consume differently; for example, people in the Far East are much more prolific savers than people in the West, who are predominately spenders. The standard of living is a good deal higher in the West, but this alone does not fully account for the huge differences in cultures.

- ✔ *Measurement difficulties with consumer basket differences.* Inflation is typically measured via a basket-of-goods currency weighted to a level value. But other nations may value their basket differently due to the resources available to that nation. Furthermore, inflation among nations is not uniformly measured in this basket format, which only increases the difficulty in measuring this intangible value.

- ✔ *Transfer costs, import taxes, and restrictions.* These restrictive measures on trade subject a cost structure into the parity condition that was never anticipated (or more likely just neglected) by the economic theorists who first postulated these theories. With costs like taxes and shipping impeded against trade, how could one expect to have a parity condition (which reflects the effect of one variable on another) hold in the short run? Time is needed to work through these additional costs.

Considering the preceding information, one may question the benefits of using the PPP in exchange rate forecasts. In the short run, PPP is not much help, partly because of the restrictions previously mentioned and the fact that exchange rates move very frequently while inflation adjusts slowly over time, But how about in the long run? Long-run exchange rate forecasting is important for two reasons:

1. Multinational businesses use these forecasts to calculate their exchange rate exposure (and the respective risk management techniques) during a given period.
2. Government policymakers utilize these forecasts when determining an effective monetary and fiscal policy plan.

As it turns out, PPP is quite intuitive in forecasting exchange rates over the long run. Empirical evidence (Hakkio, 1992) illustrates that the exchange rate will revert toward the PPP-expected rate within one to six years. Statistical tests established that exchange rates will have differing probabilities (for convergence toward PPP) for different currencies but will average about 59 percent. That is, if two currencies are presently not in parity, then one could postulate that, on average, there is a 59 percent chance that these currencies will converge within a one- to six-year time horizon. Furthermore, the number of years it takes to converge and the probability of convergence will differ between nations (currencies). For example, the U.S. dollar/British pound exchange rate has the highest probability of convergence (79 percent), as well as the shortest time horizon to converge (typically within three years).

How is all this helpful to today's investor? Assume a U.S.-based investor is evaluating a UK-based investment, and during his due-diligence correctly determines (a VFII, no doubt) that the currency effect will be a major contributing factor to the expected return of this investment. He further learns that the British pound and U.S. dollar are trading far from where their relative inflation measures would postulate (the pound is trading too cheap vs. the PPP condition). If this investor's time horizon is greater than, say, four years, then he can be relatively comfortable with the supposition that the pound will appreciate (vs. the dollar) over this horizon. If this investor enters ("puts on") this trade while the pound is trading below its parity value and then sells this investment when the pound has appreciated, he has added value to the transaction beyond that of the fundamental analysis of the security.

Mathematical Notation

$$PPP = \frac{1 + Inf\,(foreign)}{1 + Inf\,(domestic)} \times \frac{Forward\ exchange\ rate\ (fc/\$)}{Spot\ rate\ (fc/\$)}$$

Example: Inflation rate is 7 percent in France and 4 percent in the United States; if the spot rate (Euro/$) is 75E/$1, then the PPP suggests that the exchange rate on the forward market should be selling for 77.16E/$1.

Intuitively, this makes sense—prices are higher in France compared with those of the U.S., and therefore the Euro is depreciating vis-à-vis the dollar. Alternatively, it could be illustrated that the American purchasing a good in France, which has increased in price, would need the offsetting gain in currency power to permit parity.

Quick Math Method

The inflation differential between two nations is 3 percent (7% − 4% = 3%). Therefore, the Euro would need to devalue (because French inflation is higher than U.S. inflation) versus the dollar by approximately 3 percent.

$$\frac{75E}{\$1} \times 1.03 \;(3\%\ devaluation) = \frac{77.25E}{\$1} \;(Parity\ level)$$

Interest Rate Parity

Interest rate parity (IRP) states that the interest rate differential must equal the forward exchange discount or premium. Like the PPP, the IRP permits the cost of capital (interest rates) to be equal across all nations. If interest rates are higher in one nation versus another, you would think that the demand for this higher interest rate would attract so much capital that the currency would have to appreciate. Under most practical circumstances, this is exactly what happens in the short run; however, the interest rate parity condition suggests that the currency of the nation with the higher interest rate should devalue versus the other nation's currency. Arbitrage forces the IRP equation into parity, thereby permitting the most nimble currency traders to profit handsomely. However, the most popular explanation of why IRP may not hold in the short run concerns government interactions. Monetary policies of federal banks have been known to use interest rates to appreciate the valuation of their currency.

Mathematical Notation

$$\text{IRP} = \frac{1 + \text{Int (foreign)}}{1 + \text{Int (domestic)}} \times \frac{\text{Futures (or forward) exchange rate}}{\text{Spot rate}}$$

Example: The 1-year interest rate in Japan is 10 percent, and in the United States it is 4 percent; the yen is currently at a spot rate of 3,000 yen to 1 dollar. The currency is correctly priced at 3,173.07 yen on the futures market.

$$\frac{1.10}{1.04} = \frac{x}{3,000}$$

The value of x—the price of the currency on the futures market—is 3,173.07.

Quick Math Method

The percentage difference between the forward rate and the spot rate is approximated by the interest rate differential.

As in the preceding example, the interest rate differential of 6 percent approximates the devaluation of the yen:

$$3,000 \text{ yen} \times 1.06 = 3,180$$

Interest Rate Arbitrage

To understand the method by which a currency trader may expect to profit given an inequitable (non-parity) condition between two nations, consider the following example of riskless interest arbitrage (also called covered interest arbitrage).

Example: Assume that IRP is not holding and that the current spot rate is UK £ = $1.80 or .5556£ per 1 U.S. $. Furthermore, the one-year interest rates between the nations are:

$$\text{U.S. rate} = 6\% \quad \text{UK rate} = 5\%$$

Whereas the currency is trading on the futures exchange at:

$$\$1.81/1UK£ \text{ (or } .5525£/\$1)$$

Hence, a careful examination of the IRP equation would suggest that IRP is not currently holding because the future's price should be $1.8172/1£ (or .5503£/$1).

The math:

$$\frac{1.05}{1.06} = \frac{x}{.5556£/\$1}$$

The value of x (the value of the exchange rate on the futures market) should be .5503£/$1, but it is trading at .5525£/$1. The exchange rate on the futures exchange has not correctly (according to IRP) valued the British pound versus the dollar; it is trading at a discount to the value perceived by the IRP.

Quick Math Method

The United States is paying more interest than the United Kingdom, therefore, if IRP holds, the U.S. dollar should depreciate versus the pound by the equal amount of the difference between the rates (1 percent) to remain in parity. This would assign a value of approximately $1,818 (or .5501£ per $1), but as indicated $1.81/£ is not enough depreciation to make parity (which is 1.8172 or .5503£/$).

So how do the most nimble of currency traders take advantage of the situation? Consider the following steps:

1. Borrow 100£ in the United Kingdom (at 5 percent interest rate due in 1 year), because the cost of borrowing is less than that of the United States. The total due in one year is 105£.

2. Convert 100£ to U.S. dollars at the current rate of $1.80 per pound, which is $180, and invest this for one year at 6 percent to have total receipts of $190.80 in one year.

3. But we will still need to pay back the UK loan in pounds next year, and therefore you would want to hedge this currency exposure by locking in next year's exchange rate today using the

futures market. At $1.81 per pound you would have a locked-in number of pounds in one year:

$$\frac{\$190.80}{1.81} = 105.41£$$

4. All you need to pay back is 105£ so your risk-free profit per 100£ is .41£ (or .0041 per pound).

With this type of action prevalent in the foreign currency markets (probably the most liquid and intensely monitored financial market), arbitrage would force into parity any conditions that would permit a risk-less profit. The point to take home from this exercise is that the foreign exchange markets, due to their strong interlinking with the futures market, are very efficient and only the most nimble currency speculator can achieve superior results. That is not to say that a currency investor cannot profit—for the difference between a speculator and an investor revolves around the fact that the speculator has "placed a bet" and is not risk averse, whereas the investor might have mountains of research supporting his trade and is committed to a defined expected time horizon and expected return bogey.

PROBLEM SET: INTERNATIONAL PARITY CONDITIONS

Question 1

The pound/dollar exchange rate (the number of Irish currency (*punt*) per U.S. dollar) is currently (spot) 0.720£/$1, where the Irish inflation rate is 7 percent and the American inflation rate is 5 percent. Where ("at what price") should the futures on this exchange rate trade?

Answer

The purchasing power parity equation is calculated as follows:

$$\frac{1.07}{1.05} = \frac{x}{.720}$$

Algebraically, we solve the equation in the following manner:

1.07 (.72) = 1.05 (*x*). Multiply the factors on a diagonal basis

.7704 = 1.05 (*x*)

.7704/1.05 = *x*

x = .7337£ per $1

This makes sense because the interest rate differential points to an approximately 2 percent decrease in the punt versus the dollar. If you multiply 1.02 (2 percent increase in the number of punts per dollar or a 2 percent decrease in the value of the punt versus the dollar) times .72, the answer is .7334.

Question 2

Suppose that:

1. Spot dollar/KR (Denmark) exchange rate is $.39/KR.
2. The futures market for this currency is quite liquid and efficient, and a one-year futures contract is trading at 2.60KR/$.
3. The U.S. 1-year risk-free rate is 4 percent.
4. The Denmark one-year risk-free interest rate is 7 percent.

Describe how an investor can profit without taking on any risk.

Answer

The method would be interest rate arbitrage. The math works out as follows:

First calculate the IRP equation to understand where a futures contract should be trading for the exchange rate.

$$\frac{1.07}{1.04} = \frac{x}{2.5641KR}$$

$$2.7436 = 1.04(x)$$

$$x = \frac{2.6381KR}{\$1}$$

So, the futures contract to be in parity, should be traded at 2.6381KR/$ for delivery in one year. But, as in the given example, the futures contract for KR/$ exchange rate is trading at 2.60KR/$. Therein lies the opportunity to profit:

1. Borrow $100 in the United States. In one year, the debt owed is $104 ($100 + 4 percent interest).
2. Convert the $100 to krone at the current spot rate (2.5641KR/$) for a total of 256.41KR.

3. Invest these proceeds in the Danish interest rate market (at 7 percent), yielding 274.358KR in one year.

4. If the futures contract were in parity (IRP holds), then we would convert these krone to dollars (274.358KR/2.6381KR/$ = $104) to satisfy our $104 debt. But the futures contract is not trading in parity, and we are able to sell 274.358 krone today, in the futures contract, for 2.60KR/$, which would yield $105.52 in 1 year.

5. Pay the loan of $104, resulting in a risk-free profit of $1.52.

Question 3

Given the following data, calculate the real interest rate:

$$\text{Nominal interest rate} = 7\%$$
$$\text{Expected inflation rate} = 2\%$$

Answer

According to the Fisher equation:

$$\text{Nominal interest rate} = (\text{Inflation rate})\,(\text{Real interest rate})$$
$$7\% = 2\%\,(\text{Real interest rate})$$
$$7\%/2\% = \text{Real interest rate}$$
$$\text{Real interest rate} = 3.5\%$$

Investment Mathematics

I n this chapter you will learn:

✔ The present and future value of money calculations.
✔ The methodology behind net present value equation.
✔ How annuities are valued.

The idea that money appreciates in value over time is one of the oldest tenets of investment finance. Even the earliest lords and barons realized that when capital (gold or some other means of exchange) was transferred between two persons (one being the lender, the other the borrower), an additional amount, above the transferred amount, came due as a fee—now referred to as interest. Interest can be thought of, in its simplest terms, as the amount of money that is gained by giving up one's capital in an investment.

Investment finance requires a comprehensive knowledge of the values of money, some of which are:

✔ Interest.
✔ Compounding effect.
✔ Reinvestment rate.
✔ Discount rate.

Understanding the time value of money makes the reciprocal relationship—present value—become rather rudimentary. The future value equation states: "The dollar ($) value at a compounded rate of 10 percent for five years will be worth the future value"; while the present value asks the question "What is the dollar value ($) in five years at 10 percent per year worth today?"

The net present value (NPV) equation is the quantification of a cash flow diagram illustrating each movement of capital over time. In essence, the NPV is the calculation of the present value of the entire stream of movements. The following diagram should help in the understanding of this investment construct:

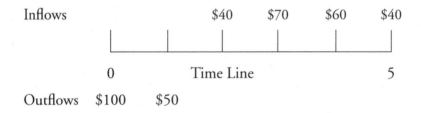

As illustrated, this hypothetical project (ranging from a company's campaign exercise in market share penetration through acquisition to a real estate venture) has an initial cost (cash outflow) of $100 and a subsequent (year 1) outflow of $50 (many projects require a continued cash outflow in the early years) and inflows (years 2–5) as described.

Typically, the corporate budgeting and finance departments of large firms use advanced versions (with decision trees and probability analysis) of the NPV diagram to determine whether a proposed project has viability. If the NPV is positive (the magnitude is not as important) then it is assumed that the project has merit for inclusion among the firm's new opportunities; however, all this depends, as it often does in finance, on the discount rate used in the diagram. If a project has a positive NPV and does so using a very conservative discount rate (meaning a high rate), this would mean that the project would have a consequently higher rate of return and thereby include more risk. The higher the risk in a given project, the higher the rate of return that must be incorporated in the project.

An annuity is a financial contract that guarantees a certain, absolutely defined cash flow. One can think of an annuity as an NPV diagram where all the payments are outflows (after an initial inflow or investment) of equal amounts.

This chapter will identify, explain, and demonstrate some important mathematical terms. Because the novice investor can learn this material much more effectively through detailed examples than from pages of theory, this chapter will emphasize examples and problem sets.

Just a word on the Present/Future Value and Annuity Tables (see Appendix): Although these tables are used in every financial text and are an accepted methodology for solving these problems, today's practitioner should become far removed from this antiquated methodology. A few hard-earned dollars and a rainy afternoon should permit, under normal circumstances, a foothold into the understandings of a financial calculator. There are few things more imposing than an investor who sports a scientific calculator while discussing an investment portfolio with his financial services provider, whose oversized metallic blue calculator looks more like a new toy than an important tool. Perhaps you can check this financial planner's work by simply "plugging and chugging"; wouldn't it be an exhilarating feeling to catch him making an error? *Now who is the advisor?*

In the problem set to follow and throughout this book, I rely on (as I do every day) the Hewlett-Packard (HP) 12C financial calculator. For the record, in no way, shape, or form do I receive any benefit in endorsing this excellent tool, except for the fact that I believe it will make any practitioner's job that much more efficient. As mentioned, a major commitment is not required to master this instrument—probably the most difficult facet is adjusting oneself to the reverse notation that is the hallmark of these calculators. It is this notation (four [4], enter, five [5], times [x]—would yield the requisite "20") that is like a secret handshake or password that only VFIIs are aware of and able to decipher. So pick one up today and begin to impress your friends with your superb understanding of this often confusing idea of the future value of money (compound interest, present value, etc.).

Future Value of Money

If an investor commits $1,000 of capital to an account that will pay an annual rate of interest of 7 percent, his first year's account balance will be $1,070 or ($1,000 × .07) = $70 worth of interest plus the principal balance of $1,000. Assume the investor leaves this investment account alone (no withdrawals or deposits) for another year (at 7 percent). The balance at the end of year two becomes $1,144.90 or $1,070 plus $74.90 worth of interest. In summary, our investor has profited by $144.90 over two years, in the following manner:

Year 1: $1,000 × 7% = $70 interest

Year 2: $1,000 × 7% = $70 interest

$70 × 7% = $4.90 interest on interest

Total = $144.90

The lender receives $70 interest from the borrower for his commitment of capital; the interest-on-interest ($4.90) is due to compounding, the single factor that separates the notions of simple interest from compound interest.

If our investor kept earning 7 percent for a total of seven years, the account balance would be $1,605.78; this amount is known as the future value. With the future value amount, the interest-on-interest or compounding factor is embedded in the calculation. The mathematical equation for future value is denoted as follows:

$$\$1,000(1.07)^7 \text{ or principal amount } (1 + \text{interest rate})^n$$

There are three methods by which one could calculate the future value of a principal amount (given the rate and number of periods):

1. Using the equation as previously shown.
2. Using a scientific calculator's (HP12C) future value (FV) function.
3. Using the future value tables (see Appendix).

The first two methods are simplified through the use of a calculator, whereas the third method utilizes the "present value factors" tabulated for several rates (1 percent–15 percent) and for many numbers of periods. Let's attempt to solve our example using this table.

We want the Future Value Factor for 7 percent and 7 periods—so we search the table (using the coordinates for n periods and $x\%$) for the corresponding factor—1.6058—and then multiply this factor by the stated dollar amount to calculate the final future value:

$$\$1,000 \ (1.6058) = \$1,605.8$$

As it is already obvious, the factors on the future value table are each equal to the equation:

$$(1+ \text{rate})^n = \text{future value factor (FVF) for } n \text{ periods}$$

Present Value of Money

"Hey Mac, I'll give you $62.27 today for $100 in 7 years; you'll earn a 10 percent rate on your money." This proposition is flawed because we know the interest rate that makes $62.27 into $100 in 7 years is only 7 percent. Algebraically, we can calculate the future value factor as:

$$FV/PV = (1 + i)^n$$

$$100/62.27 = 1.6059 \text{ so } 1.6059 = (1 + i)^n$$

$$1 + i = 1.07 \text{ and then } i = 7\%$$

Present value is what someone will pay today for a cash flow sometime in the future. This cash flow can either be a lump sum (i.e., balloon payment) or a cash flow stream spanning many periods (an annuity). Either way, the methodology is the same—what absolute dollar amount compounded at a designated rate for a certain time would equal the future value amount?

PROBLEM SET: FUTURE VALUE AND PRESENT VALUE

Question

Calculate the following amounts:

A. The FV of $1,000 in 19 years compounded at 5 percent per year.

Answer

$$FV = PV \, \{(1.05)^{19}\}$$

$$= 1,000 \, \{2.527\}$$

$$= \$2,527$$

B. The PV of $643 in 3 years compounded at 11 percent per year.

Answer

$$PV = FV/(1.11)^3$$
$$= 643/1.3676$$
$$= 470.17$$

C. If $300 is invested at a rate of 6 percent, how many years will be needed to generate an ending value of $600?

Answer

$$(1.06)^n = FV/PV$$
$$(1.06)^n = 600/300$$
$$n = 12$$

Note: in the preceding example it would be advised to either use the trial and error method (see Figure 8.8) or a financial calculator. The keystrokes for the HP12C, for this example, are as follows:

$$600 = FV$$
$$-300 = PV \text{ (PV is always inputted as a negative value)}$$
$$6 = i$$
$$0 = PMT$$
$$n = \text{the calculator will yield the answer as "12"}$$

D. Find the value of $100 invested for 5 months at a rate of .8 percent per month.

Answer

$$FV = 100(1.008)^5$$
$$= 100\,(1.0406)$$
$$= \$104.06$$

Net Present Value and Internal Rate of Return

In these cash flow problems we examine an investment with a specified diagram of the inflows and outflows of money to determine the net result or the net present value (NPV). As mentioned, this process is very useful in the evaluation of certain types of investments (real estate, bonds, and in its most basic sense, equities) as well as specific projects.

Example: A real estate project has the following cash flows (an investment is considered an outflow); is it a recommended project given the required rate of return of 10 percent?

Initial investment	$(1,500)
Year 1	$(3,000)
Year 2	$(1,200)
Year 3	$4,900
Year 4	$8,500

Graphically

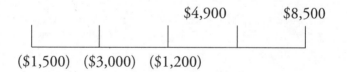

$$NPV = (1,500) + (3,000)/1.10 + (1,200)/(1.10)^2 + 4,900/(1.10)^3 + 8,500/(1.10)^4$$

$$= (1,500) + (3,000)/1.10 + (1,200)/1.21 + 4,900/1.33 + 8,500/1.46$$

Note: The denominators in this equation could also be found by taking the reciprocal (i.e., one divided by) of the future value factor (FVF) corresponding to the *n* periods and 10 percent rate on the Future Value Table. The preceding equation is equivalent to multiplying each dollar value by the corresponding present value factor rather than dividing by the future value factor. Stated empirically, PVF = 1/FVE. Getting back to the preceding equation,

$$= (1,500) + (2,727) + (991) + 3,684 + 5,805 = +4,271$$

As the example demonstrates, the resulting present value is positive and therefore is recommended for investment. It may also be useful in determining the maximum initial amount that could be invested and still expect a positive NPV—in this case it would be $4,271.

This NPV framework is used in many other areas besides real estate, but the premise is always the same; today's value of a stream of inflows and outflows given a specific capitalization rate. But assume you are given the beginning cash flow and the ending cash flow as well as all the cash flows in between, and are asked to calculate the capitalization rate that would make the NPV equal to zero. In other words, you must calculate the expected return over the life of the investment (project); this rate of return is known as the internal rate of return (IRR). The following example is a means to understand the IRR.

Example: A stock is expected to pay a dividend of $1.00, $1.50, and $2.00 in each of the next three years, respectively. At the end of the third year, the stock is expected to sell at a price of $40. The stock is currently priced at $30. What is the expected return over the next three years to an investor who buys the stock?

First dissect the problem by diagramming a cash flow table:

Year	Cash Flow
0	(–$30.00) (This represents the initial investment in the stock)
1	$1.00 (Dividends represent positive cash flow)
2	$1.50 (Same—positive cash flow)
3	$42.00 (Sale of the stock is a cash inflow or receipt plus the $2 dividend received)

Graphically the above would translate as follows:

$1.00 $1.50 $42

(-$30)

To calculate the net present value (NPV), the following equation would be employed:

$$NPV = \frac{CF0}{(1 + i)^0} + \frac{CF1}{(1 + i)^1} + \frac{CF2}{(1 + i)^2} + \frac{CFn}{(1 + i)^n}$$

In this equation, the NPV is the dollar amount resulting from the above discounting of cash flows. The internal rate of return (IRR) is the interest rate that allows the cash flow, when discounted at that rate, to be equal to a zero NPV. In some circumstances, IRR can also be known as the required rate of return, the discount rate, or the capitalization rate.

The next step is to determine the interest rate that, upon discounting each cash flow (years 1–3), would permit a positive value of $30 to thereby offset the negative value of $30 (year 0) and make the net present value equal to zero. Two methods are used to calculate this rate: (1) trial and error and (2) a financial calculator.

In the first method, we are forced to calculate each cash flow's present value using different rates to determine the rate at which the NPV is equal to zero. In our example, we initiate the calculation at 10 percent:

Year	Future Value	Present Value Factor (Table A.3)	Present Value
1	$ 1.00	.9091	$ 0.91
2	1.50	.8264	1.24
3	42.00	.7513	31.55
Total			$33.70

Using the 10 percent rate, we have calculated a positive NPV (-$30 - $33.70 = $3.70) that, in its simplest terms, reflects a profitable transaction. But we are searching for the internal rate of return (IRR) and therefore we now need to adjust the discount or interest rate to decrease the NPV to zero (an increase in the rate will decrease the present value factors and thereby decrease the NPV). This is a key concept—the higher the discount rate (or cap rate, as used in real estate as you will see in Chapter 7), the lower the resulting present value—therefore equity markets are said to be favorable in a lower interest rate environment (the lower rates yield a higher present value). An interest rate equal to 14.5 percent (the present value table only shows those factors for whole numbers; therefore, it is necessary to calculate the factor using either the extrapolation/ trial-and-error techniques or the present value factor equation shown earlier) works out to be the internal rate of return (the rate at which the NPV is equal to zero) and is therefore the rate that is embedded in this project.

If you use a financial calculator, the keystrokes are quite simple (a rudimentary understanding of the notation used is all that it takes) and would yield the same answer (14.5 percent). However, the user is cautioned to make sure that the signs of the cash flows are accurate; that is, the first cash flow must be a negative value (it is an outflow) while all other cash flows are positive. The keystrokes are as follows;

$$-30cf_o; \quad 1cf_j; \quad 1.50cf_j; \quad 42cf_j; \quad IRR \ldots 14.5 \text{ percent}$$

As mentioned, this capitalization rate takes into account the risks associated with the project and would therefore be higher (to compensate the investor) for those projects with greater risk and lower for those with less. Intuitively, one could assume that this capitalization rate may change throughout the life of the project at hand; risk is higher in the early going and then tends to decrease as the project becomes more viable. These changing inputs—both the amount and the direction (inflow or outflow) of the cash flows and the capitalization rates—make the NPV framework unique.

The process of calculating the NPV of a cash flow diagram—in this case an investment—is also used to determine the rate of return an investor would achieve given the investment parameters. As we will see in the Investment Management chapter (Chapter 8), investors in various instruments—from bonds to mutual funds—can use this construct to calculate and compare their investment returns. It is important to utilize this mathematical construct, rather than the simplistic arithmetic equation, to ensure accurate assessment of the investment's returns (using the above figures an arithmetic return would be $10 from the appreciation of the stock, and $4.50 from dividends on a $30 investment over 3 years would be 16 percent—overstating the return substantially and ignoring the time value of money—more on this, again, in Chapter 8).

Annuities

In an annuity, the cash flows and the capitalization rate are the same for the life of the investment. To value an annuity, the investor needs to discount each cash flow at the same capitalization rate to arrive at a present value. This exercise may be familiar to anyone who has been offered the choice of a lump sum or annuity payout on a retirement plan (or lottery ticket!); the choice becomes whether the investor expects to be able to invest the lump sum at a higher rate (over the period) than is assumed in the annuity.

Example: Assume that an annuity of three payments, each equal to $100 is made annually at the end of each year. (Most annuities are assumed to be "ordinary annuity" or "in arrears," where the cash flow payment is assumed to come at the end of the period. An adjustment should be made in calculating annuity with payments received in the beginning of the period). Once received, each payment is invested to earn an interest rate of 10 percent. How much will the total value of the resulting sum be worth at the end of the third year?

Here again, as with any of these cash flow problems, we begin by diagramming the cash flows:

Year	Amount	Future Value Factor	Future Value
1	$100	1.21	$121
2	100	1.10	110
3	100	1.00	100
Total			$331

The first year's $100 payment will receive two years (the full second year and third year) worth of interest and is therefore awarded the highest future value factor, while the last payment does not receive any interest (received at end of year 3 when the annuity stops earning interest).

The future value of this annuity (as shown) is simply the sum of these three calculations. Generalized, this calculation can be written for n payments (let i = interest rate and PMT = cash flow):

$$FV = PMT [(1 + i)^0 + (1 + i)^1 + (1 + i)^2 + \cdots + (1 + i)^{n-1}]$$

The arithmetic in the equation has by now grown to be somewhat intuitive. There certainly must be a better way to calculate an annuity, as I am sure you are asking yourself right now. Well, there is—the Future Value (and Present Value) of an Annuity Tables (see Appendix Tables A.2–A.5).

Before tackling the eye-distorting annoyance of those tables, it is essential to understand the algebra behind those columns of tiny figures:

$$FVFA = \text{Future Value Factor of an Annuity}$$

$$FVFA = [(1 + i)^n - 1/i]$$

So now we solve our future value problems with the following equation:

$$FV = \text{Annuity PMT [FVFA]}$$

Redoing the previous problem using this new formula:

$$FV = \$100 (3.31) = \$331$$

Note: The FVFA can be found either on Table A.4 or simply through the following algebra:

$$FVFA = [(1.10)^3 - 1/.10]$$
$$= (3.31)$$

Now look at the annuity problem for the other side, that is, present value. It can be quite advantageous to an investor to understand the value (in today's dollars) of some future, periodic, equal cash flow payments. Assume that a somewhat naive NFII is told by a more than slightly pedantic VFII that the previously illustrated annuity stream (a $100 "ordinary annuity" for three years at 10 percent per year) could be purchased today for $248. Before accepting a *sounds-too-good-to-be-true* investment, NFII asks VFII to illustrate the annuity investment in a more detailed format (this particular NFII happens to be a lawyer, just our luck, who is somewhat versed in the area of proper due diligence):

Year	Annuity PMT	PV Factor	PV
0	What we are attempting to calculate		
1	$100	.9091	$ 90.91
2	100	.8264	82.64
3	100	.7513	75.13
Total			$248.68

So, in this case, the VFII continues, "an investor need only pay $248.68 for this annuity to achieve an internal rate of return of 10 percent." The professorial VFII then goes on to illustrate the algebraic methodology behind the numbers:

PVFA = Present Value Factor of an Annuity

PVFA = $\{1 - (1 + i)^{-n}/i\}$ or alternatively, PVFA = $\{1/i - 1/i(1 + i)^n\}$

In our case, the PFVA works out to be (this can also be found in Table A.3):

$$PVFA = \{1 - (1.10)^{-3}/.10\}$$

$$= 2.4869$$

Once armed with this factor, the balance of the problem becomes rudimentary (simply apply the following equation):

$$PV \text{ (of annuity)} = PMT \text{ (PFVA)}$$

"Now for good ol' plugging and chugging," says the increasingly bombastic VFII:

$$PV \text{ (of annuity)} = \$100 \text{ (2.4868)} = \$248.68$$

This type of equation comes into play more often than one would first imagine. Let's say that you are being awarded a settlement in a personal injury lawsuit and the insurance company had agreed to pay you a certain lump sum in damages. As the negotiations progress they suddenly come back to you (and your lawyers, of course) with an annuity payout structure. Well, with a little knowledge of PVA mathematics, you can make sure that that valuation of this annuity is in line with your lump sum award—be especially careful with the assumed interest rate, for it can make a big difference (the higher the rate—that is, the higher the compounding rate—the lower the present value). A good rule of thumb might be the current rate on the 10-year Treasury bond or a similar low risk, fixed rate investment. Of course one always, especially these days, needs to be mindful of the credit worthiness of the issuer— the insurance company—as we will learn in the Credit Analysis chapter (Chapter 6).

Using the HP12C Financial Calculator

As mentioned from the outset we have no financial motivation (except for a few shares of Hewlett in a few accounts, possibly) to recommend the HP12C, but nevertheless it is an essential tool for any VFII. While its reverse notation takes a little getting used to, once you master it you will never go back. Following please find problems that we solve using the HP as a means to sharpen your skills with its use:

Question

An investor invested $10,000 into a mutual fund on 12/31/03 and on 12/31/08 it was worth $9,000, what was the average return over the life of the investment?

Answer

Plug in the following:

10000 CHS PV (this represents the $10,000 investment that we always show as an outflow by using the negative sign with the CHS button.

9000 FV (representing the future value of the fund)

0 PMT (representing no additional cash flows in between the time periods)

5 *n* (representing the 5 years of the investment)

We should now see the HP "running" and a second or two later show a –2.0852 or an average loss of 2.08 percent

Using the HP12C Financial Calculator *(Continued)*

Question

Same example as above—in each year since the initial investment was made, the investor added $1,000 (that is $1,000 added on 12/31 of 2004, 2005, 2006, 2007) and before adding it on 12/31/08, he wondered what his return had been since inception.

Answer

10,000 CHS g (blue key) and CF0 (also blue)—this represents the initial outflow

1000 CHS g CFj—this represents the next cash flow

4 g Nj represents the number of times this outflow repeats consecutively

9000 (no negative because it is a positive or current value) g CFj

f (yellow key) and IRR (also yellow) will yield the answer of –10 percent

How about some "bond math"—how can we "price" accurately a bond that is quoted to us by our FSPs? Okay, let's say that our FSP calls today (January 15, 2009) and offers us a municipal bond (more on these in Chapter 6 on Credit Analysis) that matures on April 1, 2016 at par. This bond pays an annual coupon of 3 percent and is being offered at a yield to maturity of 4 percent. What is the dollar price of the bond?

Keystrokes

4 *i* (represents the yield to maturity of 4 percent)

3 PMT (this sets the coupon rate)

g MDY (this sets the date format as month, date, year)

1.152009 ENTER (sets the purchase date)

4.012016 (represents the maturity date)

f PRICE yields the answer: 93.7872 (of par) or $937.87 per bond the "+" sign will yield the price including accrued interest ($94.8809 or $946.60)

Okay, so let's say after hearing all of this, you say to your FSP, "Hey Bob, that sounds okay, but I was looking for something more in the 4.25 percent yield range—Can you do this one for 4.25 percent YTM?" What will the dollar price of the bond have to be to yield 4.25 percent?

> ### Using the HP12C Financial Calculator *(Continued)*
>
> **Keystrokes**
>
> 4.25 *i* (representing the new yield to maturity desired)
>
> All other strokes are the same. The answer is 92.3043. Can you imagine what your FSP would say if you were doing this calculation while he was "pitching" you the bond and then you said, "Well Bob, if you can do the bonds at 92.30 so as to yield 4.25 percent, I will take 200." Two things will happen: First he will ask if he can call you back (he needs to see if the "desk" can offer the bonds at that price), and the second thing is a level of respect that will develop for you and your acumen that will serve as a goodwill factor in your relationship for years to come.

PROBLEM SET: INVESTMENT MATHEMATICS

Present Value and Future Value

Question 1

Find the future value of $100 invested for 5 years at a 6 percent interest rate.

Answer

Using Appendix Table A.2, find the Future Value Factor (FVF) for a 6 percent interest rate (horizontal axis) for 5 years (vertical axis). This factor, 1.3382, is then multiplied by the investment amount, $100, to calculate the total future value—$133.82.

Question 2

Find the present value of $500 to be received in 4 years using 8 percent as a discount rate.

Answer

Using Appendix Table A.1, find the Present Value Factor (PVF) for an 8 percent interest rate for 4 years. This factor, 0.7350, is then multiplied by the investment amount, $500, to calculate the total present value—$367.50.

Question 3

What would $100 in 10 years be worth today, assuming a discount rate of 11 percent?

Answer

This problem also calls for the use of Table A.1. The PVF is 0.3522 (on the table, given the vertical and horizontal values) and is then multiplied by $100 (as per the "given" of the table) to get a present value today of $35.22.

Question 4

This first problem requires a scientific calculator.

A. Find the rate of return that turns $200 into $300 over five years.

B. Estimate (without using a calculator) the rate of return that turns $100 into $200 in 10 years.

C. Again, without using a calculator: If $300 is invested at a rate of 6 percent, how many years will be needed to generate an ending value (FV) of $600?

Answer

Using an HP12C or similar calculator:

A. Enter the following:

−200 PV (this is the present value and is shown as a negative to represent an outflow).

300 FV (the future value or the amount expected in the future).

5 n (the number of periods or in most cases, years).

0 PMT (there have been no additions or subtractions to this stream).

i (this represents the interest rate).

You may see "running" go across your calculator.

The answer should show as 8.447 percent (this represents the internal rate of return).

B. Rule of 72: a rough estimate of the number of years it takes to double. In this case, the investment doubled in 10 years; therefore, the estimate of the average annual rate of return is 7.2 percent, because by dividing 72 by 10 you get 7.2 percent.

C. Using the Rule of 72, we can estimate that it will take about 12 years for this investment to double (72 divided by 6 is 12 years).

Annuities

Question 1

Find the future value of a 5-year annuity consisting of payments of $100 per year invested at an interest rate of 6 percent per year.

Answer

Using Appendix Table A.4, find the Future Value Factor of Annuity (FVFA) for 5 years at 6 percent. This FVFA is 5.6371; multiply this factor by the investment amount to ascertain the value of the cash flow stream (annuity). The future value is $563.71. The intuitive approach of simply adding five contributions of $100 each is not correct because of the interest each year on an increasing principal amount.

Question 2

Find the present value of a $100 per year, 10-year annuity, discounted at an 8 percent rate.

Answer

Using Appendix Table A.3, find the Present Value Factor of Annuity (PVFA) for 10 years at an 8 percent interest rate. This PVFA is 6.7101; simply multiply the investment amount (in this case, $100) by this factor to ascertain the present value of this cash flow stream—$671.01.

Question 3

For $10,000, one can buy a seven-year annuity that will pay $2,000 per year. What is the rate of return on their annuity?

Answer

Using a scientific calculator, plug in the following data:

$$-10000 \text{ PV}; 7 \text{ } n; 2000 \text{ PMT}, 0 \text{ FV}; I \ldots 9.19\%$$

Question 4

An investor is putting $2,000 per year into a mutual fund that averages a return of 9 percent per year. How many years will these payments have to be made before the fund will be worth $100,000 (rough estimate only)?

Answer

Using Appendix Table A.5, first ask yourself what factor we would need to multiply by $2,000 to get $100,000? This factor is about 50. How many years at 9 percent do we need to get a factor of about 50? By going down the 9-percent column we see that at about 20 years we get a 50 FVFA.

Question 5

A person takes out a $200,000 mortgage loan to be paid monthly over the next 360 months at an annualized interest rate of 8 percent compounded monthly. Find the monthly payment.

Answer

Using a scientific calculator, plug in the following data:

$$-200,000 \text{ PV}; 0 \text{ FV}; 8\% /12 \text{ i}; 360 \text{ n}; \text{PMT} \dots$$
"running" . . . $1,467.53

Net Present Value and Internal Rates of Return

Question 1

An investment has the following cash flow. Calculate the NPV (assume a 10 percent discount rate):

Year	Cash Flows (CF)
0	−$3,000
1	−$5,000
2	$2,000
3	$4,000
4	$6,000
5	−$1,000

Answer

$$\text{NPV} = -3,000 + \frac{(5,000)}{(1.10)} + \frac{2,000}{(1.10)^2} + \frac{4,000}{(1.10)^3} + \frac{6,000}{(1 + 10)^4} + \frac{-1,000}{(1.10)^5}$$

NPV = −3,000 + (4,545.45) + 1,652.89 + 3,005.25 + 4,098.08 − 620.92

NPV = 589.85

Question 2

An investment that costs $10,000 produces a cash flow of $3,000, $4,000, and $6,000 in each of the next three years. One could solve for the IRR using a scientific calculator:

Answer

Using a scientific calculator, plug in the following data:

> −$10000 CF0; 3000 CF1; 4000 CF2; 6000 CF3 . . .
> IRR . . . running . . . 12.71 percent is the answer.

This means that a 12.71 percent annual return over the life of the investment is earned given the cash flows described above. Now let's compare this return to what someone might estimate it to be using simple— that is, noncompounding—arithmetic. Okay, so we have an investment of $10,000 and a return of $13,000 over three years. A $3,000 profit on a $10,000 investment is 30 percent over three years, which is an "average" return of 10 percent. But of course this simple math ignores the time value of money, as well as common sense (for you could have earned interest on that $10,000 over the three years if you did not "invest" it). Therefore, the simple arithmetic equation will always undercut the value of a compounded investment.

4

Quantitative Analysis

n this chapter you will learn:

- ✔ Basic statistical constraints.
- ✔ Regression equation analysis.

In Chapters 1 through 3, we studied the tools that were, for the most part, solely tied to the investment field. This final chapter in Part 1 focuses on the scientific art of quantitative analysis. Quantitative analysis has its roots in statistics and its branches reach far into many scientific disciplines. In the investment field, the use of statistics and other more specific tools of quantitative analysis have become a critical part of the work of financial analysts. Whether your interests are merely basic investment planning or more intensive analysis, proper portfolio management and investment result presentation require the use of quantitative analysis.

In quantitative analysis, as in most mathematical fields, each piece of the discipline builds on some basic tenets. Statistics is the foundation on which we build our quantitative analysis structure.

Basic Statistics

Measures of Central Tendency

The use of statistics enables us to summarize data accurately without overwhelming the user in numerical minutia. Each of us, in our own profession, has probably come across a numerical task that leaves us fiddling with the basic arithmetic and missing the big picture. Statistics permits users the ease of seeing the big picture and then moving along to the task at hand. In the simplest of examples, consider the hypothetical company (ABC Products, Inc.) that produces widgets. ABC has several different product lines for specific market niches (each with their particular unit price) that present a confusing database for effective analysis. Note the following example:

ABC Products, Inc.—Product Analysis		
Product	Unit Price ($)	Profit Margin (%)
Consumer product	20	20
Commercial product	40	15
Government product	10	10
International product	50	30

What does the data tell us, besides the niche diversification, about the business of ABC Products, Inc.? Can we use the figures to analyze the business? Are we able to make some forecasts about future business?

When confronted with the task of quantitative analysis, the first step is to summarize the data using some basic statistical constructs. Before continuing with the ABC Products data, it is necessary to understand some of these basic constructs.

Arithmetic Mean　This is usually referred to as an "average" of a set of numerical values. The mean is the most commonly used measure of return (not compounded) in investment finance. Although its mathematical notation can seem a little frightening to those not familiar with such notation, its definition and application are understood by most third graders. We simply add all the observations together and divide by the number of observations.

Mean Equation in Scientific Notation

$$\frac{\sum_{i=1}^{N} X_i}{N}$$

The mean is the sum Σ (sigma) of all observations of X from the first (X_i) to the Nth divided by the population size (N). (Note: if it was a sample size, use $N - 1$.)

The underlying concept implied by the use of an average is that all the observations (figures) in a specific database (population) are of equal significance and are therefore represented equally by this calculated average. However, this can make the mean calculation a misleading figure; a highly diverse group of data cannot be represented by a single average that does not take into account the particular vagaries and nuances of each value.

For example, it is simple to calculate the average unit price of the widgets produced by ABC Products:

$$\$20 + 40 + 10 + 50 = \$120$$
$$\$120/4 = \$30$$

Therefore, $30 per unit is the average unit price.

What is the average profit margin for ABC?

$$20\% + 15\% + 10\% + 30\% = 75\%$$
$$75\%/4 = 18.75\%$$

Therefore, the average profit margin for ABC is 18.75 percent.

But now let's add a further nugget of information: namely, ABC sells most of its product (more than 85 percent of revenues) to the government. As such, the average unit price of $30 and the average profit margin of 18.75 percent is not really representative of the true economic performance of the company. These averages overstate the actual average unit price and profit margin of the company as a whole, because the low-price and low-margin government segment accounts for so much of the company's total revenues. It should now be obvious, if it wasn't already, how dangerous it can be to rely on strict averages without understanding their economic derivations.

Geometric Mean (Average) The main use of the geometric mean in investment analysis is to average changes over time. Once again, the mathematical notation can be quite intensive for even the most mathematically sophisticated investor:

Geometric Mean

$$[(1 + X_1)(1 + X_2) \ldots (1 + X_n)^{1/n} - 1]$$

The basic meaning behind the geometric mean is the law of compounding and therefore it is typically seen in the calculation of the compounded annual growth rate (CAGR).

In the case of ABC Products, the geometric mean of the profit margins (assuming each product is sold in subsequent years; i.e., consumer products are sold only in 2005, commercial products only in 2006, government products only in 2007, and international products only in 2008) can be calculated as follows:

$$= \{(1.20)\ (1.15)\ (1.10)\ (1.30)\}^{\wedge}.25 - 1$$
$$= \{1.9734\}^{\wedge}.25 - 1$$

Note: We use the decimal value of 1/4 (.25) in the calculation of the exponent. In calculating this equation using the HP 12C calculator, simply enter .25 and then the y^x key.

$$= 1.1852 - 1$$
$$= 18.52\%$$

Therefore, the annual compounded profit margin is 18.52 percent.

The geometric mean is expected to be slightly less than the arithmetic mean, due to the essence of compounding. This fact becomes important to the investor who is evaluating the returns of a given investment opportunity—the CAGR removes some of the volatility inherent in arithmetic average calculation.

Median   The median is the middle value in a stream of observations aligned in increasing numerical order. It is the value that divides the stream exactly in half; one half will lie above the median and the other half will lie below the median. If the data set has an *odd* number of data points, then the median is simply the value that lies in the exact middle of the stream when arranged in increasing numerical order. If the data set has an *even* number of data points, then the median is the average of the two data points that lie in the middle of the stream. Thus, in the ABC Products example, the median would be $30. The unit prices are arranged in increasing order ($10, $20, $40, $50) and the median is the average of the two middle data points (average of $20 and $40 = $30).

Mode   This statistic represents the most frequently occurring observation in a given database. It is less sensitive to extreme values in the database (outliers) than either the mean or the median.

In the ABC Products example, the mode is undefined because there is no repetitive value in either the unit cost or profit margin databases.

Measures of Dispersion

The preceding statistical constructs center around the notion of *central tendency*. Central tendency describes the tendency of data to cluster or group along a particular value. Mean (arithmetic and geometric), median, and mode all describe this clustering effect, although each has its own measurement format. This section in the basic statistics discussion focuses on the dispersion of a specific piece of data from its central value (be it mean, median, or mode). When describing the effects of dispersion on data, we turn to the following constructs:

Range This refers to the distance between the lowest and the highest data value. The range can be disrupted by extreme or unusual values; these "outliers" are often ignored to provide a remedy to this problem, but the astute investor must keep such outliers in mind to remember that, in rare occasions, extreme values are possible.

Turning to our simplistic example of ABC Products:

The range for unit prices is reflected by {$10, $50}.

The range for profit margin is reflected by {10 percent, 30 percent}.

The use of range can tell us very little about the actual dispersion around a central value given a specific data set. Therefore, we must introduce another statistical construct that becomes crucial in the study of finance, to more accurately describe the dispersion or variation in a data set. The following three measures of dispersion are most commonly used in investment finance.

Variation The difference between each value (observation) and the mean of the data set is its variation. The following notation describes this constant mathematically:

Variation Equation

$$\sum_{i=1}^{n} (X_i - \overline{X})$$

The total variation in a data set is always summed to zero: Each positive variation is canceled out by an exact negative variation in the data set. For example, consider the following simple set of observations: 10 percent (Observation 1) and 5 percent (Observation 2). From this, we can see that the variation of +2.5 (10% minus the mean of 7.5%) exactly offsets the variation of −2.5 (5% minus the mean of 7.5%). Because of this characteristic, the variation measure is not very useful except to allow a foundation for the easy calculation of other measures.

Variance   Variance is the sum (sigma) of all X observations minus the mean, (X̄) squared and then divided by the population size (N) or by a sample size N − 1.

Variance Equation

$$\frac{\sum_{i=1}^{N} (X_i - \overline{X})^2}{N}$$

This measure is calculated in the exact manner as variation, except that in variance the variation between the observed value and its mean is squared. By squaring the individual variations, all negative values are eliminated, thereby permitting a total variance value greater than 0. It is important to note that the total variance (before being divided by the population size or N) does not equal 0 as in the case of variation where the signs are positive and negative (the squaring of the individual variations eliminates the negatives). The critical interpretation feature of variance is that the higher the variance the more disperse the population. Furthermore, we now are able to use this dispersion value to some statistical significance. Or are we? (Implementing a simple spreadsheet program facilitates the number crunching.) The ABC Products data (see box on page 98) can serve as an example.

Unit Price	Mean	Variation	Variance
20	30	−10	100
40	30	10	100
10	30	−20	400
50	30	20	400

Total Variation: 0
Total Variance: 1,000
Variance: 1,000 divided by N (or 4) = 250

Although the math in the preceding statistical summary is correct, what about the interpretation? How does one describe the units in the variance value? Would we describe it as "dollars squared?" What would that mean? So while the variance equation is helpful in the calculation of dispersion by eliminating the problematic effects of the negative variation values, it introduces a new problem: definable units of measurement. However, our statistical friends also worked around this units-of-measurement problem—they took the square root of the variance in order to yield a more unit-sensitive value called *standard deviation.*

Standard Deviation Calculated as simply the square root of the variance, standard deviation was developed to provide a more realistic and definable unit of measure (it is measured in the same units as the average). A major advantage in using the standard deviation (as well as the variance) to quantify the dispersion in a data set is that it takes every value into account, not just the highest and lowest (as in the range). The following represents the standard deviation—scientific equation:

Standard Deviation—Scientific Equation

$$\sqrt{\frac{\sum_{i=1}^{n}(X_i - \overline{X})^2}{N}}$$

Standard deviation is the square root of the variance. In other words, take the sum of all the X observations minus the mean, squared, and then divide by the population (or sample size minus one) size and then take the square root.

Confidence Limits

With the standard deviation measure, we can apply probability constraints, although only when the distributions are normally distributed (that is, mean equal to 0 and standard deviation equal to entire distribution). Normally distributed data sets (or populations) are similar to a standardization—formulating the data in such a way that it conforms

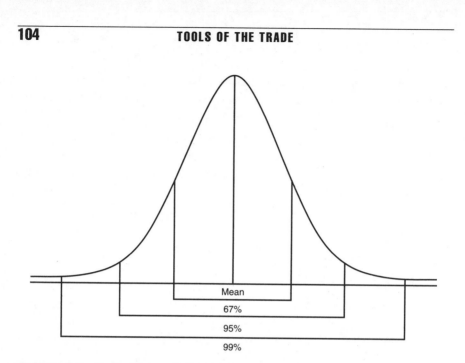

FIGURE 4.1   Typical normal distribution curve.

to a particular template so that its information may be studied under certain parameters.

Symmetrical distributions are those where the mean, mode, and median are all equal and thereby the distribution would resemble the curve in Figure 4.1. The normal distribution represents a certain kind of symmetrical relationship in which the mean is equal to zero and its standard deviation is equal to the entire distribution.
The following normal distribution curve describes the probabilistic inferences drawn from a typical data set:

- There is a 68 percent probability that an item in a population will have a value that is within one standard deviation on either side of the mean.

- There is a 95 percent probability that an item in a population will have a value that is within two standard deviations on either side of the mean.

- There is a 99 percent probability that an item in a population will have a value that is within three standard deviations on either side of the mean.

Example: If earnings per share are expected to be $5 (therefore, by definition, $5 is the mean) with a standard deviation of +/− $0.50, then we can state that:

Confidence Limits *(Continued)*

✔ There is a 68 percent chance that the actual earnings per share will be between 4.50 and $5.50:

1 standard deviation ($.50) plus observation value ($5) is equal to $5.50.

1 standard deviation ($.50) minus observation value ($5) is equal to $4.50.

✔ There is a 95 percent chance that actual earnings per share will be between $4 and $6:

2 standard deviations ($1.00) plus observation value ($5) is equal to $6.00.

2 standard deviations ($1.00) minus observation value ($5) is equal to $4.00.

✔ There is a 99 percent chance that actual earnings per share will be between $3.50 and $6.50:

3 standard deviations ($1.50) plus observation value ($5) is equal to $6.50.

3 standard deviations ($1.50) minus observation value ($5) is equal to $3.50.

The standard deviation measure can also be used in the understanding of investment portfolio risk or volatility. If a portfolio is said to have an average rate of return of 13 percent (e.g., over a 5-year period), with a standard deviation of 20 percent, then we could state the following:

✔ There is a 68 percent chance that the returns will fall between −7 percent (that is, the average return minus one standard deviation, or 13% − 20%) and +33 percent (that is, the average return plus one standard deviation, or 13% + 20%).

✔ There is a 95 percent chance (or stated differently, a 5 percent confidence) that the returns will fall between two standard deviations, or −27 percent (i.e., 13% − 2 × 20%) and 53 percent (i.e., 13% + 2 × 20%).

✔ There is a 99 percent chance that the returns will fall between three standard deviations, or −47 percent (i.e., 13% − 3 × 20%) and 73 percent (i.e., 13% + 3 × 20%).

PROBLEM SET: BASIC STATISTICS

Question 1

Consider the following set of numbers:

$$4, 23, 12, 7, 14, 7, 11, 20, 1, 25, 4, 13, 7, 2, 15$$

Calculate the following:

The mean: _____

The median: _____

The mode: _____

The range: { _____ }

The variation: _____

(*Note.* The sum of the individual variations is always 0.)

The variance: _____

The standard deviation: _____

The first step is to calculate the set of summary statistics for the above sample:

Summary Statistics		
X	(X-mean)	(X-mean)²
4	−7	49
23	12	144
12	1	1
7	−4	16
14	3	9
7	−4	16
11	0	0
20	9	81
1	−10	100
25	14	196
4	−7	49
13	2	4

Summary Statistics *(Continued)*		
X	(X-mean)	(X-mean)^2
7	−4	16
2	−9	81
15	4	16
Total 165	0	778
N 15		
Mean 11		

Now, we can use this data to answer the questions at hand (read further), as well as to extrapolate inferences into the future (see the following Regression Analysis appendix).

Answer

> Mean: 11
>
> Median: 11
>
> Mode: 7
>
> Range: {1, 25}
>
> Variation: 0 (as per definition)
>
> Variance: 51.86 (units are undefined)
>
> Standard Deviation: 7.20

Question 2

What is the geometric mean (compounded annual growth rate), arithmetic mean, variance, and standard deviation of the following set of return figures?

> 2004   9%
>
> 2005   21%
>
> 2006   11%
>
> 2007   −3%
>
> 2008   29%

	X	(X-mean)	(X-mean)^2
2004	9%	−4.4	19.36
2005	21	7.6	57.76
2006	11	−2.4	5.76
2007	−3	−16.4	268.96
2008	29	15.6	243.36
Total	67	0	595.20
N 5			
Mean	13.4		

Answer

Geometric mean: 12.87%   Variance: 119.04 (units undefined)

Standard deviation: 10.91%   Mean: 13.4%

Appendix—Regression Analysis

Regression is the analysis of the relationship between one variable and some other variable(s). In essence, regression is the means by which data (as discussed in this chapter) and the variation in that data are used to help make *predictions* (and as we know, predictions of the future are of primary concern to investors!). In regression, there are two types of variables: the dependent variable (the "explained variable," "endogenous variable," or the "predicted variable") and the independent variable (the "explanatory variable" or the "exogenous variable"). The dependent variable is thought of as the variable whose value depends on the other variable(s), and the independent variable is the variable that is being used to explain the dependent variable.

Linear regression is the technique used to determine the extent of a change in one variable (dependent variable) resulting from a change in another (independent variable). Because of the linear assumptions of regression, it is critical to first express the relationship between variables in a linear equation:

$$y = \alpha + \beta x$$

where:

y = the value of the dependent variable ascertained by the equation

α = the y axis (vertical) intercept; referred to as alpha

x = the values of the independent variable

β = a measure of covariance (relationship) between the two variables; referred to as beta

It is essential to first understand that regression begins with the variation of the independent variable around the mean, and then uses that variation to explain the variation in *another* variable (the dependent variable). This "variation analysis" is the very first step with regression where we formulate a set of summary statistics to use throughout our analysis. The example following may help shed some light on this area.

Assume that we want to see the effect of air pollution (measured in "toxic" particles per 1 millionth cubic inch of air) during the winter (in New York City) months on sales of precipitators (electrical devices that remove air particles). Precise Precipitators, Inc. has provided the following data:

Precise Precipitators, Inc.		
	Pollution	Sales
	(Particles/0.000001)	Revs ($000s)
	X	Y
Nov. 07	4,500	$95
Dec. 07	3,200	78
Jan. 08	7,500	141
Feb. 08	11,000	290

Note: The dependent variable is always X and the independent variable is always Y. Due to the small number of observations, the degrees of freedom was 0 ($N = 4$).

The first thing to do is to calculate the data's summary statistics (see Table 4.1).

Mean of pollution (X):	6,550
Mean of precipitator sales (Y):	151
Sum of variation from mean for each X variable:	0
Total variance in X:	9,032,500
Sum of variation from mean for each Y variable:	0
Total variance in Y:	6,972
Standard deviation of X:	3,005.41
Standard deviation of Y:	83.49

TABLE 4.1   Precise Precipitators, Inc.—Summary Statistics

	Data		Variation		Variance		Covariance
	X	Y	(X-mean)	(Y-mean)	x^2	y^2	xy
Nov. 07	4,500	95	−2,050	−56	4,202,500	3,136	114,800
Dec. 07	3,200	78	−3,350	−73	11,222,500	5,329	244,550
Jan. 08	7,500	141	950	−10	902,500	100	−9,500
Feb. 08	11,000	290	4,450	139	19,802,500	19,321	618,550
Total			0	0	36,130,000	27,886	968,400
Mean	6,550	151					
Total Variance					9,032,500	6,972	

Once the summary statistics are in place, we can proceed onto the calculation of some more defined statistics.

Covariance

This is a measure of correlation between sets of variables:

1. Multiply each variable's variation from its mean by the other variable's variation from its mean.

$$\text{That is: } [(X_i - \overline{X})(Y_i - \overline{Y})]$$

2. Add each of the preceding products to get total variation.

$$\text{That is: } \sum_{i=1}^{N} [(X_i - \overline{X})(Y_i - \overline{Y})]$$

3. Divide (2) by $N - 1$ (number of observations) to get covariance.

$$\text{Covariance (between } X \text{ and } Y) = \frac{\sum_{i=1}^{N} [(X_i - \overline{X})(Y_i - \overline{Y})]}{N - 1}$$

As the preceding equation indicates, some statistics need to be adjusted by the number of observations minus one (instead of dividing by N). This adjustment is not of a critical nature (without it one would yield a very similar estimate) but it should be noted that the amount subtracted from N increases with an increased number of estimates (as in multiple regression). This is referred to as "degrees of freedom."

Correlation

This measures the "goodness of fit" of a regression relationship.

$$\text{Correlation} = \frac{\text{Cov} X_1 Y}{(\text{Stan dev } X)(\text{Stan dev } Y)}$$

Correlation coefficients range between -1 and $+1$.

-1 is perfectly negatively correlated.

0 is no correlation.

$+1$ is perfectly positively correlated.

Note: In the world of finance, the extremes $+1$ and -1 are not normally observable and therefore are said to not exist. A perfectly negatively correlated hedge between two assets represents a perfect inverse relationship. The same holds true for the correlation of $+1$, which would represent a perfect direct relationship. Although much time and effort are devoted to achieving these perfect hedges (through a heavy commitment to quantitative models and financial engineering using derivatives) transaction costs and liquidity premiums (spreads between buy and sell prices) make it impractical and therefore relegated to the annals of theory.

Coefficient of Determination (or "R-squared"): This statistic calculates the amount of variation (in percent) of the dependent variable (Y variable) that is explained by the regression equation. The higher the R-squared, the stronger the regression equation.

$$R^2 = \text{Correlation squared}$$

Simple Regression Example

Note: This example is used for simple illustration purposes only. Due to its simplicity, this example serves as an excellent illustration of the basics of regression analysis. However, the reader is cautioned that the implications of this example may be flawed in a strict statistical sense. Due to the high correlation between the variables, this regression may suffer from "multicollinearity," which would dilute the model's statistical significance.

This notwithstanding, the example serves as a template to the functioning and procedure involved with regression.

As a hardware store owner, Mr. Jones wanted a better way to forecast how many snow shovels he might need for the upcoming winter season. Because snow shovels are a seasonal item and are quite cumbersome in Mr. Jones' small retail space, he felt it was critical to attempt to ascertain the very best estimate so that the store would not be burdened with storing the shovels during the off-season.

In discussions about this project with his business manager, Mr. Jones agreed that there must be some relationship between snowfall (in his area) and demand for snow shovels. This was quite obvious; but how can Mr. Jones quantify the relationship to permit a forecast? Mr. Jones's business manager suggests regression analysis. He explains that by using previous years' data of snowfall and snow shovel sales, they could extrapolate the relationship which would allow forecasting for the next winter. Once the coefficients of the equation are calculated, the anticipated snowfall for the upcoming season can be inputted and an estimate for sales calculated. Mr. Jones realizes that the variability of weather cannot be truly estimated, but feels confident in the written forecasts (for snowfall) of the *Farmer's Almanac.*

Therefore the business manager completed the following analysis:

The regression equation is $Y = \alpha + \beta X$.

Alpha (α) represents the y-intercept, or the amount of snow shovel sales if there were 0 inches of snowfall.

Beta (β) represents the slope or the ratio between the change in snowfall and the change in sales of shovels.

Using the data in Table 4.2 we first must calculate the following (note we are using the sample size calculation of $N - 1$):

Variance of X:	$221.60/9 = 24.62$
Standard deviation of X:	Square root of $24.62 = 4.962$
Variance of Y:	$1{,}606{,}010/9 = 178{,}445$
Standard deviation of Y:	Square root of $178{,}445 = 422.42$
Covariance of X and Y:	$16{,}496/9 = 1{,}832$
Correlation coefficient:	$r = 1{,}832/(4.962)(422.42) = 0.874$
Coefficient of determination:	$R^2 = (0.874)(0.874) = 0.7639$ or 76.39%

	X: Snow (inches)	Y: Shovel Sales ($)	X	Y	X^2	Y^2	XY
Month-Yr.							
Nov. 07	12	$1,020	3.8	$153	14.44	23,409	581.4
Dec. 07	15	1,300	6.8	433	46.24	187,489	2,944.4
Jan. 08	11	1,500	2.8	633	7.84	400,689	1,772.4
Feb. 08	13	1,000	4.8	133	23.04	17,689	638.4
Mar. 08	3	700	−5.2	(167)	27.04	27,889	868.4
Nov. 08	6	500	−2.2	(367)	4.84	134,689	807.4
Dec. 08	2	300	−6.2	(567)	38.44	321,489	3,515.4
Jan. 09	11	1,200	2.8	333	7.84	110,889	932.4
Feb. 09	8	900	−0.2	33	0.04	1,089	−6.6
Mar. 09	1	250	−7.2	(617)	51.84	380,689	4,442.4
Total	82	$8,670	0	$0	221.60	1,606,010	16,496.0
Mean	8.2	867					

TABLE 4.2   Jones Hardware—Regression Data and Summary Statistics

Let: x = variation from mean
   y = variation from mean
   x^2 = squared variation from mean
   y^2 = squared variation from mean
   Variance $X = \Sigma x^2/n - 1$
   Variance $Y = \Sigma y^2/n - 1$
   Covariance XY: COV$xy = \Sigma xy/n - 1$

Regression Equation: $Y = \alpha + \beta X$
   Let: α = alpha or y-intercept
   β = beta coefficient or slope
   Y = dependent variable
   X = independent variable

Now that we have calculated the summary statistics, we can move on to the coefficients of the regression equation:

Beta is calculated by the following equation:

COV/var x, which would be $1,832/24.62 = 74.4$.

Alpha is calculated by the following equation:

$$\alpha = \text{Mean } Y - \beta \text{ (mean } X)$$
$$\alpha = 867 - (74.4)(8.2)$$
$$\alpha = 256$$

Our regression equation is now $Y = 256 + 74.4X$

By inputting anticipated snowfall in inches for any given month (X), we can calculate an estimate of snow shovel sales (Y). For example, the almanac forecasted 10 inches of snowfall for the December 2009 month, which would be equal to sales of $1,000 for that month. From this information, it is assumed that Mr. Jones can estimate the need for snow shovels.

While this example is simplistic, the outcome is significant for investment analysis—the use of regression analysis to calculate the effect of one (or more—known as "multiple regression") variable(s) on another. The investor could certainly use regression analysis in his or her interpretation of an investment scenario: What would be the effect of a decrease in interest rates on new home sales? The number of high school graduates on personal computer sales? The population of 49-year olds (in the United States) on the S&P index? Due to the ability of regression analysis to forecast future trends, its use has been widespread in the investment analysis practice. While a powerful tool in its own right, regression analysis also needs to be coupled with several other factors (i.e., strong data, identifiable relationships, sensible economic framework) to avoid the many problems that can plague the regression equation (multicollinearity, autocorrelation, etc.).

PROBLEM SET: REGRESSION ANALYSIS

Question 1

The standard deviation of the independent variable is 20 percent. The standard deviation of the dependent variable is 12 percent. The covariance between these two variables is 0.0096. The correlation between the variables is:

A. 0.40

B. 0.29

C. 0.12

D. None of the above

Answer

A. The covariance (0.0096) divided by the product of the standard deviations (0.20)(0.12) equals 0.40.

Question 2

The R^2 of a simple regression of two factors, A and B, measures the:

  A. The insensitivity of changes in A to changes in B.
  B. Statistical significance of the coefficient in the regression equation.
  C. The standard error of the residual term in the regression equation.
  D. The percent of variability of one factor explained by the variability of a second factor.

Answer

  D. The R^2 measures the percent explained by the independent variable.

Question 3

Tom Sayles is the president of Southwest Steel Products, a nail wholesaler in the home construction industry. Tom believes that there is a relationship that can be estimated through regression analysis between nail sales and housing starts. He calculates the following through the regression equation

$$Y = \alpha + \beta X \,(\text{Sales} = 5.37 + .76X),$$

where:

  Y = Nail sales, in thousands (the dependent variable)
  α = Intercept (alpha)
  β = Beta estimate
  X = Housing starts, in thousands (the independent variable)
  R^2 = 0.56

    The regression statistics presented above indicate that during the period under study, if housing starts were 17 (actually 17,000), the best estimate of nail sales is:

  A. $18,290
  B. $22,290
  C. $58,290
  D. $137,000

Answer

　　A. Nail Sales = 5.37 + (0.76) (17) = 18.29 or $18,290.

Question 4

The preceding regression information indicates that for the period under study, the independent variable (housing starts) explains approximately what percent of the variation in the dependent variable (nail sales)?

　　A. 56

　　B. 29

　　C. 33

　　D. 12

Answer

　　A. The definition of R^2.

Part 2

Fundamental Financial Security Analysis

Now that we have labored through the bricks and mortar of this journey we can progress to the next phase—the valuation of securities—utilizing the tools learned (and practiced) in the first part. In Chapters 5, 6, and 7, we cover the many disciplines behind the valuation of various securities. We reduce a security to its basic blocks—those individual components that determine the value of a business. Careful attention must also be paid to the trends and industry nuances that differentiate each type of asset.

While we focus on the "fundamental" analysis and valuation methods of equity security valuation in this book, the practitioner is cautioned to note that there exist many other methods that may be used to value an equity (such as technical, or "chart-based," analysis). The fundamental methodology is chosen because it is built on previously discussed tools and it has a time-tested record of reliance. Although the markets will move from extreme to extreme over any given period, the basic tenets of the fundamental methodology will always be useful.

Credit analysis is as crucial to the investment practitioner as equity analysis. Credit analysis focuses on the ability of a company to pay on its debts. Any company that may have difficulty in this area can worry even the most steadfast investor. With credit analysis, we are thrown into a new set of ratios and quantitative constructs that are expected to yield any potential yellow flags. We will meet Myron, our faithful credit analyst, whose briefcase of specific credit analysis tools is jam-packed with quantitative equations based on the teachings in Part 1 of this book.

In addition to quantitative analysis, the analyst must also turn attention to qualitative measures that are critical to the valuation of all securities. This is the proverbial "kicking-the-tires" routine that requires the practitioner to keep an open mind and a skeptical eye at the same time. While this anatomical feat may take many years (or several market cycles) to master, without qualitative measures the true measure of a security's value can never be completely understood. The three chapters that follow have problem sets and case studies to increase your understanding of these often confusing areas.

Chapter 5

Equity Analysis and Valuation

In this chapter you will learn:

- ✔ Fundamental business analysis—the ROE equation.
- ✔ Evaluation of industry factors and management techniques.
- ✔ Growth rate and risk estimation.
- ✔ Equity valuation techniques.

Definition

An investment is the current commitment of capital for a period of time in order to derive future payments that will compensate the investor for (1) the time the funds are committed, (2) the expected rate of inflation, and (3) the uncertainty of the future payments.

The preceding definition breaks the investment equation into its three basic "needs." Any investment valuation process requires a careful analysis of each part. However, before we can do this, we first must analyze an equity investment as a business—this analysis will give us the critical background that we need to project the future payments and assess their uncertainty.

We begin the performance measurement of a business with a detailed, empirical analysis of the company's operating levers—those data points that clue the analyst into the performance of a particular firm. These levers can be thought of as a multifaceted control panel with which a company's managers report on the historical performance of the company and adjust its strategy to maximize return (in fact, some companies use a management tool called a "dashboard," which is a statistical summary report on the key levers for the company over time). Perhaps at a particular juncture in a firm's life cycle, it should leverage its business (i.e., borrow money) to achieve a larger market share or take advantage of a specific event in the industry. Accurate financial analysis would allow the investor or manager to assess the need for leverage, calculate its costs and benefits to the business, and evaluate the managers' decision.

Financial ratios such as return on equity (ROE) and return on assets (ROA) are examples of levers that serve as a means to monitor and evaluate the performance of a company's financial management and ultimately its business. We will be able to answer questions such as: *Are assets being utilized in the most efficient manner? Is a company managing its costs efficiently?* Most importantly, the ROE equation—used in conjunction with the other techniques that we will cover in this chapter—will help provide a clear picture of the eventual disposition of the asset in question, namely, *Is it a buy, sell, or hold?*

Poor financial results in the past do not necessarily mean poor future prospects. There are many examples of businesses that orchestrate successful turnarounds and begin to show strong empirical (i.e., "in the ratios") performance. This is a testament to the power of top-notch management. The definition of "good" management, however, can be subjective and difficult to quantify. As such, in this chapter we will also discuss ways to objectively assess the management of a company.

The performance of a business within its industry also deserves the attention of the financial analyst, especially the knowledge of competitive pressures within a particular industry. Questions can range from concerns over the trends in raw material prices to the current barriers to entry (environmental, regulatory, etc.). The work of Michael Porter of Harvard University serves as an excellent foundation for a careful evaluation of a particular industry's competitive forces as well as strategies to better position a

company within its industry. Porter defined fi~
influence the industry as a whole, each of wh~
definable inputs and defining characteristic~
forces in detail later in this chapter.

We also introduce the concept of growth a~
valuation process—after all, no company will grow at t~
The process is not complete, however, until the riskiness of t~
flows can also be estimated. This is a unique (to the particular ventu~
that is captured through adjustments to the Capital Asset Pricing Model~
(CAPM) required rate of return (k) estimate. Market risk—the risk that
cannot be diversified away—is captured through the statistical construct
known as beta (the covariance between the return of the specific share and
the return of the market as a whole).

After completing all the empirical detective work, the investor can at
last turn attention toward the question of valuation. (Okay, now that we
know all about Company XYZ, how do we value its equity or share price?).
This discussion revolves around the basic mathematical underpinnings of
the investment market, namely the value of the discounted (to the present
day) future cash flows of a particular financial instrument. In a nutshell:
What is the current value of next year's (and the year after, and the year after that, etc.) cash flows? That, ultimately, is the valuation of the security.

Many valuation models in financial analysis have their own particular sets of advantages and drawbacks. Analysts need to determine the
one best suited for the valuation of a particular security, or the midpoint
value among many different valuation methods. The latter often permits
the formation of a "valuation-matrix," a tool that can illustrate the range
(under specific circumstances) of values over the spectrum of valuation
methods. We will review several of the most important and commonly
used valuation methods at the end of this chapter.

After bringing all this work together, the investor must finally make
a determination about the nagging question on all investors' minds—*buy
or sell?* The answer of fair value may not be so easily summed up with an
endorsement of one transaction or another. Fair value (or undervalued or
overvalued) can depend on a long list of extenuating circumstances. As
this book stresses, investment analysis is not an exact science. Even
though it may be deeply lodged in the quantitative formats, financial
analysis still requires a good deal of the "human touch," for it is the study
of a business, not the numbers on a financial statement.

ces of Information

this chapter and those that follow, we will be referencing a variety of nancial statistics and data points about companies. Most of our examples use hypothetical data for illustrative purposes, but needless to say, in the "real world" you will need "real" information to analyze and value a security. The type of information that you will need can be found through a variety of channels, including:

- ✔ SEC filings—All publicly traded companies are required to file periodic statements with the Securities & Exchange Commission (the "SEC"), the body that regulates securities in the U.S. SEC filings can be obtained directly from the SEC, most easily through the SEC's online database known as EDGAR. These filings are the primary source of information for investors, especially for quantitative, financial data. Three of the most important SEC filings are:
  - ✔ 10-K—This is a company's main annual filing, which includes financial results for the year (income statement, balance sheet, etc.) as well as narrative reports from management about the company's operations and prospects.
  - ✔ 10-Q—This report contains similar information as a 10-K, but it is filed on a quarterly basis and covers a company's operations for the preceding three months.
  - ✔ 8-K—An 8-K is also known as a "Current Report" because it contains information on important current events of a company (known as "trigger events"). For example, trigger events include the sale of stock, an acquisition or disposition, or the resignation of a member of the Board of Directors. Thus, an 8-K provides invaluable background about recent events of note to an investor.

- ✔ Direct from the company—In addition to the reports that are required by the SEC, most companies also communicate to the public in many other ways. These efforts are often coordinated by an "Investor Relations" department, and contacting this department can serve as a great starting point for the average investor to find information. Investor relations personnel will be able to steer you to a number of information sources about a company, including press releases, investor conference calls (usually held quarterly), trade shows, the company's annual meeting, the company's annual report, and the company's web site.

✔ News outlets—It is good to hear what a company has to say, but proactive investors do not simply take a company's word at face value. Third-party news sources such as newspapers, magazines, television shows and the like can serve as valuable checks on a company's performance. The archives of individual news outlets can be searched directly, or you can take a more efficient route: search many at once at your local library or through services like Lexus-Nexus or Dow Jones Newswire.

✔ Third-party financial research and analysis—There is a worldwide industry of financial professionals who produce independent investment research and analysis reports to be used by others to make investment decisions. Examples include the bond rating agencies Standard & Poor's and Moody's, and the research arms of Wall Street firms like Goldman Sachs and Morgan Stanley. These reports usually include both quantitative and qualitative analyses. The most reputable sources often charge a fee for their services, but some are free or can be obtained through your financial advisor.

✔ The Internet—The Internet has emerged as one of the most important sources of investment information, just as it has for many other fields. A simple search of a company's name using any popular search engine is likely to start you down a path toward a wealth of information about that company, including news stories, consumer reviews about a company's products, and the like. The Internet being what it is, some of this information must be taken with a grain of salt.

✔ Direct experience—Finally, many astute investors advocate the most basic of "bottoms up" analysis: direct experience with a company's product or service. If you are thinking of investing in a restaurant, you can go out to dinner there to sample its food. If you think a company is poised to achieve strong sales growth because of a new product launch, you can strike up a casual conversation with a sales clerk at an electronics chain to find out how well the new gadget is *really* selling. The downside of this type of detective work is that such anecdotal evidence is not necessarily indicative of larger trends.

Return on Equity (ROE)

We will use the Return on Equity (ROE) equation as our primary tool to calculate and analyze the key financial and operational levers of a company. The ROE equation is so valuable because it can be broken down into its component parts through the DuPont Derivation Equation. Each of these component parts is a specific lever that helps us assess the performance of the business.

The DuPont Derivation Equation:

$$\text{ROE} = \frac{\text{Net income}}{\text{Pretax income}} \times \frac{\text{Pretax income}}{\text{EBIT}} \times \frac{\text{EBIT}}{\text{Sales}} \times \frac{\text{Sales}}{\text{Assets}} \times \frac{\text{Assets}}{\text{Equity}}$$

$$\text{ROE} = \frac{\text{Tax}}{\text{burden}} \times \frac{\text{Interest}}{\text{burden}} \times \frac{\text{Operating}}{\text{margin}} \times \frac{\text{Asset}}{\text{turnover}} \times \text{Leverage}$$

Definitions

Net Income. The bottom line of the income statement. This figure takes into account all the expenses related to running the business (including: depreciation and amortization, taxes, and interest charges).

Pretax Income. The amount of income before taxes are taken out. The corporate tax rate is levied against this amount to yield the income tax expense. Interest on debt payments (cost of debt financing) is tax deductible; it is removed from pretax income and therefore is not being taxed (often referred to as the "interest tax shield").

Earnings before Interest and Taxes (EBIT). The operational income of the business before any effects of interest and taxes. This line item reflects the costs involved in operating a business (marketing expenses, cost of goods sold, salaries, fixed costs, etc.) but does not include such items as taxes and interest expense.

Revenues. The measure that combines all recorded sales within the firm. Sales are considered to be the inflow of capital resources to the firm from the disposition of goods or services. There are several nuances to the major methods of revenue recognition depending on the industry in question; however, each must follow the underpinnings of the *Statement of Financial Accounting Concepts (SFAC) 5,*

"Recognition and Measurement in Financial Statements of Business Enterprises." SFAC 5 calls for the satisfaction of the following two conditions for revenue to be recognized:

1. The completion of the earnings process (in addition to a measure of the costs needed to complete a given project).

2. A quantification of the amount of revenues (or other benefit) expected to be received.

Assets. The balance sheet's "Total Assets" amount, combining both current and noncurrent assets. An asset is anything having commercial or exchange value that is owned by a business, institution, or person. It may be tangible (a factory) or intangible (a patent).

Equity. Also a balance sheet item reflecting the firm's net worth. It is calculated with the simple arithmetical notation: Assets – Liabilities = Equity. In an investment sense, equity refers to the ownership interest possessed by shareholders in a corporation.

Before the advent of this derivation, financial executives at major industrial companies were, more or less, at the mercy of the "machine." Although the machine provided for their livelihoods, it would give no details to how it might be run more efficiently. No sense of where (what division) or when it would need more oil (liquidity) or more fuel (leverage). The machine just ran its course and the financial management team was there only to put out fires when they arose. However, with the derivation of the return-on-equity ratio, the financial executives at DuPont (in the mid-1950s), and later many industrial firms, were able to fine-tune the performance of the company and its operating divisions by adjusting the individual levers to achieve maximum efficiency and profitability. This "tweaking" of the company's financial ratios gave rise to the importance of financial managers who were able to quantify their expertise and rationalize their commitment. No longer would excuses like "cyclical downturns in the industry" satisfy the board of directors, and later the shareholders. They demanded more statistics:

If the economy (or industry) is slowing, perhaps we should reduce our leverage so as not to compound the slower revenue pace? Or, given the demise of our largest competitor, perhaps now is the time to increase leverage so as to capture market share?

The correct answer? It depends; in some circumstances either strategy would yield the desired return. With the ROE, however, the investor (or manager) can perform *what if* testing. We can estimate growth (or lack thereof) that would, given some other assumptions, yield the targeted ROE. This exercise practically resembles the composition of a symphony, where each note, placed in sequence with others, will result in a different sound. If we, as conductor, strive for a certain harmony, achieving it may take several permutations of the same instruments. A little tweaking here and there can surprise even the most musically inclined.

Investment practitioners (yes, I mean you!) can use the ROE derivation to seek further information about the company's performance in comparison with its peers. *If* Company A has a larger asset turnover than its peer group, one could hypothesize that the firm is being managed at a higher efficiency level. Why would this company yield a higher amount of sales for a given unit of assets than another company in the same industry? Perhaps the management of Company A has striven for a higher level of productivity from its asset base and therefore, yields a higher amount of sales for a given unit of assets, or perhaps a company just hired 50 new salespeople. Each of us, in our personal peer group (of equally earning friends and relatives), could think of a person who seems to get so much more assets out of his earnings than the rest of us (*How does my brother-in-law afford all those luxuries?*). In our peer group, however, debt (leverage) may be (incorrectly) seen as an asset when it is not; again, the importance of the equity portion of the ROE equation.

Financial analysis is also aided through the use of *common-size financial statements*. Common-size statements express each line item as a percentage of the relevant total (for a common-size income statement, the relevant total is revenue, while for a common-size balance sheet, the relevant total is total assets). For example, to calculate cost of goods sold on the common-size income statement, the dollar value of cost of goods sold on the normal income statement is divided by the dollar value of revenue on the normal income statement. This calculation is done in turn for each line item on the income statement (i.e., dividing each one by total revenue). These financials permit analysis of each contributory item to total revenues and assets and easy comparison across peers (*Why is cost of goods sold 65 percent of revenue for Company ABC but 75 percent of revenue for Company XYZ?*). Please see Table 5.1.

TABLE 5.1	Company ABC (Common-Size Statement) (shown in percentages)		
Income Statement	*12/31/XX*	*Balance Sheet*	*12/31/XX*
Revenues	100.00	Cash and equivalents	7.41
− Cost of goods sold	65.00	Trade receivable	16.7
= *Gross profit*	35	Inventory	28.23
−Operating expense	25.31	Other	3.38
= Operating profit	9.69	Current assets	55.72
−Other expenses	3.15	Fixed assets (net)	44.28
= Profit before taxes	6.54	Intangibles	0
−Tax expense	2.33	Other	0
= *Net income*	4.21	Total assets	100.00
		Notes payable	12.27
		Current portion LTD	0
		Trade payables	11.22
		Income tax payables	0.39
		Other	5.44
		Current liabilities	29.32
		Long-term debt	15.87
		Deferred taxes	0
		Other noncurrent liabilities	0
		Total liabilities	45.19
		Equity	54.81
		Total liabilities and equity	100.00

The ROE Equation

We now move on to a more detailed look at each of the five components of the ROE equation.

    1. Tax Burden. This is the percentage of pretax income which falls to the bottom line as net earnings; therefore, 1 − tax burden = tax rate paid by company. Well-established firms expect a nonvolatile tax burden; however, with loss carryforwards and related tax-shielded policies, many small firms witness a volatile tax burden. The prudent analyst must be aware of a small firm with seemingly high ROE but a rather high tax burden (therefore a low tax rate): What will happen to ROE when the tax advantages are fully exhausted?

2. **Interest Burden.** This lever indicates the financial strain on the company caused by the costs of leverage. Although debt has its advantages, they are not without costs; debt service can become a stifling obligation to even the strongest firm, especially if expected sales performance is not achieved. Like the tax burden, the interest burden also provides a figure that is not quite a "burden," but rather an additive to ROE. The interest burden's calculated value is the percentage of EBIT that flows down to the pretax income line; the calculation of one minus the interest burden is the true drag to the company due to the costs of leverage.

3. **Operating Margin.** This ratio evaluates the company's operating margin or the company's effectiveness at minimizing costs. It measures the true efficiency of the management at running the company. By using Earnings Before Interest and Taxes (EBIT) (instead of net earnings, where the ratio would be known as the net profit margin), we get a true read on the firm's operating efficiency without the effects of leverage or taxes.

4. **Asset Turnover.** This measures the asset utilization efficiency of the firm. How many times do the assets need to be turned to produce the level of sales? This lever will certainly differ dramatically between industries; an airline manufacturer (capital intensive and therefore greater amount of assets needed to produce a sales amount) will definitely have a lower ATO than that of a janitorial supplies firm given a similar level of sales.

   Other Turnover Ratios. Asset turnover is a relatively general measure because it refers to all of a company's assets. In practice, two more "refined" ratios are also used.

   1. Accounts Receivable Turnover: Sales divided by average accounts receivable (average of beginning and ending balance of accounts receivable for the period). This measures how efficiently a company collects its sales on credit. Often the "accounts receivable collection period" is calculated as well (this is 360 days divided by accounts receivable turnover). The result is the number of days that it takes the company, on

average, to collect on its credit sales. Contractual terms in many industries require payment within 30–45 days.

2. **Inventory Turnover:** Costs of goods sold divided by average inventory (average of beginning and ending balance of inventory for the period). This measures how efficiently a company uses its inventory. Like the accounts receivable collection period, the "days to sell inventory" is calculated as 360 days divided by inventory turnover.

5. **Leverage.** The ratio between total assets and equity (assets minus liabilities) provides the analyst with the ability to recognize the firm's position on leverage. A firm growing at x percent without debt (no leverage) could likely grow at a faster rate than x given an initial (or increased) amount of debt, because this debt could be used to fund the purchase of additional equipment, supplies, and so on. But be wary of too much leverage, especially in a cyclical firm, for it could lead to financial distress. What is the optimal amount of debt that a company should undertake? The answer to this hypothetical question is not so easily obtained (although the academic work of Miller & Modigelani has made strong progress in this area). However, suffice it to say optimal leverage depends upon many factors, including industry outlook, current business operations, cashflow constraints, each of which need to be investigated carefully by management before an increased leverage scenario could be endorsed. (An alternative measure of leverage is the debt-to-equity ratio, calculated as total debt divided by total equity.)

Other ROE Derivations

Now that the ROE derivation is firmly in memory, it is time to consider other derivations of the equation that are often seen in the work of financial analysts. For example:

Return on Assets (ROA)

$$\frac{\text{Net income}}{\text{Sales}} \times \frac{\text{Sales}}{\text{Assets}}$$

or

$$\text{Profit margin} \times \text{Asset turnover}$$

As shown earlier, this statistic can isolate the efficiency of a company in the use of its resources. This ratio includes debt as an asset (inasmuch as it does not reflect the assets as net, i.e., after debts) whereas the ROE equation does reflect these net assets.

Net Return on Equity

$$\frac{\text{Net income}}{\text{Sales}} \times \frac{\text{Sales}}{\text{Assets}} \times \frac{\text{Assets}}{\text{Equity}}$$

or

$$\text{Net profit margin} \times \text{Asset turnover} \times \text{Leverage}$$

Here we are only losing the "burden ratios" (Tax and interest burdens) and thereby combining the first three levers into one.

With the preceding derivations as well as the other ROE-related levers at one's disposal, the proactive investor is able to simply (yes, I mean simply) "plug and chug" to achieve the desired result. As the examples make obvious, the equations are all "chain-linked," so that pieces cancel out and the entire equation collapses into a more simplified model. As mentioned, the ROE (and ROA, etc.) derivation provides a more detailed look into the company's performance and financial management practices.

Using Financial Statement Footnotes

The numbers that are reported on a company's income statement, balance sheet and cash flow statement are used extensively in the ROE equation (and its many derivations) that we have just reviewed. However, they do not always tell the entire story. Using the tools we have identified above, you can thoroughly assess the performance of a company, but there are sometimes additional details lurking behind the scenes. These details can be found in the footnotes to the financial statements, which always follow the financial statements themselves in a company's 10-K filing. It is critical for the investor to not stop at the financial statements as presented, but instead to delve into the sometimes mysterious world of footnotes to gain a complete understanding of the reported numbers.

Footnotes are important because they contain details that are not required by GAAP to be included in the financial statements themselves (i.e., directly on the income statement), but are nevertheless important enough to be disclosed to the public. Thus, they are "buried" in the footnotes. Footnotes can drag on for pages and pages, sometimes making up the bulk of the entire filing. They are dense with facts and figures and do not make for terribly exciting bedtime reading, but sometimes it is these "unexciting" facts that are key to the evaluation of a company.

Through the careful study of footnotes, some savvy investors were able to see the warning lights well in advance of catastrophes like the fall of Enron and the subprime mortgage crisis. Following is a list of important items that can be ascertained within the footnotes.

- ✔ Off-balance sheet liabilities—The term "off-balance" sheet is used to describe items that, due to the complexities of GAAP accounting, are not required to be reported as a liability on the balance sheet of a company. Thus, the calculation of financial metrics using the numbers reported on the balance sheet is not inclusive of these liabilities. Nevertheless, they may be very important liabilities that should not be ignored. For example, sometimes the full pension commitments of a company are not completely factored into the balance sheet. Similarly, a commitment to build a new plant or to lease some types of manufacturing equipment may not be carried on the balance sheet in full. What is an investor to do? Look to the footnotes! There, information on these liabilities will be disclosed. If appropriate, the financial metric calculations should then be adjusted to account for these liabilities.

- ✔ Use of derivatives—Derivatives are financial instruments that have become increasingly complicated but also increasingly common in their usage. For example, many airlines now use derivatives—in the form of hedge transactions—to try to manage their exposure to changes in oil prices. In the footnotes, these strategies must be described. This allows the proactive investor to review them and determine if they pose any threat (*What if oil prices change unexpectedly? Will this airline incur a huge unexpected cost due to its usage of derivatives?*).

✔ Accounting policies—GAAP accounting rules give company managers discretion over certain accounting decisions. These are described in the footnotes, and can be assessed to determine if management is being aggressive or conservative in its use of accounting policies.

✔ Schedule of debt maturities—The footnotes show a detailed schedule of when a company's debts come due over time, meaning that the company must have the resources at that time to repay the debt. For example, two companies may have exactly the same amount of debt and cash on their balance sheet. But if Company A must repay all its debt next year, while Company B does not need to repay its debt until five years from now, Company A has a much bigger problem on its hands.

✔ Stock compensation plans—Stock compensation plans are similar to off-balance-sheet liabilities in that they are not always incorporated fully into the operating results of a company. Companies might rely heavily on paying their employees in stock or stock options, instead of in cash, leading to an undercounting of the true "salaries" on the income statement. The footnotes must always describe the details of any stock compensation plans, allowing investors to ascertain their impact on the company.

✔ Breakdown of items—Much like the DuPont Derivation Equation breaks down the ROE into its component parts, other items on a company's financial statements can also be "broken down" into smaller parts. For example, the balance sheet may show that a company has $1,000,000 in inventory, but the footnotes will show how this is broken down between raw materials, works in process, and finished goods. Similarly, property, plant, equipment, and investments can also be broken down in this way. The operating results of a company are also often broken down into different "Operating Segments," as defined by the company's management. Operating Segments might be determined geographically (e.g., North America, South America, Asia, etc.) or by type of product (cars, trucks, buses, etc.).

✔ Investments/dispositions—Finally, the footnotes will often provide further details on any investments or dispositions that a company undertook during the year, including the timing and price paid. This can provide a key insight into the growth of a company. Did the company increase its sales in a given year by selling more products itself, or by buying a competitor?

Management Analysis

When exploring a company's prospects, an investor should be quite attuned to the management—those who are at the helm. Today's investors must feel comfortable speaking with (and even inquiring of) top management about the future prospects of the enterprise; after all, that is where the money is—the discounted value of future cash flows. As equity owners, investors have a vested stake in the way the company is managed. With effective management in a good operating environment, any company should have many positive net present value (NPV) projects. As discussed earlier, positive NPV projects translate into achieving the required rate of return, which in turn permits an efficient valuation.

Clearly, management plays an important role in the growth sequence of a firm. But how does one evaluate management? Is there a quiz that all members of the management team must pass to be considered effective? Besides the empirical analysis of the firm, are there other methods we can employ to value solely the management team's efforts?

In many cases, the investor can get a "gut feeling" about the people who run a particular company. For example, investors can join in a company's quarterly conference calls (open to all investors) or attend the company's annual meeting. Are the managers generally open to questions and highly knowledgeable in their answers, or are they evasive and aloof? Do top managers own many shares—a potentially positive indication that they believe strongly in the future of the company? Or did they recently sell all their holdings—a potentially negative indication that they have lost faith?

Gut feelings alone cannot suffice, however. They may tell you a little something about the leadership of an organization, but good management is about so much more than the CEO whose face appears on television. The evaluation of management is not an exact science. There is, however, a very wide body of literature that has developed over time to assess and evaluate overall management effectiveness. This comes from both the academic sphere (researchers at universities and think tanks) and the more practical arena (managers themselves, consultants and other practitioners who advise based on their real world experience "in the trenches"). Some of the most lasting and impactful management "gurus" in recent years include Tom Peters, Peter Drucker, Warren Bennis, James MacGregor Burns, Marcus Buckingham, Malcom Gladwell, Stephen Covey, Amy Edmondson, and Rosabeth Moss Kantor. For further reading on the topic of leadership and management, the works by any of these authors would be a good place to start.

Since every company is different, it is nearly impossible to put forth any general rules as to what is "right" or "wrong" in management—it depends on the specific situation of the company in question. However, in the list following we offer a general outline of the key areas that define how a company is managed, for better or for worse. By assessing the management of a company across each of these areas, a more complete picture of the effectiveness of management can be ascertained than through a simple "gut check" of the CEO.

- Centralization vs. decentralization—The level of centralization refers to a company's management hierarchy and the concentration of power. It is essentially a spectrum of control, with the most "centralized" organizations concentrating power in the hands of the few at the top of the organization, and the most "decentralized" organizations delegating significant responsibility to workers throughout the organization. For example, in a highly decentralized factory, a frontline employee might have the authority to stop the production line and implement an improvement in the process without any special permission required, while in a more centralized factory, the employee would have to go through layers of management before getting the sign-off required from the "boss" to implement the idea. Over time, the benefits of decentralization have been increasingly extolled by many management theorists, since frontline employees are "closer" to the day-to-day activities of the business, and therefore in a better position to make day-to-day decisions, while higher-level managers are squirreled away in their ivory tower offices writing budget reports and conducting meetings. As such, more decentralized organizations are considered to be more nimble, efficient, and innovative. Decentralization is also thought to boost employee morale, since it gives employees greater responsibility and autonomy to make decisions. The flip side of decentralization, however, is the risk of quality deterioration, which can result when too many changes have been implemented incongruously, thereby undermining the value of certain brands or products. Weighing this balance of control versus agility for a particular company will be important in determining management effectiveness.

✔ Organizational structure—Organizations can be structured in many different ways, each offering both advantages and disadvantages. Consider a company that produces two lines of products, baseball bats and golf clubs. One way to structure this company would be by "product line," meaning that the baseball bat division and the golf club division operate almost like two smaller, independent companies within one larger holding company. Each would have their own production equipment and employees, sales teams, human resources groups, accounting teams, and so on. Alternatively, the company could be divided by "function," meaning that there would be only one production team (producing both bats and clubs), one sales team (selling both products), one accounting team (preparing the books for both product lines), and so on. The company might also be segmented by geography, with a "domestic" division covering all the U.S. operations and an "international" division encompassing all the international operations. The optimal organizational structure can only be determined by understanding the underlying dynamics of the company and its industry.

✔ Innovation—Even in the most mundane and mature businesses, innovation drives performance. It can mean anything from cutting costs, to developing a new product, to finding new customers. The most innovative companies are willing to take risks, recognizing full well that some may fail. Almost all companies talk about being innovative, but the best actually *do it*—they encourage employees to take risks by offering incentives for positive outcomes and not overly penalizing risks that fail. Often, innovation and decentralization go hand in hand, since decentralization gives employees greater authority to take risks if they so choose. Some downsides of mishandled innovation are the loss of focus on core competencies and the risky allocation of scarce resources.

✔ Customer Service—A business succeeds when it offers something of value to its customers and is paid in return. Thus, it is important to assess a company's relationship with its customers. Is a company close to its customers? Does it elicit their feedback and incorporate it into its operations? Does it treat its customers with respect and dignity? Does it meet or exceed its customers' expectations? Or is the business model based on low-cost products, and therefore there is minimal customer interaction beyond the point of sale?

✔ Oversight—Oversight has become an increasingly hot topic in the wake of the financial scandals of the last few decades. A company's Board of Directors plays a critical function in this regard. A good Board must be composed of a wide variety of people representing different backgrounds, cultures and areas of expertise. It should be truly independent in its decisions, not composed of entrenched insiders who may not be willing to make difficult decisions. Financial controls are also important—namely, what check and balance systems are in place to adequately manage the business and detect any fraud or misappropriations?

✔ Values and Culture—A company's values and culture are a critical component of its success; in many ways, they underlie all the previous ideas that we have discussed. If a company truly values respect and justice for all, this will be reflected in its strong demonstration of decentralized authority, safe risk-taking and an obvious commitment to fair hiring and compensation practices. If a well-managed company is truly driven by a worthwhile mission to serve others, this will be reflected in its excellent customer relationships and high employee satisfaction. And if the culture of a company encompasses both teamwork and a sense of healthy competition, employee morale and work ethic are sure to benefit.

As we have seen, there are no clear answers as to how to best manage a business. Likewise, it would be incorrect to assume that any particular management technique will necessarily be highly predictive of future investment results. Just because a company exhibits great customer service and decentralized risk-taking doesn't mean the stock is sure to go up. But in combination with our other analysis techniques, such factors are important in helping to inform the overall investment decision.

Industry Analysis

Once we have a handle on the somewhat nebulous concept of management evaluation, we need to turn to the evaluation of the industry in which a particular company competes. This industry competition is synonymous to the soil conditions that a farmer would be subject to in cultivating a crop: If the land is hilly and the soil is full of rocks, the farmer certainly needs to evaluate his crop-growing scenario to maximize his output. Similarly, the corporation needs to evaluate its environment to maximize the profit that can be generated. This evaluation consists of surveying the competition within the industry, regulations which can impact the profitability of a firm within an industry, and the potential substitutes that can wreak havoc on even the most established firms.

Michael E. Porter of Harvard Business School reigns as the czar of industry analysis. His five competitive forces serve as a template for the evaluation of the environment in which firms conduct their business. Porter's competitive forces are detailed in the following schema, often known in business jargon as "Porter's Five Forces":

1. Bargaining power of buyers—In this context, "buyers" refers to the customers for a company's products, and the degree of bargaining power refers to how much leverage buyers have in dealing with the company. For example, a buyer with high bargaining buyer would be in a better position to demand a price concession from the company. As such, from the standpoint of the company in question, it is generally preferable for the bargaining power of its buyers to be lower. (Of course, from the standpoint of the buyer in question, they would be happy to have as much leverage as possible!)

   How to assess: Companies often footnote (or will provide upon request) a list of their top 10 or 20 customers, along with how much they buy from the company. Using this, you can determine if the company's buyers are financial powerhouses (higher leverage) or smaller organizations (lower leverage). Also, you can calculate whether the company's top buyers account for a small or high percentage of the company's total sales.

2. Bargaining power of suppliers—This is a complement to the bargaining power of buyers, with suppliers being those companies

that sell inputs (raw materials, equipment, etc.) to the company in question. Similarly, it is preferred (from the company's perspective) for the bargaining power of suppliers to be lower, since that means they will have less leverage to demand harmful concessions.

How to assess: Lists of the top suppliers to a company can also usually be obtained from the company. Also, consider the nature of the inputs that suppliers provide. Are they highly complex products that only one or two specialty manufacturers can offer? If so, then those manufacturers probably enjoy greater bargaining power. On the other hand, if a company is a particularly big purchaser of a readily available commodity, then the company probably enjoys the advantage.

3. Threat of new entrants—New entrants are those who are not currently competing in the market, but may enter the market to offer the same product. As such, a high threat of new entrants is an undesirable factor, since it means that the potential for increased competition is great. And increased competition is almost certain to bring with it lower prices, lost sales, and lower market share.

How to assess: An industry's *barriers to entry* are a critical factor. For example, is it extremely costly to acquire the expertise or equipment needed to offer a product? Does a company have a patent that prevents others from utilizing its technology? These constitute high barriers, and thus a decreased threat of new entrants. Government rules or environmental regulations can also pose significant barriers to entry. Read up on press releases or newspaper articles about the industry, and the annual reports of potential competitors—they may also disclose new competition in the works.

4. Threat of substitute products or services—Substitutes are products or services that may arise to *take the place of* the existing product offered by a company. The threat of substitute products is just as detrimental as the threat of new entrants, as it also portends the possibility of lower prices, lost sales, and lower market share. A leading seller of cassette tape players may have faced a low threat of *new entrants* in the 1980s, but this did not prevent the downfall of the cassette tape industry due to the threat of *substitute products*—namely, compact discs.

How to assess: Barriers to entry, such as those described above, are also informative about the threat of substitutes. In addition, trends in technology must be monitored closely, since technological breakthroughs often lead to the creation of substitute products. After all, it was a technological breakthrough that led to the transition from cassette to CD, and yet another breakthrough that led to the transition from CD to MP3 players.

5. Rivalry among existing firms—This refers to the level of competition among existing firms, such as pricing (how much do competitors charge?), location (is the nearest competitor down the street or across the country?), and so on. Few companies enjoy true monopolies, particularly in the United States, so there are bound to be competitive forces at work in almost any industry.

   How to assess: A key measure of rivalry among firms is a company's *market share,* measured as the company's total sales divided by the total sales in the entire industry. This is often readily available in company and industry reports. Consider the market share of the company in question as well as its peers. Is market share fairly evenly divided, or do a few companies enjoy the lion's share? Also note the trends over time. If market share was once dominated by a single major firm but has been slowly transitioning to a more even playing field, this points to increased rivalry among firms. Automakers in the U.S. are a prime example of market share trends. The U.S. auto market was once dominated by "The Big Three" automakers (GM, Ford, and Chrysler), who collectively held a huge share of the market, but the market share of the Big Three has since dwindled due to new entrants (Toyota, Honda, etc.).

These five forces interact to determine the profitability conditions within a particular industry. An analyst would be expected to survey the industry in which a specific firm is operating to identify how these forces are affecting (or may affect) the ability of the firm to continue growing. If a firm is in a monopolistic industry, its market share will be far less penetrable by competitors unless a substitute product is introduced. The company that brings this substitute product to market can employ a strategy of undercutting the leader to gain market share. However, the monopoly would be expected to retaliate (and should have the margin advantage or staying power to permit a concerted retaliation effort) to force out this threat. Technological advantages take an important role in this competition; if a substitute product is more efficient or provides greater utility, then it is likely that it will survive the pressures of the monopoly.

PROBLEM SET

Question 1

The following problems will allow you to practice your understanding of the ROE equation and its derivatives, management effectiveness, and industry analysis.

Parrot Computers Inc. Balance Sheet (in thousands)			
Assets		*Liabilities and Equity*	
Cash	$ 300	Accounts payable	$ 400
Accounts receivable	200	Debt	250
Inventory	700	Common stock	1,000
Fixed assets	1,200	Retained earnings	750
Total assets	$2,400	Total liabilities and equity	$2,400

Parrot Computers has A/R terms of net 30 days (i.e., payment is due within 30 days)

At the beginning of the year, accounts receivable were $175, inventory was $600, assets were $2,200, common stock was $900, and retained earnings were $650.

Parrot Computers Inc. Income Statement (in thousands)	
Sales	$6,000
Cost of Goods Sold	(4,000)
Depreciation & Amortization	(300)
EBIT	$1,700
Interest expense	(100)
Pretax income	1,600
Taxes	(640)
Net income	$ 960

Use the financial statements above for Parrot Computers Inc. to compute the following ratios.

A. Return on assets

B. Return on common shareholders' equity

C. Leverage ratio

D. Asset turnover

E. Debt-to-equity

Answer

    A. Return on Assets: Net income/average assets

        ROA = 960/((2,200 + 2,400)/2)

        ROA = 41.7%

    B. Return on common shareholders' equity: (Net income—Preferred dividends)/Average common equity

        ROE = 960/((1,550 + 1,750)/2)

        ROE = 58.1%

    C. Leverage ratio: Assets/Common equity

        Leverage = 2,400/(1,000 + 750)

        Leverage = 1.37

    D. Asset turnover: Sales/Assets

        Asset turnover = 6,000/2,400

        Asset turnover = 2.5x

    E. Debt-to-equity = Debt/Equity

        Debt-to-equity = 250/1,750

        Debt-to-equity = 14.3%

Question 2

Is the company achieving its stated AR terms of net 30 days? How does its accounts receivable collection period compare to its days to sell inventory?

Answer

To answer the first part of this question, we must calculate accounts receivable turnover and then the accounts receivable collection period.

Accounts receivable turnover: Sales/Average accounts receivable

    Accounts receivable turnover = 6,000/((175 + 200)/2)

    Accounts receivable turnover = 6,000/187.5

    Accounts receivable turnover = 32

    Accounts receivable collection period: 360/AR turnover

    Accounts receivable collection period = 360 days/32

    Accounts receivable collection period = 11.25 days

The accounts receivable collection period shows that, on average, the company collects its accounts receivable within 11.25 days. This is well within its stated terms of 30 days.

Now we can calculate the days to sell inventory to compare it to the accounts receivable collection period.

Inventory turnover: Cost of goods sold/Average inventory

Inventory turnover = 4,000/((600 + 700)/2)

Inventory turnover = 4,000/650

Inventory turnover = 6.15

Days to sell inventory: 360 days/inventory turnover

Days to sell inventory = 360 days/6.15

Days to sell inventory = 58.5 days

This shows us that it takes just under two months, on average, for the company to sell its inventory. This is significantly longer than the AR collection period, meaning that the company collects on its sales more quickly than it is able to sell its inventory.

Question 3

What information might you find in the company's footnotes to its financial statements that would cause you to re-evaluate the ratios that you calculated in Questions 1 and 2 above?

Answer

Helpful information that might be disclosed in the footnotes could include:

- ✔ Off-balance sheet liabilities—For example, the company might have significant pension liabilities or a commitment to build a new plant that is not included in the total debt that is stated on the balance sheet. As such, it would be preferable to add these liabilities to the stated debt and re-calculate the leverage ratios.

- ✔ Accounting policies—Parrot Computers appears to collect its AR in a relatively short period of time (11.25 days), but perhaps it is using a questionable accounting policy to make its numbers look more favorable. The footnotes must disclose such accounting policies.

- ✔ Breakdown of items—If the footnotes disclose information about different product lines or geographic regions, then the ratios could be re-calculated for the specific product lines (or regions) identified. We saw above that the total number of days to sell inventory was 58.5 days. However, provided the breakdown by product line, you might find that inventory for one type of product sells at a different rate than inventory for a different type of product (e.g., maybe an older, less popular product is selling very slowly and thus "dragging down" the average for the company).

✔ Acquisitions/dispositions—If the company bought or sold businesses during the year, then the historical ratios calculated above might not be applicable to the business going forward. For example, suppose Parrot Computers recently acquired a business that generates lower ROE. Thus, the ROE for the new, combined company (Parrot plus the new business) will be lower next year than was the ROE for Parrot alone in the year that just ended.

Question 4*

Refer to the Analyst Notes (AN) for Mento Machines (following) and evaluate the competitive structure of the router industry using Porter's five competitive forces. For each of these forces, cite three items of evidence from the Analyst Information Package that justify your evaluation.

Mento Machines—Analyst Notes

1. Network environments are very complex due to the hardware and software technology and the lack of common standards. Routers are needed to connect computers with diverse operating systems ("languages"). The two industry leaders' routers accommodate 25–30 such "languages" whereas newcomers' routers support five or fewer.

2. The two industry leaders have substantial research and development budgets, patents, and technology and design expertise.

3. The two industry leaders have extensive direct sales and service organizations.

4. Theoretically, routers would not be needed if all computers had compatible systems and could communicate easily with each other.

*Industry Analysis CFA 1994 Level 2 Exam. Copyright 1994 by AIMR, Reprinted with permission.

5. New research and development and the adoption of universal "languages" may eventually eliminate the need for routers, but that is not expected to happen for many years.

6. Other pieces of equipment frequently perform some functions of routers, but this is not yet significant nor is it anticipated that they will be able to duplicate all the functions of today's routers.

7. The cost of routers is a small percentage of the total cost of a computer network.

8. A high quality router can significantly increase the efficiency of a network system relative to the router's cost.

9. Customers prefer a single supplier of routers.

10. Customers who switch to another supplier's routers face high costs related to the change.

11. Router industry leaders subcontract the manufacturing of their products to companies whose services are plentiful and commodity-like.

12. Routers are assembled mostly from commonly available electrical components.

13. Some of the components used to assemble routers are proprietary to a single supplier but these are currently insignificant.

14. 80 percent to 90 percent of sales of the two router industry leaders are to repeat customers.

15. Competition in the router industry is based on product features. Price is secondary. The two industry leaders have different sets of product features.

Answer

Following is a discussion of each of Porter's five forces for Mento Machines.

Threat of New Entrants   Barriers to entry are high and rising because of the unique nature of the router market. The two industry leaders have established significant leads in understanding complex customer needs, developing technology, building a highly trained sales and service staff, and building reputations for proven product liability (AN 1,

2, 3). Any new entrant will have difficulty overcoming any of these factors alone and extreme difficulty overcoming all of them at once. The threat of new entrants is therefore low, as a result of the extensive skill sets required at the outset to compete effectively.

Threat of Substitutes   This threat is currently low, mainly because of the lack of unifying protocol (AN 4, 5), but it is rising somewhat because of the selective provision of some router functions by other pieces of equipment (AN 6). Longer term, the threat of complete substitution may come in the form of a unified protocol rendering a router obsolete.

Power of Buyers   Buyer power is low and will remain low because of the high costs to switch (AN 10). Preferences for a single vendor (AN 9), the low cost of routers relative to whole systems (AN 7), and the importance of increasing overall network efficiency (AN 8) contribute to low buying power.

Power of Suppliers   Supplier power is low as a result of the commodity-like nature of the components and required manufacturing capabilities, as well as the multiple vendors of each supplier (AN 11, 12, 13).

Rivalry among Existing Firms   Rivalry does not seem too intense; the two main suppliers do not even compete for 80–90 percent of their sales (AN 24, 29). When they do compete, they compete on a basis other than price and are known for different product sets (AN 30).

Evaluating Growth

Another critical input in the valuation of an equity security is growth. After all, it is hoped that future cash flows will grow over time (at least as much as inflation), since it is these future cash flows that are discounted to present value, leading to the ultimate valuation of the security. Many techniques are used to analyze and track growth. We will start by reviewing what is considered to be a company's theoretically "sustainable" growth rate. We will then move on to the strategies for achieving actual growth. Finally we will cover how to analyze historical growth and project growth into the future.

Sustainable Growth

The sustainable growth rate theory starts with defining growth as:

$$\text{Growth} = \text{Return on equity} \times \text{Retention ratio}$$

$$g = \text{ROE} \times b$$

where the retention ratio (b) is calculated as follows:

$$\text{Retention (plowback) ratio} = 1 - \text{Dividend payout ratio}$$

$$b = 1 - p$$

This equation for growth makes some intuitive sense—ROE is the return on the book equity of a firm and the retention ratio is the amount of those earnings (return) that is not paid out to shareholders, but rather retained and "plowed back" into the firm for growth (positive net present value) projects. The following example illustrates this important financial tenet:

Company A posts net income of $500,000. The Board of Directors decides to pay $100,000 in dividends to shareholders. Therefore Company A's dividend payout ratio is 20 percent ($100,000/$500,000) and the retention ratio or plowback ratio is 80 percent ($400,000/$500,000).

Net income:	$500,000	% of net income:	100%
Dividends paid:	100,000	% of net income:	20 (dividend payout ratio)
Retained earnings:	400,000	% of net income:	80 (retention ratio)

This growth product (g) is often referred to as sustainable growth (g^*) for the simple fact that dividend payout policy is typically unlikely to be volatile, because sticky dividends and the signaling effects of dividend changes reduce volatility. The sustainable growth framework allows corporate officers to develop critical firm strategies based on the relationship between sustainable growth and actual growth. To show this, we will consider the following two scenarios.

Scenario 1: Sustainable Growth Less than Actual Growth (g* < g)

Suppose that Company X has a sustainable (calculated) growth rate of 12 percent but has an actual growth rate (in sales or in earnings) of 15 percent. This would mean that Company X's financial management would need to develop strategies to raise capital or decrease (yes, *decrease*) actual growth (for not doing so could lead to a severe cash crisis—the demise of many financial managers at fast-growing companies).

If this situation is expected to continue and is not an industry-wide phenomenon, then one option the firm might consider would be *reducing its payout ratio*. This would *increase* the retention ratio and thus the sustainable growth rate, bringing it closer to actual growth. The firm could also consider *selling new equity* or *increasing leverage*. These two methods of raising capital would generate additional resources for the firm to increase its sustainable growth rate. However, both have their drawbacks. Selling equity is an expensive proposition that dilutes earnings, and increased borrowing increases the risk of financial distress. Finally, the firm might consider *profitable pruning*, which is the sale of marginal operations to plow the capital back into the remaining businesses.

Scenario 2: Sustainable Growth Greater than Actual Growth (g* > g)

Conversely, we can consider the other side of the growth paradigm, when sustainable growth is greater than actual growth. *Ignoring the problem* will not simply make it go away—it will leave the company ripe for the picking by a corporate raider or competitor who recognizes the underlying sustainable growth prospects of the company and will seek to acquire the company to unlock the hidden growth. As such, the company must start with some soul-searching to identify and remove any internal constraints on company growth. This can be a painful exercise resulting in organizational restructuring.

Failing this, when a company determines that it is unable to generate sufficient growth from within, it might consider *increasing its payout ratio*. At first this might seem like a good thing, since it returns more money to shareholders, but it is controversial in practice. Some investors might actually frown upon an increased dividend, because it raises the uncomfortable question of why the company's management does not believe they can invest the money back into the company more profitably. If an investor simply wanted a high dividend payout, they might have invested in a bond, or another stock. In addition, increasing the dividend at one point in time might raise problems if the company later decides that it wants to decrease the dividend at some point in the future to plow back more funds into the company. At that point, investors who have come to rely on the steady dividend payout ratio at the higher rate might punish the stock for lowering the dividend rate.

Growth Strategies

In the preceding discussion, we took the actual growth rate as a "given" and compared it to the sustainable growth rate to arrive at strategies for addressing divergences between the two. We will now review the key strategies that can be utilized to drive actual growth, some requiring minor tweaks and others requiring major organizational shifts.

- ✔ Existing Product Line Growth—The most basic definition of revenue (volume of units sold × price per unit) points to two of the levers that can be managed to drive growth in a company's existing product line. First, managers can try to increase the volume of units sold. This involves the marketing, sales personnel and advertising arms of a company strategizing to either sell more products to existing customers or attain new customers. For example, a clothing retailer might try to sell two shirts to a customer instead of just one, or it might open a new location in a market where it has not previously operated. Second, managers can try to increase the price per unit, especially if they are in a strong position relative to their buyers (see Porter's Five Forces above). Of course, there is an inverse relationship between price and volume that must be finely tuned. If prices are dropped too much to try to attract new customers, the overall impact on growth may be negative, and if prices are raised too much, customers may be lost.

✔ New Product Development—Revenue growth may also be achieved by developing new product lines. Across the world, companies spend billions of dollars every year in their efforts to develop new products. The pharmaceutical industry is a prime example. In this highly regulated industry, prices are often sticky and patents eventually expire, leading companies to search for years for the next new "blockbuster" drug that they will add to their existing line of drugs for sale.

✔ Cost Reductions—Revenue growth, often known as "top line" growth, is not the only way to grow. A company might have the exact same revenue year after year, but it still may achieve growth in net income through cost reductions. Astute managers are ever vigilant in their pursuit of cost savings strategies that will allow the company to boost profit margins and thus increase the amount of net income earned per dollar of revenue.

✔ Acquiring Growth—In the annals of financial history, countless corporate raiders and ambitious managers have pursued aggressive acquisition strategies to grow their businesses year after year by buying other companies. Some stay within the same line of business by buying a competitor or the producer of a related product, and others have built huge conglomerates of completely unrelated companies, all in the name of growth.

Analyzing Historical Trends and Projecting Future Performance

The growth strategies that we reviewed above point to the questions that must be asked to analyze the growth of a company. Consider a company that has achieved earnings growth of 10 percent over the past year. This data point is only the *start* of the analysis. The investor must ask a series of questions to ascertain and quantify the true, underlying "drivers" of this growth. Let's walk through a hypothetical series of questions that would be asked to arrive at a true understanding of a company's observed growth. Please see Figure 5.1.

By asking these questions and uncovering the corresponding facts and figures, total growth can be broken down into its component parts. The goal is to be able to quantify how much each component contributed

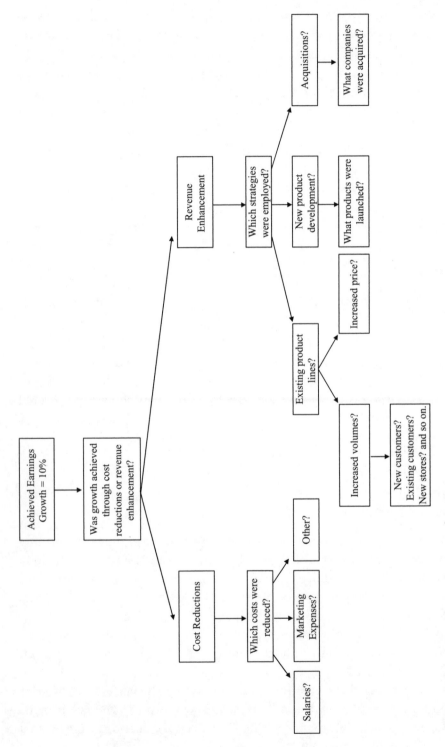

FIGURE 5.1 Hypothetical Series of Questions.

to the total growth rate. For example, was the growth of 10 percent split fairly evenly between the components (e.g., 1 percent through cost reductions, 2 percent through volume increases, 2 percent through price increases, 3 percent through new products, and 2 percent through acquisitions)? Or was it highly skewed toward one of the components (e.g., 9 percent through the acquisition of a major competitor and only 1 percent through everything else)?

With these answers in hand, we can make more accurate projections of future growth, and thus more accurate investment valuations. In practice, many analysts use historical growth trends to extrapolate into the future. In other words, if a company has grown at an average rate of 10 percent over the past five years, then growth of 10 percent serves as the baseline for projected future growth. But we all know that past performance is no guarantee of future results. As such, we can use our analysis of the drivers of historical growth to make the necessary adjustments to our predictions of future growth.

For example, consider a company with a consistent track record of launching successful new products, year after year. This has accounted for two-thirds of the company's average growth rate of 15 percent over the past five years. However, we have uncovered the following facts through our research: (1) A recent change in management has stifled the culture of risk-taking at the company, (2) Spending on research and development has decreased significantly over the past five years, (3) Barriers to entry in the industry are low, with many new firms starting up and offering competitive products, and (4) Rivalry among existing firms has increased, with many competitors beginning to launch new products of their own. Based on these facts, it appears that the company's strategy of achieving growth through new product development is in jeopardy. Since new product development accounts for two-thirds of the company's growth, the past growth rate of 15 percent is unlikely to be achieved going forward.

PROBLEM SET

Question 1

The following are selected financial data (growth rate in sales represents end-of-year data; all else is beginning-of-year policy data) for the Widget Corp., a New Jersey based retailer of specialty products for the engineering market:

	2006	2007	2008
Profit margin (%)	1.77	1.65	1.16
Retention ratio (%)	91	90	81
Asset turnover (×)	2.51	2.35	2.38
Financial leverage (×)	2.36	2.72	2.72
Growth rate in sales (%)	10.04	14.54	7.28

A. Calculate Widget's sustainable growth rate in each year.

B. What is Widget's payout ratio for each year?

C. Comparing the company's sustainable growth rate with its actual growth rate in sales. What growth problems does Widget appear to have faced over the 2006–2007 period?

D. In 2008, what strategy did Widget seem to employ to remedy the growth problem highlighted in Part C?

Answer

A. The sustainable growth rate for the following periods:

2006	2007	2008
9.55%	9.49%	6.08%

Note that while we were not given the ROE directly in this example, we are able to calculate it using our knowledge of the DuPont derivation. Specifically, using the information provided, we can calculate ROE as Profit margin × Asset turnover × Financial leverage. Then we multiply ROE × Retention ratio to arrive at the sustainable growth rate.

B. The payout ratios for the following periods:

2006	2007	2008
9%	10%	19%

By definition, payout ratio is calculated as 1—retention ratio for each year.

C. During this period Widget's actual sales growth is greater than its sustainable growth rate. Thus, Widget Corp. is growing too fast; to sustain this growth, management would need to adjust the company's financial "levers." In 2007, management seems to begin this task by decreasing the asset turnover ratio, net profit margin ratio, and retention rate. However, the significant increase in financial leverage more than offsets these decreases and the increase in actual sales is again greater than the sustainable growth rate.

D. In 2008, management again toyed with the financial levers of Widget Corp. in order to permit a more sustainable growth strategy. A significant decrease in the net profit margin and the retention ratio coupled with only a slight increase in asset turnover ratio and a flat leverage ratio yielded a sharp decrease in actual growth that was much closer to the sustainable growth rate. In subsequent years, further fine-tuning of these levers should permit Widget Corp. to achieve strong, sustainable growth without the problems that too much growth can bring.

Question 2

Company ABC has exhibited average growth of 10 percent over the past five years. Based on this historical performance, a financial analyst is projecting growth of 10 percent for the next five years. What adjustments would be necessary to this projection (up or down) given the following information?

Case 1: The majority of growth over the past five years has been achieved through acquisitions. This year management has indicated that it has identified no viable acquisition candidates for the future.

Case 2: Growth has been achieved through increased pricing and increased sales to existing customers, with no new store openings. Over the next five years, management plans to double the number of stores around the country, while continuing to increase pricing and sales to existing customers.

Case 3: The company has consistently achieved price concessions from its suppliers, helping to reduce costs (and thus boost earnings growth) by the equivalent of 2 percent per year. However, an analysis of Porter's Five Forces indicates that the bargaining power of suppliers increased substantially last year due to a merger between two key suppliers.

Answer

Case 1: Decrease growth forecast to account for the lack of acquisition activity.

Case 2: Increase growth forecast to account for the new store openings.

Case 3: Given the increased bargaining power of suppliers, price concessions are now less likely to be achieved. Thus, the growth forecast must be decreased.

Evaluating Risk

We have now seen how to measure and evaluate the financial performance, management techniques, industry characteristics, and growth of a company. However, before moving on to the final step of equity valuation, we must first formulate a measurement process for the risk of a firm.

Any discussion of risk in investment finance must focus on an assessment of the required rate of return (i.e., the rate of return that is necessary to compensate the investor for the risk that is undertaken by investing in the company). This required rate of return is what will be used to discount the future cash flows of the company to their present value.

The Capital Asset Pricing Model

The Capital Asset Pricing Model (known as CAPM) is the leading theory of equity investment risk and required return, among both academics and practitioners. A fundamental element of CAPM is the risk measure known as beta, which is specific to each and every stock. Beta represents the covariance between the returns of that stock and the market as a whole. A beta of one would perfectly correlate with the market, whereas a beta of two would mean that the particular equity would be twice as volatile (if the market increased or decreased by 10 percent, then this equity would increase or decrease by 20 percent). An investment that is perfectly negatively correlated with the market (beta $= -1$) represents a perfect hedge and is not possible under practical circumstances. Consequently, the search for a perfectly negative correlation between assets has spawned activities in the derivatives market to create a synthetic hedge that approaches such a correlation.

The required rate of return is also referred to as the discount rate or capitalization rate. Under the theory of CAPM, this rate incorporates the risk of that particular equity security (measured in the context of the market) as well as the risk-free rate available in the market. The CAPM theory is summarized in the following equation, which is used to calculate the required rate of return (k):

$$k = r_f + \beta \, (r_m - r_f)$$

where:

β = Beta (the covariance of returns between that particular equity and the market portfolio)

r_f = risk-free rate (typically represented by the current U.S. Treasury rate)

r_m = the return on the market portfolio (typically based on a historical average of a basket of equity securities)

The logic of the CAPM equation is that it starts with the risk-free rate and adds to it an adjustment factor to reflect the fact that equity is not a risk-free security (in the parlance of CAPM, this is known as adding a "market risk premium" to the risk-free rate). The adjustment factor incorporates the specific risk of the security in question, as measured by beta, to result in a required rate of return that is specifically tailored to the equity security in question. Once the required rate of return (k) is calculated in this way, we can utilize it as a discount-rate mechanism in the valuation exercise of the present value of future cash flows for an equity security.

Sample Problems

Using the CAPM theory, what is the required rate of return for the following equities given the following data?:

U.S. Treasury bond yield = 5 percent and historical market return = 12 percent

SEC Corp.	Beta = 1.45	(Answer: k = 15.15%)
IRS Corp.	Beta = .85	(Answer: k = 10.95%)
FBI Corp.	Beta = 1.00	(Answer: k = 12.00%)

Note that the answers make intuitive sense. SEC Corp. is riskier than the market (as measured by beta), resulting in a higher required rate of return than the market return; IRS Corp. is less risky than the market, resulting in a lower required rate of return; FBI Corp. is exactly correlated with the market (the implication of a beta of 1), resulting in a required rate of return that is exactly equal to the market rate of return.

Equity Valuation

We have now assessed the equity on the grounds of performance (the ROE equation, industry analysis, and management techniques), growth prospects (sustainable growth, the components of growth, and future growth projections), and risk (under the construct of CAPM). Now it is time to pull all this together and value the equity.

How is an equity security valued? This is the ultimate reason we study fundamental equity analysis—to determine the financial security's "true value" and decide if it is a "buy" or a "sell." As we have noted already (but it bears repeating), equity valuation is as much an art as it is a science. As such, a variety of techniques are used, ranging from simplistic rules of thumb to detailed discounted cash flow models. We will start with the use of ratios in equity valuation and move on to the more complicated discounted cash flow techniques.

Valuation Using Ratios

While strict financial theory holds that the only way to truly value a security is by discounting its expected future cash flows to the present day, in practice, valuation ratios are commonly used as a shortcut technique. Ratios are heuristics or "rules of thumb" that point to the value of a security in a much more simplified way than discounted cash flow models. The advantage of ratios is that they can quickly and easily be assessed for the company in question, its competitors and the market as a whole, both today and over time. It could also be argued that the use of ratios is a self-fulfilling prophecy—no matter what financial theory might say, the fact of the matter is that ratios are used by investors the world over, and therefore, they are indicative of value.

Common Ratios   The following ratios are the most commonly used by investors. They may sound familiar to you already, as both financial professionals and the mainstream media frequently cite them.

✔ Price-to-Earnings (P/E)—Perhaps the most popular valuation ratio of all, this is calculated as stock price/earnings per share (EPS). A stock trading for $20 with $2.00 in EPS would have a P/E ratio of 10.

✔ Forward P/E—Instead of utilizing a stock's *current* EPS, this ratio utilizes a stock's *expected* or *future* EPS. If the same stock mentioned above were expected to generate $2.50 in EPS next year, the stock would have a Forward P/E of 8 ($20/$2.50).

✔ Price-to-Book Value—"Book value" is just another term for shareholder's equity or owner's equity on the balance sheet. It is the sum of all of a company's assets minus the sum of all of its liabilities. The ratio is calculated as stock price/book value per share.

✔ Price-to-Sales—This is similar to P/E, with sales per share in place of earnings per share.

✔ Enterprise Value-to-EBITDA—The enterprise value (EV) of a firm is the sum of its stock market capitalization *plus* preferred stock, debt, and any minority interest, *minus* cash and cash equivalents. EBITDA is the accounting shorthand for "earnings before taxes, interest, depreciation, and amortization." The ratio is calculated as EV/EBITDA. Proponents of this ratio argue that EV is a more comprehensive picture of the value of a firm as a whole (since it includes all components of the firm's capital structure, not just stock) and EBITDA is a better gauge of the performance of the underlying business (since it excludes non-operating expenses and non-cash charges).

Using Ratios   Ratios are not used in a vacuum; they are benchmarked against other ratios to arrive at a valuation conclusion. If a ratio is "out of line" with its benchmarks, it may signal a buy or a sell opportunity. This is based on the theory that the stock price will change to bring the ratio back "in line" with its benchmark. (If a stock's P/E ratio is 10 but you believe it should be 15, then the price—being in the numerator of the calculation—must go up to result in a higher P/E ratio.)

What's important to note is that ratios do not necessarily point to an *answer* about a stock's value, but rather to a situation that requires further investigation. A ratio may be "out of line" for a very sound reason. Good investment opportunities are those in which the ratio appears to be out of line simply because the stock is priced wrong, not because of some fundamental issue with the business. (For simplicity, we'll use P/E in our list following, but the same techniques could be utilized with any of the ratios listed previously.)

✔ Benchmarking over time—One common technique is to compare a valuation ratio to its historical trend. For example, suppose a company currently has a P/E ratio of 10, but over the past five years, it has had an average P/E ratio of 15. Is this a buy signal (i.e., the stock price is experiencing a temporary downturn, but it will go up in the future to bring the P/E ratio back in line with the historical average)? Or is the P/E below its historical average for a very good reason (i.e., maybe the company just lost a major customer, meaning that EPS is going to decline next year)?

✔ Benchmarking against peers—Ratios are also compared against the ratios of peer companies. For example, if you were valuing an airline stock, you would compare the P/E of the stock in question to the average P/E of all other airline stocks. You would note any divergence between the individual stock and its peers, and determine if this divergence was justifiable or if it presented an investment opportunity.

✔ Benchmarking against the market—A third technique is to compare a ratio against the market as a whole, such as the average ratio for the entire S&P 500 or the entire Dow Jones Industrial Average. Does it make sense that a particular stock has a lower P/E than that of the S&P 500 as a whole based on the company's ROE, management, growth prospects, and so on?

✔ Standardizing ratios—A common pitfall in any type of ratio analysis is the comparison of two ratios that are actually not directly comparable (comparing "apples to oranges"). For example, all P/E ratios are not created equal—one company might *exclude* unusual, one-time charges in its EPS figure, while another might *include* such charges. As such, the ratios will be different for that reason alone, not for any fundamental, underlying business reason. In practice, analysts generally like to use earnings figures that *always* exclude one-time charges or other such unusual items; this makes the ratios comparable across different companies. Whenever you see a ratio cited by a company or the media, be sure to check the underlying calculation so you understand exactly what the ratio includes or excludes. Otherwise, you could be misled by incomparable data.

Valuation Using Discounted Cash Flow Models Discounted Cash Flow (or "DCF") models are the most comprehensive valuation technique. They involve projecting all the cash flows of the security into the future and discounting them at the appropriate discount rate—the resulting net present value of all the cash flows represents the value, or price, of the security. According to financial theory, this is the one "correct" way to accurately value a stock.

In the classical sense, the cash flows to be discounted are the dividends paid to common stockholders. Thus, we have used the term *dividend* and the notation "DIV" to represent the cash flows in our examples. However, dividends may not be the correct measure of cash flow. For example, what about a company that pays no dividends? As an alternative, "free cash flow to equity" is used, calculated as: Net Income + Depreciation and Amortization—Net Capital Expenditures—Changes in Net Working Capital. Additionally, simplifying assumptions are often used to make DCF models quicker and easier to calculate. In the following section, we will start with the most simplified of DCF models and then "layer on" increasing levels of complexity.

Dividend Discount Method (aka Gordon's Constant Growth Model)

$$P_0 = \frac{DIV_0\,(1 + g)}{k - g} = \frac{DIV_1}{k - g}$$

where:

P_0 = Price today (i.e., the value of the stock)

DIV_t = Dividend at time t (e.g., t of 0 = today, t of 1 = next year)

k = Required rate of return calculated using CAPM

g = Growth rate (of dividends, free cash flow, etc.)

As its name implies, this model assumes one, constant growth rate for the entire projection period. This makes it easy to calculate, but also fairly unrealistic in practice. How many companies grow at one rate for their entire lifetime?

H Model

$$P_0 = \frac{D_0(1 + g_n)}{k - g_n} + \frac{(D_0)(H)(g_a - g_n)}{k - g_n}$$

P_0 = Price today

D_0 = Today's value of dividends

g_a = Abnormally high growth rate

g_n = Long-run growth rate

H = Number of years it is expected that the abnormally high growth rate will last

The H model adds to the realism of the projection by dividing the life cycle of a company into two periods: one of faster growth and one of slower growth. This is a trait exhibited by many companies in the real world—when they are young, they grow at a fast pace as they launch their products and gain market share. This continues for some period of time, but then their growth slows to a more sustainable, long-term rate once they have matured and saturated the market.

Multistage (2-Stage) Model

$$P_0 = \underbrace{\frac{DIV_1}{(1+k)^1} + \frac{DIV_2}{(1+k)^2} + \frac{DIV_3}{(1+k)^3} + \frac{DIV_4}{(1+k)^4} + \frac{DIV_5}{(1+k)^5}}_{\text{Stage 1}} + \underbrace{\frac{P_5}{(1+k)^5}}_{\text{Stage 2}}$$

where:

$$P_5 = \frac{DIV_6}{k-g} = \frac{DIV_5(1+g_{long})}{k-g_{long}}$$

P_0 = Price today

DIV_t = Value of dividend at time t (1, 2, 3 . . .)

k = Required rate of return calculated using CAPM

g_{long} = Long-run growth rate

The multistage model allows for the most customized or "explicit" cash flow projections. In Stage 1, the cash flows are projected individually, on a year-by-year basis. There is no single, specific growth rate chosen—growth could be 5 percent in year one, 10 percent in year two, 15 percent in year three, −10 percent in year four, 7 percent in year five, and so on. In addition, Stage 1 can last for as many years as the analyst sees fit, from three years to 300 years. In practice, a five- to ten-year period is usually used (as in this example, which has a five year period for Stage 1).

In Stage 2, a simplified calculation based on a long-term growth rate is incorporated. Notice that the value of P_5 in Stage 2 simply utilizes the constant growth method that we reviewed in method #1 above. The idea behind the multistage model is that growth can be explicitly forecast for a few years, but beyond that, it is impossible to predict the future with a high degree of accuracy, so a simplified assumption is more appropriate. The Stage 2 value is sometimes known as the "terminal value" or "exit value," since it is the value of all the cash flows that accrue at the "end" of the explicit assumption period (i.e., after Stage 1). It can also be thought of as the price at which the asset could be sold at that point in time.

Sensitivity Analysis and IRR

While our ratio valuation and DCF techniques may appear precise, they all involve uncertainty. What if the discount rate chosen is too high or too low? What if earnings growth is slower or faster than projected? Uncertainty is impossible to eliminate, but it is also improper to simply ignore. Sensitivity analysis can be used to understand the implications of uncertainty in a valuation, and IRR analysis can be used in cases in which the discount rate is not given.

Sensitivity Analysis   Sensitivity analysis is a technique by which key assumptions are varied, and the resulting impact on valuation is quantified. For example, growth rate is a key assumption in any DCF model—the faster the growth, the more valuable the stock, all else being equal. You may have a best guess as to the future growth rate, but you can never know for certain. As such, you can calculate the value of the stock using a *range* of growth rates, centered on your best estimate. This would result in a *sensitivity table* like the one in Table 5.2.

TABLE 5.2 Sensitivity Table			
	Downside	*Best Guess*	*Upside*
Growth Rate	2%	7%	15%
Stock Value	$20	$30	$80

So, our best estimate of the stock's value is $30 per share. But with sensitivity analysis, we can also see a range of values using different assumptions for growth. Even in a "downside" case, the stock is still worth $20, and if growth is much faster than expected, the stock's value will shoot up significantly.

Internal Rate of Return   As defined previously, the internal rate of return (IRR) is the discount rate that causes the present value of a stream of future cash flows to be exactly equal to zero. Thus, calculating IRR is like a DCF valuation in reverse. It takes the projected stream of future cash flows as a given, but it does not use CAPM to *input* a discount rate into the model—instead, the *output* of the model is a discount rate (the discount rate that sets the present value to zero). If the actual discount rate is less than the IRR, then the NPV will be positive; if the actual discount rate is greater than the IRR, then the NPV will be negative; and if the actual discount rate is equal to the IRR, then the NPV will be zero (by definition).

CAPM is a theoretical construct that has its own inherent uncertainties—How is beta calculated? What is the correct risk-free rate of return? What is the correct market rate of return? All of these answers are subject to debate. Therefore, investors can use IRR as a "gut check" or "hurdle rate" in evaluating an investment. The higher the IRR, the better, generally speaking. Many investors will set a target IRR for all of their investments—say 15 or 20 percent. An investment must meet this hurdle rate in order for funds to be committed.

Equity Valuation—Sample Problems

Given the preceding data (from the CAPM problem set), in addition to the following information, calculate the intrinsic value of each security:

1. SEC Corp.
   Current dividend = $2.50
   Long-term growth rate = 12%.
   Intrinsic value = ($2.50 × 1.12) divided by (.1515—12) = $88.89
2. IRS Corp.
   Current dividend = $1 and is expected to grow at 5 percent per year for the next two years and then increase to a long-term growth rate of 9 percent.

$$\text{Value} = \frac{\$1 \times 1.05}{1.1095} + \frac{1 \times 1.05^2}{1.1095^2} + \frac{(DIV_2 \times 1.09) \text{ divided by } 0.019}{1.1095^2}$$

Value $= \$49.52$

Case Study: Equity Valuation

In the following case study, much of the preliminary detective work is not addressed. This is not to say that the analysis techniques that we covered in this chapter are not applicable in practice. Rather, we assume that the background research has already been performed—financial performance, industry analysis, management techniques, growth prospects, and the like. This allows us to take the "inputs" as given and focus on the procedure and overall methodology behind the valuation process.

Following is a summary of the important background and metrics for our (fictitious) case study company: Hamilton Enterprises.

Company and Industry Background

Hamilton Enterprises is on the forefront of the "green revolution." The Boston-based company designs, manufactures, and distributes solar energy panels used by private consumers and businesses to lower their electricity usage. Hamilton Enterprises is an industry leader. It was the first to develop solar technology and has invested heavily in building manufacturing plants that meet the government's strict regulatory requirements. The company enjoys significant leverage as the largest solar panel producer in the country, and its only peers are smaller, start-up firms. Recently, federal, state, and local governments have taken a keen interest in solar technology. They have passed tax incentives to defray the costs of designing panels and building manufacturing plants, and they are loosening their regulatory guidelines for producing solar panels.

Growth Forecasts
Analysts have been impressed by the company's growth track record (15 percent average growth over the past five years), and most expect growth of 15 percent to continue for the next five years, before settling down to a long-term growth rate of 7 percent. However, one

Company and Industry Background (*Continued*)

analyst is particularly optimistic, projecting even faster growth of 20 percent for five years, followed by 8 percent in the long run. Another analyst is more pessimistic than most, projecting growth of only 10 percent for the next five years, followed by 5 percent for the long run.

Key Statistics
($ in millions)

Revenues	$606.0
Cost of Goods Sold	$215.0
Gross Profit	$391.0
Selling, General & Administrative Expenses	$230.0
Operating Income (aka EBIT)	$161.0
Interest Expense	$ 19.0
Income before Income Taxes	$142.0
Income Taxes	$ 31.0
Net Income	**$111.0**
Supplemental Information	
Number of shares outstanding (millions)	41.6
Current stock price per share	$27.00
Dividends per share	$2.00
Depreciation & Amortization ($ millions)	$24.00
Beta	1.25
Balance Sheet Information	
Cash (millions)	$50.0
Debt outstanding (millions)	$500.0
Market Information	
Peer Group Average P/E	14.5
Peer Group Average EV/EBITDA	11.0
Risk-free rate	5.0%
Historical market return	12.0%

Ratio Analysis

Let's start by using two of our ratios to analyze the current stock price.

1. P/E Ratio—To calculate the P/E ratio, we first calculate earnings per share (EPS). This is $111.0 million divided by 41.6 million

shares = $2.67 EPS. Now we divide the current stock price of $27 by $2.67, for a P/E of 10.1. Comparing this to the peer group average of 14.5, we see that the stock would be considered *undervalued* according to this metric. To be more in line with its peers, the stock price would have to rise to $38.72, resulting in a P/E ratio of 14.5 ($38.72/$2.67).

2. EV/EBITDA—The company's enterprise value is its stock market capitalization (41.6 million shares × $27 = $1,123.9 million) plus its debt outstanding ($500 million) less cash ($50 million), for a total of $1,573.9 million (or $1.6 billion). Its EBITDA is calculated as its EBIT ($161.0 million) plus depreciation & amortization ($24.0 million), equal to $185.0 million. Thus, its EV/EBITDA ratio is $1,573.9 million divided by $185.0 million, or 8.5. Like its P/E ratio, this ratio is also below that of its peers. A new stock price of $38.08 would result in an EV/EBITDA ratio of 11, like its peers.

Discounted Cash Flow Model

We've seen that the company appears undervalued according to two of our ratios. Now we'll use a DCF model to provide an alternate view of valuation. Specifically, we'll use the multistage (2-stage) model.

$$P_0 = \underbrace{\frac{DIV_1}{(1+k)^1} + \frac{DIV_2}{(1+k)^2} + \frac{DIV_3}{(1+k)^3} + \frac{DIV_4}{(1+k)^4} + \frac{DIV_5}{(1+k)^5}}_{\text{Stage 1}} + \underbrace{\frac{P_5}{(1+k)^5}}_{\text{Stage 2}}$$

where:

$$P_5 = \frac{DIV_6}{k-g} = \frac{DIV_5(1+g_{long})}{k-g_{long}}$$

Step 1: First, we'll need to calculate the discount rate, and for that we'll use CAPM. From the data provided above, we have all the necessary inputs for the CAPM equation:

$$k = r_f + \beta\,(r_m - r_f)$$
$$k = 5.0\% + 1.25 \times (12.0\% - 5.0\%)$$
$$k = 13.75\%$$

Step 2: Now we can move on to the value of Stage 1, the initial period of "abnormal" growth. What growth rate shall we use? For now, let's use the average analyst prediction of 15 percent for five years.

	Year 1		Year 2		Year 3		Year 4		Year 5
Stage 1 Value =	$\dfrac{\$2.00}{(1 + 13.75\%)^\wedge 1}$	+	$\dfrac{\$2.30}{(1 + 13.75\%)^\wedge 2}$	+	$\dfrac{\$2.65}{(1 + 13.75\%)^\wedge 3}$	+	$\dfrac{\$3.04}{(1 + 13.75\%)^\wedge 4}$	+	$\dfrac{\$3.50}{(1 + 13.75\%)^\wedge 5}$
Stage 1 Value =	$\dfrac{\$2.00}{1.1375}$	+	$\dfrac{\$2.30}{1.2939}$	+	$\dfrac{\$2.65}{1.4718}$	+	$\dfrac{\$3.04}{1.6742}$	+	$\dfrac{\$3.50}{1.9044}$
Stage 1 Value =	$1.76	+	$1.78	+	$1.80	+	$1.82	+	$1.84
Stage 1 Value =	$8.99								

Step 3: On to Stage 2, the terminal value, using the long-run growth rate. Again, we'll use the average estimate of 7 percent to start.

$$P_5 = \frac{\$3.50 \times (1 + 7.00\%)}{(13.75\% - 7.00\%)}$$

$$P_5 = \frac{\$3.74}{6.75\%}$$

$$P_5 = \$55.45$$

$$\text{Stage 2 Value} = \frac{\$55.45}{(1 + 13.75\%)^\wedge 5}$$

$$\text{Stage 2 Value} = \frac{\$55.45}{1.9044}$$

$$\text{Stage 2 Value} = \$29.12$$

Step 4: Finally we add Stage 1 plus Stage 2 for a DCF valuation of $38.10.

$$\text{DCF Valuation} = \$29.12 + \$8.99$$

$$\text{DCF Valuation} = \$38.10$$

At first glance, it appears that we have a clear conclusion to our analysis: the stock is **undervalued** and should be a **buy**. Our P/E ratio and EV/EBITDA calculations implied that the stock price should trade at about $38–$39, and our DCF model also supported a price in that range. However, let's conduct a sensitivity analysis before finalizing our conclusion.

Sensitivity Analysis

Since we have a range of analyst growth estimates (pessimistic, average and optimistic), our sensitivity analysis will vary the growth rates and assess the impact on valuation. To build the table following, we simply "plug and chug"—that is, repeat steps 2 through 4 above, substituting the pessimistic and optimistic growth rates in place of the average growth rates.

Case	Pessimistic	Average	Optimistic
Growth	10% for 5 years, then 5%	15% for 5 years, then 7%	20% for 5 years, then 8%
Valuation	$26.68	$38.10	$50.71

Now we have added some intrigue to our earlier conclusion: If the pessimistic analyst is to be believed, then the stock is not undervalued at all, it is *fairly valued*. The DCF valuation of $26.68 is right in line with the current stock price of $27.

Conclusion

We have reached an impasse that is all too common in practice, where valuation is more an "art" than a "science." There is no truly "right" answer to this question; only time will tell the future price. However, this does not mean that all is lost, for this is exactly where all your additional detective work comes into play. What industry forces are at work here? Is management strong and credible? Are the organizational structures and culture conducive to innovation? What is the company's strategy for growth? (Price increases, acquisitions, international expansion?) How do the company's financial metrics compare to its peers? (ROE, operating margins, asset turnover?) Is the company appropriately leveraged? Your answers to these questions will be your guide to the final conclusion.

In our current case study, we do have some clues. First, we should note that a significant industry force is rearing its head—the threat of new entrants. In fact, the government is helping to increase this threat through its tax incentives and regulatory reforms. These changes are alleviating barriers to entry, such as high start-up costs and tough regulatory re-quirements, making it easier for new entrants to prosper. Increased rivalry among firms is likely to ensue, including price concessions and lower market share.

Second, we know that Hamilton Enterprise's peers are much younger, start-up companies. Thus, we must question the validity of us-ing their P/E and EV/EBITDA ratios as points of comparison. All else equal, younger companies enjoy brighter growth prospects than more mature companies, as they launch new products and grab market share. This could be the reason that Hamilton Enterprises has lower ratios than its peers. The company's stock is not mispriced; it is simply more mature and thus not directly "comparable" to its peers.

Putting all these facts together, our pessimistic analyst may be right after all: the stock is appropriately priced at around $27. This is also a sit-uation that is all too common in practice. Market efficiencies mean that many more companies are fairly valued than are mispriced, and it takes great skill and determination to uncover the hidden gems.

Chapter

Credit Analysis

I n this chapter you will learn:

- ✔ Basics of bonds.
- ✔ Types of fixed income securities.
- ✔ Credit analysis tools and techniques.
- ✔ Credit ratings.

Credit analysis, for the exclusive purpose of making loans, is one of the oldest arts in investment finance. As an example, assume that centuries ago, benevolent overlords (yes, they did exist, albeit, in the minority to their tyrannous brethren) would determine whether a minor lord was deserving enough for a loan (Did he work hard? Was he knowledgeable about his craft—be it artisan or agrarian? Did he possess any collateral?). This loan was to be used by the minor lord to produce goods that could be later sold to earn enough currency (or other goods) to repay the loan with interest. The credit analysis function didn't really take form during these early years for the simple reason that brutal force and cruel punishment prevented any serious defaults.

The concept illustrated by this somewhat far-fetched example is important for our discussion of credit analysis—the relationship between the two "investment parties" (lender and borrower) is very different from the relationship shared by equity owners and the company. With the equity relationship, the players seek a mutually beneficial outcome: the capital growth of the firm and consequently the increase in the share price. Therefore, it is in the best interests of the shareholder (who has limited claim to the assets of the company, but rather only the future growth prospects) to hope and even assist (perhaps this is a bit utopian—shareholders promoting the company's prospects; or is it?) in the future growth of the company. In the case of the bondholder and the company, however, the relationship is not as mutually synergistic because the bondholder simply desires (read: is only entitled to) the stated interest payments on a timely basis and the eventual repayment of principle at maturity. Therefore the agency relationship that exists between bondholder and company is more consistent with the relationship between a company and its raw material supplier ("Just pay me for my goods promptly and we will be satisfied"). It is important to realize that a bondholder (as well as the equity holder) is also a supplier to the company—a supplier of capital. But because the bondholder is "entitled" to some portion of the assets of the firm upon default (depending on the terms embedded in the bond issuance) he or she is less interested in any future growth and more concerned about current net worth and business policies—in other words, everything that goes into the ability of the borrower to repay the loan in full.

In early modern times, the analysis of lending practices was *the* investment science. Only over the past 100 years or so have equities entered into the picture. Proponents of this "paper financing" could easily value its worth; they would charge an exorbitant fee for their compensation to outweigh any risks of forfeiture. This fee was eventually renamed to the more euphemistic "debt service" or "interest." In addition, the early covenants of these loans granted the lender many rights and liberties (perhaps the takeover of a business, the sale of assets, or a management reorganization) to such a degree that the sheer power rendered by these financiers could force the reconciliation of any outstanding loan.

As the financial markets became more standardized and regulated, these financiers were forced to succumb to more realistic interest terms. In addition, with the advent of equities, firms in need of capital could now seek it without submitting to unfair practices by the lending financiers. Hence the birth of the formal study of credit analysis. Lenders needed to make up for the "margin squeeze" created by these external forces. If the amount that was being charged to borrow capital was under pressure (decreasing), then it stands to reason that the "default cushion" that the lenders had enjoyed was also diminishing. Therefore, the need grew for a more prudent methodology to assess default rates. Because lenders needed to become more discriminating, they employed analysts to scrutinize a borrower's current business, industry position and trends, current financial picture (ratio analysis), and collateral (assets) before considering the holding of any bonds (granting credit). Furthermore, the analyst would attempt to rationalize the reason the company was seeking credit:

> Were the company's expansion plans warranted? Did the planned acquisition make economic sense given the current environment?

In addition, the analyst would be concerned about the company's balance sheet:

> Does the company have any noncurrent assets held at book value that have a significantly higher market value? How about the liability side of the balance sheet—what is the amount (percentage of pension assets) of unfunded pension liabilities? What is the company's current debt level?

These are the musings of a credit analyst; they have certainly come a long way. And, they indicate what the savvy potential investor should look for.

Basics of Bonds

Definition

Throughout this chapter, we will use terms like "bond," "credit," and "fixed income security" interchangeably, because they generally mean the same thing. As the nomenclature suggests, a fixed income security is a security that provides for fixed cash flows between the borrower and the lender. The legal relationship between the borrower and lender outlines the terms for the repayment of the borrowed money at some future date (the maturity date) along with interest payments at various times during the life of the loan. So a bond, just as it sounds, is one person's promise to do something (repay borrowed funds) within a given amount of time.

The cash flows of the bond may not necessarily stay the *same* over the life of the bond or be known *exactly* in advance, but they are "fixed" in the sense that they are based on pre-determined, contractually defined payment terms.

The contractual agreement is detailed in a legal document known as an *indenture*, which defines the rights and obligations of the borrower and the lender with respect to the bond. As we'll discuss later, the credit analyst must carefully examine the indenture as part of the credit review, searching for any provisions that might be beneficial and/or detrimental to the bondholder (i.e., the lender). These provisions can cover such areas as additional debt issuance (the lender would want to limit the borrower's ability to increase its outstanding debt until its existing bond is extinguished), sinking fund requirements (moneys escrowed by the borrower to assure future repayments), and sale and leaseback transactions (protecting the lender from the borrower's sale or lease of assets that would be viewed as security to the lender).

Key Components

Following are the key components of a typical bond:

Coupon. This represents the percentage paid to the security owner as a periodic (typically monthly, quarterly, or semiannually) cash flow. This cash flow is calculated by multiplying the stated coupon by the bond's *par value* (or *face value*), which is the amount that will be repaid at the maturity date (5 years, 10 years, etc.). For example, if a bond is offered at a par value of $1,000 with a coupon of 8 percent, the annual cash flow that is generated would be $80 (8% × $1,000).

Price. Whatever a bond's par value, it often trades in the market at a *discount* or *premium* to par. For example, a bond with a par value of $1,000 might trade for $1,020, in which case it would be "quoted at 102." The discount or premium to par reflects both market conditions and the creditworthiness of the issuer.

Current Yield. This is the current cash flow divided by the current price of the bond (remember again, the price is usually different from the par value). Continuing our example above, an 8 percent coupon on a bond priced at $1,020 would result in a current yield of 7.8 percent ($80 divided by $1,020). Note that in this case, the yield of 7.8 percent is lower than the coupon of 8 percent. In fact, there is always an inverse relationship between the price and yield of a bond: the higher the price, the lower the yield (and vice versa). This inverse relationship is best described by the actions of a seesaw—as the price goes up, the yield goes down. This makes sense intuitively. The more money you need to pay up front to buy the bond, the more that price will reduce your return (the yield).

Yield to Maturity. Unlike the current yield, the yield to maturity calculation calculates the fixed income security's return using the security's maturity value as an ending cash flow. The yield to maturity (YTM) calculation is simply an internal rate of return (IRR) equation, where the price paid for the bond is the initial, negative outflow, the coupon cash flows represent the periodic inflows, and the maturity value is the final value at termination.

Types of Fixed Income Securities

Following is a list of some of the common types of fixed income securities available in the market.

Corporate Bonds. When a corporation wants to borrow money from public investors (for example, to build a new plant or to buy another company), it "issues" a corporate bond—which is to say that it sells the bonds to investors. The corporation thus becomes the "borrower," and all those investors who buy the corporate bonds are the "lenders." All manner of corporations borrow money in this way, from casinos to construction companies, and these bonds trade on the open market just like stocks.

Alternatively, a corporation might seek a *private loan* directly from a bank or other lender. Many businesses are too small to issue bonds to the public, but they borrow money from banks everyday to pay for inventory, raw materials, and so on. Such loans may be packaged together into a security that trades on the open market, or they may simply be held by the bank as a private loan. Either way, the same principles of credit analysis apply just as surely to them as they do to corporate bonds.

Municipal Bonds. Municipal bonds are issued by local public agencies or municipalities, rather than by private corporations. Examples of entities that issue municipal bonds are state governments, city governments, and local transportation agencies. Two main subsets of municipal bonds are *revenue bonds* and *general obligation* ("GO") bonds. Revenue bonds are backed by a specific project, like a toll road, while GO bonds are backed by an entire municipality (most importantly, its taxing authority).

A key advantage of municipal bonds is that they are exempt from both federal and state taxes (in the state in which they are issued). This permits the issuer to raise capital at a lower rate due to the tax-free cash flow generated. Because of this government subsidy, investors (especially those in high tax brackets) can enjoy a higher after-tax return than otherwise may be available (on an after-tax basis) on taxable securities. To evaluate between these different securities, an investor needs to calculate the taxable equivalent yield (TEY).

$$\text{TEY} = \frac{\text{Tax free yield}}{(100\% - \text{Tax rate})}$$

Municipal bonds are not to be confused with *U.S. Treasuries,* which are backed by the full faith and credit of the United States *federal* government. U.S. Treasuries are classified based on their maturity (one year or less is a T-Bill, between one and 10 years is a T-Note, and over 10 years is a T-Bond). They usually have the lowest yield of all comparable bonds because they are viewed as essentially risk-free (i.e., there is a very, very low probability that the U.S. federal government will default on its bonds).

The relationship between the yields of U.S. Treasuries and municipal bonds can fluctuate. At times, municipal bonds may yield less than U.S. Treasuries, owing to their tax-free status, but in extremely risky market circumstances, municipal bonds may yield more than U.S. Treasuries as investors flee to the ultimate "risk-free" safety of U.S.-backed securities.

High-Yield Bonds. Also known as "junk" bonds, these securities became notorious in the 1980s as the medium of choice for corporate raiders and takeover specialists, but they are now more of a mainstream vehicle for even the average investor. As their name implies, the yields on "high-yield" bonds are higher than those of other bonds. This is due to the risk/return trade-off that is fundamental to all of finance: the higher the risk, the higher the required return. In the case of high-yield bonds, they offer higher returns (in the form of yield), because they are deemed to be riskier than other bonds.

Typically, "investment grade" securities are those rated AAA to BBB- (using the Standard & Poor's rating system) and "high-yield" are those rated below BBB-. (We will cover bond ratings later in this chapter.) Due to their high level of implied risk, high yield bonds are often analyzed from an equity perspective as much as they are from a traditional credit analysis perspective.

Convertible Bonds. A convertible bond is a "hybrid" security, somewhere between an equity and a bond. The holder of a convertible bond receives a periodic cash flow (represented by the coupon) as well as the ability to exchange the bonds into common stock at some given exchange rate (number of shares per bond).

To illustrate, we consider the following convertible bond issue (par value of $1,000):

Coupon:	7%
Maturity:	10 years
Current market price of bond:	$1,050
Current market price of stock:	$55
Conversion ratio:	15.75
Dividend on common stock per share:	$1.00

The *conversion ratio* represents the number of shares of common stock for which each bond can be exchanged within the given period of the bond (maturity date). The premium (or discount) of a convertible bond is calculated by multiplying the conversion ratio by the current stock price (to ascertain the current value of conversion) and comparing this value to the bond's current price. In this example, each bond would result in 15.75 shares of common stock, each valued at $55 per share, for a total value of $866.25 (15.75 × $55). This is a $183.75 discount to the current price of the bond ($1,050 − $866.25). Furthermore, the convertible bond issue is providing a higher level of coupon (7 percent) versus the common stock dividend payout yield ($1.00/$55 = 1.82%). In dollar terms, the cash flow generated on the bond is currently $70 per bond, whereas the common stock would only generate $15.75 per each bond converted (15.75 shares × $1.00 dividend per share). Thus, it would seem imprudent and unjustified for an investor to convert his or her bond holdings at this time (while shares are trading at $55).

Credit Default Swaps. Credit default swaps (CDS) have become part of the lexicon of the financial meltdown of 2008/2009 in much the same way that high-yield bonds were synonymous with the corporate raiders of the 1980s. Credit default swaps are not investments directly in fixed income securities; rather they are *derivatives* whose cash flows are based on an underlying fixed income security. A CDS transaction is structured so that the holder of a bond ("Party A") receives protection against a default by the issuer of the bond. Specifically, Party A pays a semi-regular protection premium to another party ("Party B"), who in turn assumes the risk of default. (Party A and Party B are known as the *counterparties* of the transaction.) If the issuer defaults, Party B must compensate Party A for its loss. If the issuer does not default, then Party B profits by receiving the semi-regular protection premium payments from Party A.

For this reason, credit default swaps are often likened to insurance, with Party B being the "insurer" (the company that must pay out in the event of a loss), just like a car insurer must compensate a car owner in the event of an accident. However, before 2008/2009, a key ingredient in the world of CDSs that was often overlooked was the financial health of the insurer (i.e., the "counterparty," Party B). Companies playing the role of Party B stretched themselves too thin and assumed too much default risk from other parties. Thus, defaults became a financial catastrophe for them, just as a huge earthquake would be a financial catastrophe for a home insurer if the insurer were not properly capitalized (as they are required to be under U.S. insurance regulations).

Credit Analysis Tools

The bond basics we have just covered are essentially the first steps in the credit analysis exercise. As a precursor to using the tools described below, it is essential to understand the type of security, the key terms, the seniority in the capital structure and the collateral backing the security. Two bonds from two different companies may look identical using our credit analysis tools below, but if one has a higher seniority than the other, that fact must certainly factor into the evaluation as well.

So now let's meet Myron—our stereotypical green eye-shaded credit analyst. Myron is gainfully employed (although he seems to spend most of his money on computer games, Spiderman comics, and lettuce for his pet rabbit) at a major commercial bank's credit department. So what does Myron do all day at work? Let's open his briefcase and see what's inside. Although many of the tools used by Myron have already been covered in Chapter 5, many are used primarily, if not exclusively, by those like Myron who are seeking to analyze credit instruments.

Introduction

The fundamental question that must be answered by any credit analyst is a deceptively simple one: *Can this borrower repay the loan in full, including all interest and principal?* The answer to this question involves answering a subset of intertwined questions: How much debt has the company borrowed? Does the company have the flexibility to continue to pay its debt in a downturn? Will the company miss market share opportunities because its debt is too burdensome?

We'll turn to each of these questions as we move forward, but first we'll start with a simple case study. Assume for a moment that you are a lending officer at a local bank (perhaps not the most pleasant daydream, we know) and you are deciding which application to approve for a $10,000 loan (assume you can only approve one):

✔ *Applicant A.* Has a commission-based sales position within the fast-growing telecommunications industry in which he has recently attained a high degree of success:

Average taxable income of $100,000 over the past two years ($80,000 in the first year and $120,000 in the second).

Household debt (credit card balances, student loans) of $35,000.

Home value (recently assessed) is $235,000 (floating-rate mortgage of $200,000).

Investment and savings (net of retirement accounts) account balances are $3,500.

✔ *Applicant B.* Has a middle management position (recently promoted) in a large conglomerate, which he has held for several years:

Average taxable income of $60,000 over the past two years ($55,000 & $65,000, respectively).

Household debt of $1,000.

Home value (recently assessed) of $150,000 (with a fixed-rate mortgage of $95,000).

Investment and savings (net of retirement accounts) account balances of $10,000.

Although an argument could be made for either of these applicants, the more solid candidate for a loan would be Applicant B. Applicant B has more fiscal restraint (less debt and more modest tastes) and therefore, a greater level of financial flexibility. Although Applicant A has grown his earnings at a faster pace than Applicant B, he is also in a more volatile position (sales in a "new" industry). If A's business contracted next year, his commission-based income would suffer. With only $3,500 in savings to cushion his $35,000 in household debt and $200,000 in mortgage debt, he might not have the financial wherewithal to withstand such a downturn. Furthermore, A's floating-rate mortgage debt subjects him to further possible volatility in his cash flows.

Now back to Myron's briefcase. In it we will find a variety of tools to analyze and quantify all of the decision-making factors that we intuitively recognized above. As we'll see, *ratios* are a particular hallmark of the credit analysis function. There are ratios to assess the amount of leverage, liquidity, financial flexibility, and operating efficiency, among other things. Each ratio answers one or more of the questions that we posed earlier, and ultimately leads to the final answer: whether or not a borrower is creditworthy.

It is critical for the discussion in this chapter to recall the importance of not relying on the single value of any ratio but rather to look at trends over time as well as comparisons within industry groups. We must also remember our earlier review of financial statement footnotes—be sure to review them for any supplemental disclosures that might affect the ratios covered in the following section.

How Much Leverage Does the Company Have?   Our first question ascertains a company's current level of borrowing. Several variations of "leverage ratios" answer this question, including:

- ✔ Total Debt/Total Equity
- ✔ Long-Term Debt/Total Equity

✔ Total Debt/Total Capitalization (where Total Capitalization = Total Debt + Total Equity)
✔ Total Debt/Total Assets
✔ Total Assets/Total Equity

Additionally, the amount of cash on the balance sheet can be subtracted from the amount of debt, and the resulting "net debt" is substituted for total debt in the ratios above. The assumption is that, theoretically, the cash on the balance sheet could be used to pay down debt and decrease the amount of leverage.

In these ratios we are looking at a snapshot of the total capitalization of a company—how much is made up of debt and how much of equity? Generally speaking, the higher the leverage, the riskier the debt. A debt-to-equity ratio of 3 to 1 illustrates a company that is leveraged to the tune of three times its equity's current market value. However, herein lies an irony (and significant importance) of credit analysis—equity is valued daily (with the movement of stock prices) whereas debt is usually held on the balance sheet at historical cost (subject to ever-changing GAAP guidelines). Thus, the credit analyst would be wise to re-price (to market) the company's outstanding debt to get a more realistic picture of true leverage.

How does one mark-to-market the debt of a company? By comparing the value of the debt currently, to what it would cost if it was to be issued today. As the interest rate environment and the company's financial condition changes, so do the required price that the market demands for the debt. For example, a 10-year corporate bond may have required a yield of 10 percent when issued, while only an 8 percent yield would be required if the bond were to be issued in the marketplace today. Therefore, the issuer would be able to save by refinancing the debt. By re-pricing the debt, the analyst can get a more accurate understanding of the true leverage of the company, and therefore, gain a better handle on its financial flexibility.

What Is the Company's Liquidity Position? *Liquidity* refers to the ability of a company to run its business on a day-to-day basis and meet its short-term obligations—that is, to pay its suppliers, pay its rent, pay its employees, sell its inventory, collect its sales on credit, and so on. It should be obvious that liquidity is crucial to the credit analyst. If a company is not in a comfortable short-term liquidity position, then its ability to repay its long-term debts is likely compromised as well (or will be when the debts come due).

Working Capital = Current Assets − Current Liabilities. Current assets and liabilities are those that are most easily converted to cash. Thus, this calculation shows how much readily available cash (current assets) the company has to meet its upcoming payment needs (current liabilities). If the number is positive, sufficient assets are available; if negative, short-term liquidity is in question.

Current Ratio = Current Assets/Current Liabilities. This is a variation on the working capital calculation. In this case, the resulting figure is a ratio. If the ratio is one or higher, readily available cash is sufficient to meet upcoming payments. If it is less than one, readily available cash is insufficient.

Cash Ratio = (Cash + Cash Equivalents)/Total Current Assets. Not all current assets are created equal—some may be more "readily" converted into cash than others. In recognition of this fact, this ratio indicates how much of a company's current assets are actually held in cold, hard cash. As the saying goes, "Cash is king."

Acid Test = (Current Assets − Inventory)/Current Liabilities. This is another variation that accounts for the potential difficulties in converting current assets into cash. Specifically, inventory is subtracted from current assets because items in inventory may be very difficult to sell, especially during market downturns. Inventory might be of little real value if it is simply collecting dust in a warehouse. (This ratio is also referred to as the "Quick Ratio.")

Days to Sell Inventory and Accounts Receivable Collection Period. These ratios were covered in Chapter 5. As discussed, they are another technique to assess the ability of a company to generate short-term cash. The lower the number of days, the more quickly, on average, the company is turning its current assets into cash.

Can the Company Afford to Service Its Debt? The leverage and liquidity ratios discussed above essentially assess the financial position of a company at a given snapshot in time—that is, as of today. We now turn to the ability of a company to service its debt over time—that is, can the company comfortably afford to pay all required interest and principal payments into the future?

This is primarily addressed through what are known as "coverage" ratios. Coverage ratios are calculated in different ways, but they all serve the same purpose: to compare a company's fixed expenses to its cash flow generation capability. Thus, the ratio illustrates the "margin of safety" that exists. If a company generates much more income than its fixed expenses, then it has a greater ability to withstand unexpected hardships. The company's income could fall and it would still have plenty left to pay its expenses. On the other hand, if the margin of safety is low, then any small misstep or financial turbulence could sink the company. These ratios also offer a clue as to a company's flexibility. All else equal, if a company generates plenty of cash to cover its fixed expenses, then it has greater flexibility to pursue new business opportunities and the like.

Here are several variations of coverage ratio calculations. In practice, analysts usually refer to several of them in their analysis, rather than focusing on any single measure.

- ✔ EBIT/Interest Expense: Utilizes earnings before interest and taxes so as to capture the underlying operating performance of the company.
- ✔ EBITDA/Interest Expense: Adds depreciation and amortization back to EBIT since they are "non-cash" expenses.
- ✔ (EBIT + Long-Term Lease Payments)/(Interest + Long-Term Lease Payments): Incorporates long-term lease payments, since they are similar to interest payments in that they are regular charges on a pre-determined schedule that are used to finance a purchase.
- ✔ Operating Cash Flow/Fixed Charges: A comprehensive measure that incorporates many factors of a company's cash flow, specifically:
  - ✔ Operating Cash Flow = Pretax income + Depreciation and amortization + Deferred income taxes + Minority interest income − Undistributed earnings from subsidiaries − Increase in receivables − Increase in inventories + Increase in accounts payable − Decrease in accrued taxes
  - ✔ Fixed Charges = A catch-all that varies by company and is meant to incorporate any "fixed" expenses, such as interest,

lease payments, rent payments, insurance premiums, pension obligations, etc.

Schedule of Debt Maturities. Another factor to keep in mind in assessing a company's ability to repay its debt is its schedule of debt maturities. This is not a calculation per se, but rather a schedule that can be found in the footnotes to the financial statements (as discussed in Chapter 5). The schedule lists, on a year-by-year basis, exactly when a company's debts are coming due (i.e., when the entire principal balance must be repaid, usually in one lump sum). Just because a company can comfortably afford to pay its regular debt service (as shown through its coverage ratios), doesn't mean that it can necessarily afford to repay or refinance the entire debt when it comes due. If Company A's debts all come due at the same time in two years, while Company B's debts are spread out evenly over 10 years, then clearly Company A faces a more imminent repayment issue. If the schedule of debt maturities shows a high level of debt coming due in the near future, then the analyst must pay careful attention to the amount of resources the company has available to pay the maturing debt and/or its ability to refinance the debt (for example, by borrowing a new loan or raising equity).

What Are the Company's Underlying Business Fundamentals? Here we are referring to the type of analysis that we reviewed in Chapter 5 to assess the heart of a company's performance, namely ROE, industry analysis, management analysis, and growth. These factors are key for the credit analyst as well. After all, once the means of financing—equity, bond, option, and so on—is removed from the equation, what remains is a *business*. Whether it is a local grocer or a multinational conglomerate, a careful and skeptical eye must be cast on the actual business. The difference between a credit analyst and an equity analyst is one of perspective, as we shall see.

Growth and Stability. When we covered equity analysis, we were primarily concerned with the level of future growth—will a company be able to grow at 5 percent per year? 10 percent? 20 percent? The higher the growth, the more valuable the stock. In credit analysis, we are more concerned with a company's *stability* of income than we are with the absolute *level* of growth. This is because lenders do not share in the income upside of a business. Lenders receive their contractually obligated interest payments of $XX no matter how fast the company grows, be it 5 percent or 500 percent. A lender's bigger concern is whether the company's income could *decline* to an extent that it is unable to pay its current debt service (or not grow fast enough to pay higher debt service in the future). In fact, an argument could even be made that too much growth is *detrimental* to a lender. High growth requires investments in inventory, property, plant, and equipment that use up valuable cash—cash that could otherwise be saved as a financial cushion to pay debt service.

Recall the issues that we analyzed regarding growth in Chapter 5. In credit analysis, we must review the same concepts of sustainable growth and the underlying drivers of growth (new product lines, new customers, cost reductions, acquisitions, etc.). But now we answer these questions from the perspective of financial stability. Do the company's growth strategies subject it to the potential for high volatility in its income? Has the company grown at a steady rate in the past, or does growth swing wildly in one direction or another? What will happen to interest coverage if the company's growth strategies do not succeed as planned?

Attention must also be focused on the underlying functioning of the entire economy, and the company's correlation to the rest of the economy. Does the company tend to grow when the economy grows, and contract when the economy contracts, or does it move in the opposite direction? Is its growth more volatile than the rest of the economy (e.g., it grows a lot even when the economy only grows a little) or less volatile? As mentioned in Chapter 2, the overall economy tends to move through boom-and-bust periods, known as the economic cycle. Industries that tend to be particularly sensitive to the economic cycle are called *cyclical*. Examples include capital goods, heavy industry manufacturers, and financial intermediaries.

Financial and Operational Performance (Analyzed using ROE). In Chapter 5 we used ROE (and its DuPont derivation) to analyze the key financial and operational metrics of a business, and these types of tools are information for credit analysis as well. Companies with strong financial and operational performance are better positioned to repay their debt. As usual, all such analysis must be considered with regard to industry averages and historical trends over time. When it comes to credit analysis, it is especially important to note if financial and operational performance is relatively stable over time or fluctuates wildly.

We must also remember that reported financial data are not always what they seem, so be sure to review the footnotes to the financial statements for anything unusual or questionable. When applying U.S. Generally Accepted Accounting Procedures (GAAP) standards, companies have a margin within which they can report their accounting data. Management's hand can mold reported numbers in areas such as depreciation methods, pension liabilities, revenue recognition, bad debt reserves, and intangible items. The use of conservative versus liberal accounting practices is sometimes referred to as the "quality" of a company's earnings. Companies that use straightforward, conservative principles are said to have "high quality" earnings, a good sign for the credit analyst. After all, debt service ultimately cannot be paid through an accounting gimmick—it must be paid with cold, hard cash.

Industry Analysis. Just as we saw in equity analysis, Porter's Five Forces are critical to the credit analysis arena. As discussed in Chapter 5, they are: bargaining power of buyers, bargaining power of suppliers, threat of new entrants, threat of substitute products or services, and rivalry among existing firms. How competitive is the industry in question? Are the players out to gain market share at the expenses of profits? Is the industry trending toward consolidation, making small companies vulnerable to large companies? A tough regulatory environment can serve as a helpful barrier to entry, or new regulations may serve to ruin management's best-laid plans.

Management Analysis. Once again, an assessment of those who are at the helm of a company is just as important to credit analysis as it is to equity analysis. Of course, it remains hard to quantify exactly what makes for "good" versus "bad" management, but the management traits we reviewed in Chapter 5 are a helpful guide. Over time, management analysis is something that becomes more intuitive to seasoned investors.

What Legal Protections Exist to Benefit the Lender?   Now we turn to an assessment of the "worst-case scenario." What protects the lender against financial difficulties or poor business decisions, if anything? Legal protections primarily take the form of seniority, collateral, and covenants.

Seniority. A bond's "seniority" refers to its position within the capital structure. You can think of a company's capital structure like a deck of playing cards, with different securities being different cards at different positions in the deck (in fact, industry insiders often use the term "the stack" to refer to a company's capital structure).

- ✔ The securities at the top of the deck are known as the most *senior* securities (usually debt). They are the safest and most likely to retain all of their value.

- ✔ At the bottom of the deck are the riskiest securities, those facing the highest probability of loss in value, but also the highest possibility for upside gain (usually common stock or equity).

- ✔ In the middle can exist a hodgepodge of specialized securities. For example, preferred stock is above common stock, but below debt. In addition, a company will often have two levels (or "tranches") of debt, a higher level called "senior debt" and a lower level called "subordinated debt." Other terms for middle layers of debt include "mezzanine debt" or "junior debt." Whatever the terminology employed, the implication is the same— the debt is below the senior debt in the capital structure, and thus at a greater risk of loss.

What determines a security's position within the capital structure? Why is one bond called "senior" and another called "junior"? The key element is *the ordering of the legal claims* that exist on the company's assets. In other words, who gets paid first, second, third, and so on in the event of financial difficulties. We'll illustrate this with the extreme example of a bankruptcy liquidation. Suppose a company has outstanding senior debt of $35, subordinated debt of $40 and equity of $25, for a total capitalization of $100. Now let's consider three cases:

1. After the liquidation of all its assets (i.e., selling all its inventory, raw materials, buildings, etc.), the company has $85 remaining. This would be distributed as $35 to the senior debt, $40 to the subordinated debt, and $10 to the equity. Thus, all bondholders have been repaid in full, but the equity holders have only been paid $10 of their $25.

2. After liquidation, the company has $60 remaining. This would be distributed as $35 to the senior debt, $25 to the subordinated debt, and $0 to the equity. Now, the lower position of the subordinated debt within the capital structure has forced the subordinated bondholders to absorb some of the losses (along with the complete loss of the equity holders), while the senior debt is still repaid in full.

3. After liquidation, the company has $30 remaining. This would be distributed entirely to the senior debt. Now the senior bondholders must absorb some losses, but only after the equity and subordinated debt holders have been completely "wiped out."

Collateral. An element that is related to a bond's seniority is the *collateral* that backs the bond. Collateral is comprised of the cash on hand, property, buildings, materials, inventories, and anything else that the bondholder may claim in the event of default (sometimes referred to as "pledged assets"). Company A might issue a bond that is collateralized by its manufacturing plant, while Company B issues a bond that is not collateralized by its plant. In the event of default, Company A's bondholders could seize the plant and sell it to pay themselves back, while Company B's bondholders could not do so. In financial parlance, a *secured bond* is one that is backed by hard collateral of some type, while an *unsecured bond* is one that is only backed by the general creditworthiness of the company, with no specific pledged assets. Needless to say, a bond that is secured by high quality collateral is viewed as safer, all else equal.

Covenants. A covenant is a binding commitment that a borrower has made as part of a loan agreement. Covenants can be financial or non-financial in nature, and they can be prohibitive (something that *cannot* be done) or mandatory (something that *must* be done). In addition to understanding the covenant itself, it is also necessary to understand what happens if the covenant is violated or "breached." In other words, what remedies can the lender pursue? Remedies may include legal warnings, financial penalties, and, in the extreme case, bankruptcy or foreclosure. There is also usually some amount of leeway allowed for a borrower to correct a covenant breach, known as a "grace period." Following are a few examples of typical covenants. (Note that these are for illustrative purposes—not all loans include the examples listed here.)

- ✔ Leverage—Maximum leverage, measured by debt-to-equity or a similar measure (e.g., maximum of 50 percent). This limits how much debt a company may borrow.

- ✔ Coverage—Minimum required coverage, measured by EBIT/ Interest or a similar measure (e.g., minimum of 1.2×). This covenant is meant to keep an eye on the operations of the company; if the minimum coverage is violated, it is indicative of an operating problem that must be addressed.

- ✔ Prohibitive covenants—For example, without the consent of lenders, sometimes borrowers may not be allowed to make an acquisition, buy a piece of property, enter into a contract of a certain size, take on any additional debt, or distribute excess cash to equity holders.

- ✔ Mandatory covenants—First and foremost, it is obviously mandatory that a borrower must pay all its debt service obligations on time. In addition, borrowers must usually report any material developments at the company in a timely manner, prepare audited financial statements at least one time per year, and take other such actions to protect or inform the lender.

Buy, Sell, or Hold? Finally, we must answer the question on every investor's mind: is this particular fixed income security a good investment? Like all investments, the underlying question here is: does this investment compensate me adequately for the risks undertaken? For a fixed income security, we more or less know the "compensation" part of the equation—it is the yield on the security (subject to the obvious caveat that the yield is not *guaranteed* income due to the possibility of default, bankruptcy, etc.). Thus, the question becomes: is the given yield adequate compensation for the inherent risks?

A key means of answering this question is by considering the *spread*. A spread is the differential between the yield on two different securities. Often, a spread is calculated between a particular security and a benchmark rate, like the yield on a U.S. Treasury of the same duration. For example, suppose you are considering an investment in a 5-year corporate bond yielding 8 percent and the current yield on a five-year U.S. Treasury Note is 5 percent. In this case, the spread would be 3 percent (8% − 5%). Spreads are usually measured in basis points (or "bps"), where one basis point corresponds to 1/100 of a percentage point. So a spread of 3 percent is equivalent to 300 basis points. If the corporate bond were yielding 5.5 percent instead of 8 percent, the spread would be 0.5 percent, or 50 basis points (5.5% − 5%).

Spreads are used as a reference point for comparative valuation, much like P/E ratios are used for comparison of stock prices. Spreads are usually considered relative to other securities or historical trends:

- ✔ *Relative to other securities.* Example: Suppose you believe that two corporate bonds are of similar quality (based on all our tools discussed above), but Bond A has a spread of 300 bps over treasuries while Bond B has a spread of 500 bps over treasuries. This would make Bond B the better investment, since it generates a higher yield for the same level of risk. Similarly, you could consider the spread on a particular bond relative to its industry average or some other specific industry benchmark.

- ✔ *Relative to historical trends.* Example: You notice that the spread on a particular bond has decreased recently, from 500 bps over the past several years to 300 bps today. (In bond parlance, it would be said that the spread is "tightening" or becoming more "tight." Conversely, when spreads increase, they are "widening.") In the case of tightening spreads, the market is indicating that the bond is becoming less risky for some reason—perhaps the company just won a major new customer contract. However, suppose you don't believe the hype—you think that the new contract is going to be cancelled due to weak market demand. This would make the bond a poor investment, or a possible short sale opportunity, because now the compensation is too low for the given level of risk.

Credit Ratings

As we've seen previously, credit analysis is both an art and a science, just like equity analysis. Not surprisingly, many firms provide third-party debt recommendations to investors, just as many firms provide third-party equity research and analysis. The most visible of these firms are known as the "rating agencies," which provide independent assessments of the creditworthiness of a debt issue, known as a "credit rating." The two largest rating agencies—Standard & Poor's (S&P) and Moody's—

dominate the industry, but other smaller players have also carved out a niche market as alternatives to the two giants, including Duff & Phelps and Fitch Investors Service.

How do the rating agencies assess creditworthiness? By using all the tools we've just discussed, from leverage and interest coverage ratios to liquidity and legal terms. The resulting credit rating indicates the likelihood of default on a bond's interest and/or principal payments. The better the rating, the lower the probability of default. The different rating agencies each have their own unique rating definitions and assignment protocol. For example, one agency might use a certain leverage ratio versus another, or one might hold a company's management in higher regard than another.

Both S&P and Moody's primarily use letters in their credit ratings. Just like back in high school, ratings in the "A" category are the best, and they get subsequently worse with each letter in the alphabet (B, C, etc.). However, the exact ratings are specific to the agencies. At Moody's, the highest rating is Aaa and numbers are also used to further differentiate ratings, while at S&P, the highest rating is AAA and "+" or "−" is used for further differentiation. For illustrative purposes, following are the official rating definitions and guidelines used by Standard & Poor's.

Standard & Poor's Issue Credit Rating Definitions

A Standard & Poor's issue credit rating is a current opinion of the creditworthiness of an obligor with respect to a specific obligation. It takes into consideration the creditworthiness of guarantors, insurers, or other forms of credit enhancement on the obligation and takes into account the currency in which the obligation is denominated. The issue credit rating is not a recommendation to purchase, sell, or hold a financial obligation, inasmuch as it does not comment as to market price or suitability for a particular investor.

Issue credit ratings* are based, in varying degrees, on the following considerations:

 ✔ Likelihood of payment—capacity and willingness of the obligor to meet its financial commitment on an obligation in accordance with the terms of the obligation

Source: Standard & Poor's.

✔ Nature of and provisions of the obligation

✔ Protection afforded by, and relative position of, the obligation in the event of bankruptcy, reorganization, or other arrangement under the laws of bankruptcy and other laws affecting creditors' rights

AAA

An obligation rated AAA has the highest rating assigned by Standard & Poor's. The obligor's capacity to meet its financial commitment on the obligation is extremely strong.

AA

An obligation rated AA differs from the highest-rated obligations only to a small degree. The obligor's capacity to meet its financial commitment on the obligation is very strong.

A

An obligation rated A is somewhat more susceptible to the adverse effects of changes in circumstances and economic conditions than obligations in higher-rated categories. However, the obligor's capacity to meet its financial commitment on the obligation is still strong.

BBB

An obligation rated BBB exhibits adequate protection parameters. However, adverse economic conditions or changing circumstances are more likely to lead to a weakened capacity of the obligor to meet its financial commitment on the obligation.

BB, B, CCC, CC, and C

Obligations rated BB, B, CCC, CC, and C are regarded as having significant speculative characteristics. BB indicates the least degree of speculation and C the highest. While such obligations will likely have some quality and protective characteristics, these may be outweighed by large uncertainties or major exposures to adverse conditions.

BB

An obligation rated BB is less vulnerable to nonpayment than other speculative issues. However, it faces major ongoing uncertainties or exposure to adverse business, financial, or economic conditions that could lead to the obligor's inadequate capacity to meet its financial commitment on the obligation.

B

An obligation rated B is more vulnerable to nonpayment than obligations rated BB, but the obligor currently has the capacity to meet its financial commitment on the obligation. Adverse business, financial, or economic conditions will likely impair the obligor's capacity or willingness to meet its financial commitment on the obligation.

CCC

An obligation rated CCC is currently vulnerable to nonpayment, and is dependent upon favorable business, financial, and economic conditions for the obligor to meet its financial commitment on the obligation. In the event of adverse business, financial, or economic conditions, the obligor is not likely to have the capacity to meet its financial commitment on the obligation.

CC

An obligation rated CC is currently highly vulnerable to nonpayment.

C

A C rating is assigned to obligations that are currently highly vulnerable to nonpayment, obligations that have payment arrearages allowed by the terms of the documents, or obligations of an issuer that is the subject of a bankruptcy petition or similar action which have not experienced a payment default. Among others, the C rating may be assigned to subordinated debt, preferred stock, or other obligations on which cash payments have been suspended in accordance with the instrument's terms.

D

An obligation rated D is in payment default. The D rating category is used when payments on an obligation are not made on the date due even if the applicable grace period has not expired, unless Standard & Poor's believes that such payments will be made during such grace period. The D rating also will be used upon the filing of a bankruptcy petition or the taking of a similar action if payments on an obligation are jeopardized.

Plus (+) or Minus (−)

The ratings from AA to CCC may be modified by the addition of a plus (+) or minus (−) sign to show relative standing within the major rating categories.

NR

This indicates that no rating has been requested, that there is insufficient information on which to base a rating, or that Standard & Poor's does not rate a particular obligation as a matter of policy.

The Rating Process

A credit rating is usually initially assigned at the request of a borrower upon a new issuance of debt. Why would a borrower *request* a credit rating? It is desirable to a borrower because it serves as an enticement for investors to buy the debt. Since we live in a world of imperfect information, the credit rating is viewed as a "third-party endorsement" about the quality of the debt. In addition, some capital pools, like pension funds, are restricted from investing in debt that does not have a minimum rating, or is not rated at all. Ratings are easy to understand, easily accessible and nearly universally accepted, making them a virtual requirement for any company seeking to issue debt.

To secure a credit rating, the borrower contracts with the rating agency (one or perhaps more) and pays a fee to the agency. The payment of a fee brings about an important potential conflict of interest—if the borrower is *paying* the rating agency, is the rating agency truly objective in its opinion? The answer to this question is hotly debated, but suffice it to say, the financial relationship that exists between the issuer and the rating agency is something that should always be kept in mind. (At the time of this writing, various regulatory reforms are under discussion that could significantly impact the rating process and the relationship between the borrower and the rating agency.)

In exchange for the fee, the rating agency takes on the job of investigating the company, its industry (competitive position, etc.), its financial ratios, and ultimately, its ability to service its debt. It is important to realize that a rating pertains to only a specific debt issue and not to the overall company itself. The final rating is not some mechanical, mathematical equation that is simply an exercise in number crunching (otherwise companies could calculate the equation themselves!). Rather, it is a function of the professional judgment of the analyst(s).

If the issuer doesn't agree with the rating agency's opinion, it might choose to appeal the rating in a negotiation process involving the issuer and the rating agency (as well as the underwriter, whose fee is dependent on getting the deal done). In this negotiation, the terms of the offering may be amended to achieve the desired rating. For example, a more restrictive leverage covenant might be added, or more valuable collateral might be posted as security, so as to boost the rating from A to AA. Additionally, there may be a guarantor (a company, such as a parent organization, that agrees to guarantee the payment of the debt in the event of default by the subsidiary) or credit insurance (a third-party financial insurer that agrees to guarantee the debt in exchange for a premium payment). These are commonly known as "credit enhancers."

Changes to Credit Ratings

A rating is not fixed for the life of a bond any more than a stock price is fixed for the life of a stock. Bond ratings do not move everyday like stock prices, but the rating agencies do attempt to keep an eye on the bond and update their ratings when necessary. Usually, that means when newly released external information becomes available or material business trends become evident. For example, if ABC Corp. is rated AA+ by S&P, but last night the company announced a major acquisition that is expected to significantly increase leverage and impact current cash flow, it follows that the rating will be re-assessed by the rating agencies and may change.

Fixed income securities that are under review for potential rating changes are said to be on the "watch list." (For example, the bonds of ABC Corp., above, would likely go on the watch list after the acquisition was announced.) Once the review is complete, the rating may be downgraded (e.g., from AA+ to A), upgraded (e.g., A to AA+), or it may stay the same. Rating agencies also indicate their position on a particular security through their "outlook," which may be "positive" (a future upgrade is possible), "negative" (a future downgrade is possible), or "stable."

The threat of a credit rating downgrade is not a meaningless threat, but quite a real one with major implications for the company. If an issue is downgraded, its market price is sure to be negatively affected, and consequently, the issuing company's debt service for subsequent debt offerings could increase. This can impede a company's financial situation as well as its flexibility. A downgrade below the "investment grade" dividing line of BBB- (Standard & Poor's) or Baa3 (Moody's) may find the corporation without the all-important institutional market for its bonds. Some institutions and fiduciary funds are prohibited, either by policy or legal constraints, from participating in non-investment-grade investments, thereby removing this major buyer of debt from the pool of available capital for a non-investment-grade issuer. As we know from basic economics, less demand for a good or service will, invariably, lead to a lower price. In the case of a bond, the lower price is reflected in the higher yield that the issuer must pay to attract capital.

It is important to remember that credit rating actions can also have a strong spillover impact on a company's stock price. When a company is placed on the watch list or downgraded, equity investors are likely to be influenced by the same information that is concerning the rating agencies. Thus, some attention must be paid to credit ratings even if your main interest is a company's stock. A sharp decline in a company's stock price due to a ratings downgrade could reflect a fundamental business issue…or a good buying opportunity. Fortunately, much fixed income research (from Moody's, S&P and many other sources) is usually obtainable for the asking through your representative at the company.

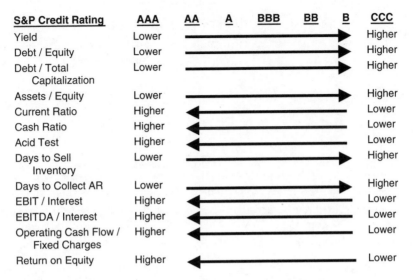

FIGURE 6.1 The Impact of Credit Statistics on Credit Ratings.

The Relationship Between Credit Ratings and Key Metrics

Tying together all our lessons from this chapter, we can summarize the dynamics of the credit markets with two rules of thumb. In general, bonds with higher credit ratings will tend to exhibit: (1) lower yields, and (2) stronger credit statistics. Figure 6.1 illustrates this dynamic for several key metrics.

PROBLEM SET: CREDIT ANALYSIS

Question 1

Use the Parrot Computers data below to compute the following ratios:

Leverage

Total Debt/Total Equity

Total Debt/Total Capitalization

Assets/Equity

Liquidity

Current Ratio

Acid Test

Coverage

EBIT/Interest Expense

EBITDA/Interest Expense

Parrot Computers Inc. Balance Sheet (in thousands)			
Assets		*Liabilities and Equity*	
Cash	$300	Accounts payable	$400
Accounts receivable	200	Debt	250
Inventory	700	Common stock	1,000
Fixed assets	1,200	Retained earnings	750
Total assets	$2,400	Total liabilities and equity	$2,400

Parrot Computers has A/R terms of net 30 days (i.e., payment is due within 30 days).

At the beginning of the year, accounts receivable were $175, inventory was $600, assets were $2,200, common stock was $900, and retained earnings were $650.

Schedule of debt maturities: $0 in Year 1, $25 in Year 2, $75 in Year 3, $75 in Year 4, $50 in Year 5, $25 in Year 6.

Parrot Computers Inc. Income Statement (in thousands)	
Sales	$6,000
Cost of Goods Sold	(4,000)
Depreciation & Amortization	(300)
EBIT	$1,700
Interest expense	(100)
Pretax income	1,600
Taxes	(640)
Net income	$960

Answers

Leverage

Total Debt/Total Equity = 250/1,750 = 14.3%

Total Debt/Total Capitalization = 250/(250 + 1,750) = 12.5%

Assets/Equity = 2,400/1,750 = 1.37

Liquidity

Current Ratio = Current Assets/Current Liabilities = (300 + 200 + 700)/400 = 3.0

Acid Test = (Current Assets − Inventory)/Current Liabilities = (1,200 − 700)/400 = 1.25

Coverage

$$\text{EBIT/Interest Expense} = 1,700/100 = 17.0$$
$$\text{EBITDA/Interest Expense} = (1,700 + 300)/100 = 20.0$$

Question 2

Following are the average statistics for companies with the given credit rating:

	AAA	AA	A	BBB	BB
Debt/Equity	9.0%	15.0%	25.0%	35.0%	50.0%
Current Ratio	4.0	3.0	2.0	1.0	0.5
EBIT/Interest	22.0	15.0	10.0	5.0	0.7

A. Based on the preceding information, make a recommendation for a credit rating for Parrot.

Answer

Here is where Parrot falls in relation to each of the statistics:

Debt/Equity	Slightly better than AA (14.3% vs. 15%)
Current Ratio	In line with AA (3.0 vs. 3.0)
EBIT/Interest	Slightly better than AA (17.0 vs. 15.0)

Thus, based on these statistics alone, it appears that Parrot is deserving of an AA credit rating.

B. Do you believe that these statistics are sufficient for a complete assessment of Parrot's credit? If not, what other information would you like to ascertain?

Answer

These statistics offer a useful guide to the quality of Parrot's credit, but other information is necessary for a full understanding, both qualitative and quantitative in nature. Specifically, information regarding the company's underlying business fundamentals and the credit's legal protections would be especially helpful. What is the seniority and collateral backing the security? Are there any covenants to protect the lender? What has been the trend in growth over the past several years—are earnings relatively volatile or stable? Is the company's management trustworthy and knowledgeable?

Question 3

Below are the financial statements for Parrot's main competitor, Robin Computers Inc. Based on this information, do you believe that Robin also deserves an AA credit rating?

Parrot Computers Inc. Balance Sheet (in thousands)			
Assets		**Liabilities and Equity**	
Cash	$250	Accounts payable	$380
Accounts receivable	330	Debt	300
Inventory	900	Common stock	1,200
Fixed assets	1,400	Retained earnings	1,000
Total assets	$2,880	Total liabilities and equity	$2,880

Parrot Computer has A/R terms of net 30 days (i.e., payment is due within 45 days)

At the beginning of the year, accounts receivable were $200, inventory was $800, assets were $2,500, common stock was $1,000, and retained earnings were $900.

Schedule of debt maturities: $275 in Year 1 and $25 in Year 2.

Robin Computers Inc. Income Statement (in thousands)	
Sales	$7,039
Cost of Goods Sold	(4,700)
Depreciation & Amortization	(350)
EBIT	$1,989
Interest expense	(125)
Pretax income	1,864
Taxes	(750)
Net income	$1,114

Answer

We can start by comparing Robin's credit ratios to the averages:

Debt/Equity = 300/2,200 = 13.6%

Current Ratio = 1,480/380 = 3.9

EBIT/Interest = 1,989/125 = 15.9

Each of Robin's ratios is better than the average ratio for a AA credit rating. By these measures alone, it would appear that Robin is similar to Parrot and also deserves a AA rating. However, this question illustrates the importance of looking "beyond the numbers." In this case, we cannot ignore the footnote to the financial statements regarding debt maturities. Parrot has a low and steady level of debt maturing each year, with none maturing in the first year. Robin, on the other hand, could have a severe liquidity crisis in the near future. It has $275 of debt maturing in the upcoming year, but only $250 of cash on the balance sheet. How is Robin going to manage this situation? Is it going to be able to refinance the maturing debt with a new loan? If so, what will be the terms of the new loan? What if it needs to use all of its cash to repay the debt? How will it fund the purchase of raw materials and the payment of salaries? Without knowing the answers to these questions, we cannot comfortably assign the same credit rating to Robin as we can to Parrot.

Question 4

True or False? After reviewing the legal terms of Parrot's debt, you discover that the debt is collateralized by the manufacturing plant that Parrot owns. This means that the debt has the most senior position in the capital structure.

Answer

False. The type of collateral is not necessarily indicative of a security's position within the capital structure. From this information we know that the debt is *secured*, but we do not know if it is the most senior in the capital structure.

Question 5

You observe the following data for three bonds.

	U.S. Treasury Note	Parrot	Robin
Par Value	$1,000	$1,000	$1,000
Price	$975	$950	$1,150
Coupon Rate	5.0%	7.0%	8.5%

A. Your friend advises you to buy Robin's bonds. He states, "I calculated the debt-to-equity ratio, coverage ratio, and current ratio for both companies and they are very similar. But Robin has a higher coupon rate than Parrot, so it must be a better deal!" Do you agree with your friend's analysis?

Answer

Step 1: First, we must remember that the coupon rate does not tell the whole story. We must take the bonds' prices into account and calculate their yields to compare their returns on an apples-to-apples basis.

Yield = (Coupon Rate × Par Value)/Price
Parrot's Yield = (7.0% × $1,000)/$950 = 7.4%
Robin's Yield = (8.5% × $1,000)/$1,150 = 7.4%

Step 2: Next we can calculate their spreads relative to the observed U.S. Treasury Note.

U.S. Treasury Yield = (5.0% × $1,000)/975 = 5.1%
Parrot's Spread = 7.4% − 5.1% = 2.3% or 230 bps
Robin's Spread = 7.4% − 5.1% = 2.3% or 230 bps

Step 3: Now we can make a conclusion—your friend is mistaken! Both Parrot and Robin have the same spread relative to the U.S. Treasury, implying that they both have a similar level of risk versus the U.S. Treasury. But we know that this is not the case, since Robin has a much higher level of risk due to its upcoming debt maturity and possible liquidity crisis. Therefore, it would make no sense to buy Robin's bonds. In fact, you could make the opposite argument—buy Parrot's bonds to enjoy the same yield with lower risk.

Question 6

The most critical aspect of a municipal revenue bond rating is:

A. The management of the agency seeking the financing.
B. The demographic shifts occurring in the municipality.
C. The cash flow expectations from the project being undertaken.
D. The annual tax revenues of the municipality.

Answer

The correct answer is (c). The most important factor in a *revenue* (not a *general obligation*) issue is the cash flows that are expected from the project. This makes intuitive sense from the standpoint that the revenue bond does not carry any taxing authority and is a contract between the agency and the investor. Each of the other three choices can be considered factors involved in the evaluation of general obligation (GO) municipal bonds.

Question 7

A $1,000 face value New York City General Obligation bond is currently trading at par and has a coupon of 5 percent. What is the taxable equivalent yield that an investor needs to receive (assuming a 40 percent total tax rate) to be equally compensated?

Answer

The bond is trading at par, which means that the market price is currently $1,000 per bond and the cash flow generated is $50 per bond (5 percent coupon), making the yield 5 percent. The tax equivalent yield is calculated using the following equation:

$$\text{TEY} = \frac{\text{Tax free yield}}{(100\% - \text{Tax rate})}$$

So given the 5 percent tax-free yield, we would require a taxable equivalent yield (assuming the 40 percent tax bracket) of 8.33 percent (5 percent DIVIDED by 60 percent).

Chapter

7

Real Estate

I n this chapter we cover:

- ✔ The fundamentals of real estate assets.
- ✔ Real estate loans.
- ✔ Mortgage-backed securities.
- ✔ Real Estate Investment trusts.

Real estate investments are all around us. You probably woke up in a real estate investment this morning: be it a single-family home, multi-family apartment, condominium complex, or hotel. Office buildings, industrial warehouses, shopping malls, and big-box retail destinations—these are all real estate investments as well. In each of these examples, the investor in the real estate may be as simple as one person or it may be a tangled web so complicated that even the investors themselves have trouble unraveling it. It is straightforward enough to imagine a single person or company, with the help of a single loan from a friendly neighborhood banker down the street, who purchases a home or office building. We would describe this as an investment in a "hard" or "bricks and mortar" real estate asset—it is a direct investment in a tangible piece of real estate. However, financial engineering has proliferated over time to create real estate securities that are one or more steps *removed* from the physical asset. These securities derive their value from or are backed by the underlying real estate, but they are not investments *directly* in the real estate itself.

In this chapter, we start with reviewing the fundamentals of real estate and "hard" real estate assets—what they are, what drives their value, and how they are analyzed. We then apply that knowledge to analyze some of the less tangible securities that derive their value indirectly from hard real estate assets, starting with real estate loans, and proceeding on to mortgage-backed securities and Real Estate Investment Trusts.

Types of Real Estate

The overall "real estate" designation is generally broken down into one of seven categories. These categories account for the majority of real estate assets, with the remainder being other smaller, more specialized types of real estate.

Residential

This category of real estate covers where people live. Single-family homes are the largest category of residential real estate in the United States, comprising about 65 percent of the total housing stock. They may be detached (the typical suburban home that stands alone on a private lot) or attached (a row house or townhouse that is connected to others). Multi-family residential consists of more than one housing unit within the same building. Overall, multi-family homes account for about 25 percent of the total housing stock, and they are much more common in urban areas than they are in suburban or rural areas (over 50 percent of the homes in New York, for example, are multi-family, but under 15 percent of the homes in Idaho are multi-family). The remaining 10 percent of residential real estate consists of mobile homes, houseboats, and other less common types of homes.

Office

This category covers where people generally work, meaning anything from the gleaming skyscrapers of a big city's downtown financial district, to a sprawling suburban office park that is miles from the nearest skyscraper. Investors often segment the office real estate market based on a building's (1) quality and (2) geographic location. The shorthand for the quality of an office building is its "Class": Class A, Class B, or Class C. Class A properties are the premier, "trophy" buildings with the best views, best services, best lobbies, best heating and cooling systems, and so on. Class B properties are inferior to Class A (a Class B building might have an older heating system that doesn't always function perfectly), and Class C properties are inferior to Class B. In terms of location, buildings that are in the core, downtown area of a city are described as being in the Central Business District or CBD. Office buildings that are in outlying areas, such as a suburban office park, are non-CBD assets. About two-thirds of all the available office space in the United States is non-CBD.

Retail

This category covers where people generally shop for goods and services. Retail assets can be clumped together in a densely packed city—think of New York's Fifth Avenue, with its block after block of storefronts selling everything from souvenirs and fast food to Tiffany diamond earrings. They might be in suburban malls, where merchants line up in row after row on one level or more. They might be stand-alone, "big-box" retail stores that are many times larger than the size of a typical store in a mall, like Best Buy and Wal-Mart, or they might be small, "Mom-and-Pop" shops in a strip mall or rural location.

Lodging/Resorts

This category covers establishments where people stay for a short period of time. Hotel chains are a common example, many of which are publicly traded companies in their own right, such as Hilton and Marriott. Beyond your average hotel, there are also a wide range of "boutique" assets and stand-alone lodging establishments in this category. One factor that distinguishes the lodging sector in the world of real estate is that owning a hotel is considered closer to running an operating business than other types of real estate. For example, the owner of a hotel must consider branding strategies and advertising campaigns much more thoroughly than the owner of an office building, who may consider them little, if at all.

Industrial/Warehouse

This category covers where tangible goods are stored or processed. Unlike homes, office buildings, or hotels, successful warehouses are not known for their gleaming finishes or nearby restaurants. Rather, the best warehouses provide for efficient storage and transportation in large quantities. Huge warehouses with millions of square feet of space are situated throughout the outlying areas of cities like Los Angeles and Chicago. There, everything from coffee beans to video games are processed and stored before taking their next step toward reaching their end users. The industrial sector is closely aligned with the availability of transportation infrastructure, since warehouses must be able to accommodate huge volumes of goods moving in and out on a regular basis.

Healthcare

Healthcare facilities are a large segment of the real estate industry, and growing in importance every year as the population of the U.S. ages and demand increases for healthcare services. The healthcare category covers all manner of healthcare facilities, such as independent or assisted living facilities, retirement communities, skilled nursing facilities, hospitals, and medical office buildings.

Self-Storage

Self-storage may seem like a mundane business—it means little more than the provision of simple storage areas in large buildings for private individuals and businesses. Still, it accounts for a non-trivial portion of the real estate investment world. In fact, a company called Public Storage (NYSE: PSA), specializing in self-storage facilities, is one of the largest REITs in the world, dwarfing many others that specialize in residential, retail, office, and the like.

Other

We've now covered the most prominent sectors in the real estate industry, accounting for a great majority of real estate investment and development activity. But we could go on. There are a variety of other, even more specialized real estate markets in which fortunes are made and lost every day. Some examples include land, student housing, military housing, and academic institutions (classrooms, research space, etc.).

Ownership versus Rental

Within most of the categories above, there is a further distinction between ownership and rental. The owner of a unit holds the legal claim to the property (the "title" or "deed") and rents it to another party for a definitive rate and period of time. The renter has the right to utilize the premises for the period of the lease, while the underlying title to the property remains with the owner. This is a common distinction in the residential world (do you own your home or rent an apartment?), but it is also applicable to other types of real estate. For example, a large company might decide it would prefer to own its office headquarters or storage warehouse, rather than rent space from a third party.

Real Estate Financial Statements

The Operating Statement

In general, the accounting principles that guide the preparation of financial statements for real estate are similar to the principles that are applicable to other types of businesses, but there are certain real-estate specific nuances. The typical real estate operating statement (sometimes known as a "set-up") combines elements of both a traditional income statement and a cash flow statement. (Remember that in this section we are referring to the financial statements for a specific hard real estate asset, not for securities that are backed by real estate assets, but many of the same principles apply for real estate securities as well. We will cover other specific financial metrics for specialized real estate securities later in this chapter.)

Revenue

- ✔ Rental or sales income—This is the principal source of revenue in real estate. It is the income generated by renting a space or selling it outright.
- ✔ Reimbursements—These accrue when tenants must pay for some of the building's operating costs, such as a charge for cleaning services.
- ✔ Parking—The cost that must be paid to a landlord to buy or rent a parking space on the landlord's property.

- ✔ Profit sharing—Common for retail leases, this accrues when the landlord receives a certain percentage of the tenant's sales or profits (known by the term "percentage rent").
- ✔ Vacancy Loss/Bad Debt Reserve—Revenues must be offset by the possibility of (1) vacancy in the building (known as *vacancy loss*), and (2) defaults by tenants or buyers who are unable to pay the agreed upon price (known as *bad debt reserve*). A small percentage of total revenue is usually estimated for these items, around 1–2 percent each.

Operating Expenses

- ✔ Real estate taxes—Real estate taxes that must be paid to the local government are often one of the biggest operating expenses.
- ✔ Operations and maintenance—These include:
    - ✔ Landscaping (snow removal, floral decorations)
    - ✔ Routine repairs (repairing cracks, fixing leaks)
    - ✔ Cleaning/Janitorial
    - ✔ Utilities
    - ✔ Insurance
    - ✔ Security
    - ✔ Fire & Life Safety
    - ✔ Administrative (salaries and supplies for property managers who collect the rent, etc.)

    Revenue–Operating Expenses = **Net Operating Income** or **NOI**

Capital Expenditures/Non-Operating Costs   These are one-time, non-routine costs, in contrast to operating expenses, which are more regular, recurring costs.

- ✔ Building improvements—One-time upgrades or projects are generally classified as "building improvements" rather than operating expenses. For example, the cost of repairing a broken window air conditioner would be an operating expense (repairs), while the cost of replacing it with a brand new central air system would be a building improvement.

✔ Tenant Improvements—These are capital projects undertaken to prepare a space for use by a new tenant, such as the cost to re-paint the walls of an apartment or build new office partitions.

✔ Commissions—Commissions are payable to agents upon the completion of a transaction, such as a 2 percent fee payable to a residential sales agent upon the sale of a home.

✔ Legal—The fees associated with legal representation for purchase and sale agreements, leases, and the like.

$$\text{NOI} - \text{Capital Expenditures/Non-Operating} = \textit{Cash Flow Before Financing} \text{ or CFBF}$$

Financing Costs

✔ Loan Payments—Many real estate owners use loans to finance the purchase of a property. If so, loan payments of interest and/or principal are due to the bank on a regular basis. This is also known as *debt service.*

✔ Financing Transaction Costs—Financing arrangements have their own set of transaction costs, such as sales commissions (if a mortgage broker is used) and closing fees or "points" for the loan.

$$\text{CFBF} - \text{Financing Costs} = \textit{Cash Flow After Financing} \text{ or CFAF}$$

The Development Capital Budget

The Operating Statement captures the financial performance of a building once it has been built. A Development Capital Budget, on the other hand, captures all the costs that go into building something from the ground up. Development costs are broken into two categories:

Hard Costs These are the tangible or direct costs that go into the final product.

✔ Land acquisition

✔ Demolition—Materials, equipment, labor

✔ Construction—Materials, equipment, labor

✔ Site Improvements—Such as creating a parking lot

✔ Infrastructure—Such as new sewer systems or telecommunications lines that are necessary for the building

Soft Costs   These are "indirect" costs that are not literally tangible products, but are necessary for the construction process.

✔ Architectural and Engineering—Known by the shorthand A&E.
✔ Legal.
✔ General and Administrative.
✔ Leasing and Marketing.
✔ Carrying Costs—These are the operating and financing costs that must be borne during the construction period.
✔ Government Fees.
✔ Contingency—All development budgets should include a contingency, which is a reserve set aside in case certain costs are higher than anticipated.

Investing in Real Estate: Hard Assets

The most direct way to invest in real estate is by buying it outright. We refer to this as an investment in a "hard" real estate asset because it is a direct investment in a tangible piece of property. If you are the owner of an office building, apartment complex or plot of developable land, you own a real asset that you can touch and feel, and that you must manage or develop profitably. That being said, a direct investment in hard real estate is probably the least practical for the average investor, as it involves significant up-front costs and management time. However, we start here by reviewing the characteristics of cold, hard real estate, because that is what underlies the more exotic securities we will turn to next.

Location, Location, Location

Location, location, location. It is a popular refrain about real estate value that is repeated again and again. But what does this really mean? What really drives the value of a piece of real estate? When you think about "location, location, location," the idea is to think about the many factors that make a given location what it truly is.

Physical   The physical attributes of different pieces of real estate often require a high level of specialized knowledge to understand completely (mechanical, structural, architectural, etc.). Even the most experienced real estate investors usually hire independent, outside consultants to help them evaluate the physical condition of a building. Potential hidden dangers, such as asbestos or mold, can be extremely costly to mediate, heightening the need for an expert evaluation. The long list of physical attributes that must be considered includes the windows, floors and foundations, roof, façade (the exterior faces of the building), entry and exit ways, elevators, heating, ventilation and cooling systems (HVAC), electrical systems, and plumbing systems.

Demographic   The demographics of the area where a piece of real estate is located will say a great deal about the demand for that real estate, both now and in the future. The U.S. Census Bureau offers a wealth of demographic data to help assess the condition of a local market, as do local government agencies (e.g., the local Mayor's office) and private sources. Important demographic topics to consider include: (1) Population (is it growing or declining?), (2) Income levels, (3) Educational attainment, and (4) Age (young couples or aging baby boomers?). For example, building a development of pricey, luxury mansions in an area dominated by college students and young couples might not be a wise investment.

Economic Conditions   Local economic conditions will impact all segments of the real estate market, from the selling price of a home, to the number of guests staying at hotels in the area, to the number of workers filling up downtown office buildings. The strength of the local economy is measured by several key statistics including: (1) Employment (measured by job gains/losses and the unemployment rate), (2) Economic output (measured by Gross Domestic Product), and (3) Key industries (what industries dominate the local economy and what is the outlook for these industries?).

Area Amenities   These are the elements of a neighborhood that contribute to its quality of life, for better or for worse. Unlike some of the factors cited previously, area amenities are often less tangible elements that aren't easily captured by statistics or charts. Such amenities include cultural activities (museums, theatre), entertainment (movies, concerts, nightlife), shopping (restaurants, malls), schools, community engagement, crime rates, sports, outdoor activities, and weather.

Infrastructure   Infrastructure refers to all of the underlying structures and systems that support society. Infrastructure is something that is often taken for granted in everyday life—until it breaks down, that is. Examples include transportation (roads, bridges, airports, mass transit), water and sewer systems, electricity, gas, waste management, and telecommunications systems (phones, cable television, internet). For new developments, providing infrastructure can be a very costly proposition, and the burden is often shared between the private and public sectors. It is essential to consider the cost of infrastructure in any new development proposal.

Political   Political circumstances can sometimes play the most important role of all, especially for new developments. Some local governments and community residents are eager for real estate projects and allow developers to quickly and easily construct new projects, while others are wary of too much density and try to restrict new development. The *permitting process* is the term used to describe the steps necessary to create a new development. Cumbersome permitting is detrimental to new developers, but it conversely rewards the owners of existing buildings by limiting new supply—and it also rewards those developers who are savvy or well connected enough to make their way through the process and get their project approved for construction. (In the jargon of Michael Porter's Five Forces, a high level of political resistance to new development would constitute a *barrier to entry*.) Politics also impacts the real estate market through government spending on services and projects in the community.

Supply and Demand Statistics

At the fundamental level, the real estate market is like any other in a capitalist system—it is driven by the relative levels of supply and demand that exist for the product. For example, if the local government is very restrictive of new development, then new supply will be limited, but if the area is attracting many new families due to its great local amenities and thriving job market, then demand will be robust. As a result, low supply and high demand will translate to higher prices, all else equal.

Current Supply We start with the statistics that offer a snapshot of the current supply in the market. The *inventory* of real estate is simply a tally of the number of homes in a market, the amount of square feet of office space, the number of hotel rooms, and so on. This can be further refined to *inventory on market*, meaning the amount of real estate that is being actively offered for sale or rent. Another key metric is the *vacancy rate*, which is calculated as (1) currently unoccupied space divided by (2) total amount of inventory.

For example, if a hotel has 100 rooms and 90 of them have guests for the night, then 10 rooms are unoccupied and the vacancy rate is $10/100 = 10$ percent. Generally speaking, the lower the vacancy rate, the greater the bargaining power of the owner of the real estate, since it implies high demand relative to the level of supply.

In commercial markets such as office, industrial, and retail, *sublease availability* is a related metric of great significance (sometimes called "shadow space" in real estate jargon). A sublease is space that is leased by one tenant, but due to a change in the needs of that tenant, the tenant has offered it for lease to another party. This is especially important to consider during times of economic difficulty, when many tenants may be downsizing and no longer need excess space. The sum of sublease availability and the vacancy rate gives the *total availability* in a market.

Pipeline of New Supply Real estate supply is never static. The new supply that is expected to come "on line" in the future is called the *pipeline*. Even if inventory and vacancy statistics are very low, new supply might overwhelm demand and drive prices down. Real estate can take a long time to develop, so there are metrics to track pipeline at each stage of the development process. The number of *building permits* issued in a market is a leading indicator of new supply, since new developments require a permit before work can begin. The number of *building starts* tracks the new supply that is under construction. Finally, the number of *building completions* tracks the new supply that has been finished and is now "open for business." An element related to the pipeline of new supply is the availability of undeveloped land. Locales like Boston and Midtown Manhattan have a very limited stock of undeveloped land remaining, while areas like Phoenix and Las Vegas have a ready supply of land on which to build.

Level of Activity in the Market In the housing market, real estate professionals anxiously await the monthly government statistics for *new home sales* and *existing home sales.* These are counts of the number of home sales that have closed in a given period of time. If the number is high or trending up, it is indicative of strong or increasing demand, while if the number is low or trending down, it is indicative of low or weakening demand. Similarly, the number of sales or leases completed is tracked in the other segments of the real estate market (e.g., there were 50 shopping malls sold last quarter or 90 office leases signed in a certain city last month), usually compiled by private companies that specialize in that market.

A related data point is known as *absorption,* a statistic which is calculated as (1) the amount of formerly vacant space now occupied less (2) the amount of newly vacant space. For example, suppose that in your town, there were 20 homes that were vacant at the beginning of the year. Over the course of the year, 15 of those homes were purchased by newcomers to the community, but in the meantime, a local developer has completed construction of 10 new homes and put them up for sale. The calculation of absorption would then be $15 - 10 = 5$. On the other hand, if 3 of those 15 home sales were purchased by people who already owned homes in the community (i.e., moving from one existing home to another existing home), then the calculation of absorption would be $15 - 13 = 2$.

Absorption is critical because it points to the level of *new* demand for real estate and is distinct from demand that consists of the same person or entity simply moving from one space to another. A high level of absorption points to a robust or "seller's market" in which many new users are clamoring for real estate, while a low (or even negative) level of absorption points to a weak or "buyer's market."

Average Time on Market The *average time on market* is the number of days or months that a given piece of real estate is available for sale or rent before a transaction is completed with an end user to buy or rent the space. Low time on market generally signals strong demand, and vice versa. In commercial and/or rental markets, the phrase *downtime* is often used in place of average time on market, but it has essentially the same meaning.

Price Levels One of the most commonly cited statistics in real estate is the *comparable sale* (also known as a *sales comps* or just *comp* for short). A comp is the selling price of another piece of real estate that is similar in quality to the real estate that you are considering. Choosing comps is as much of an art as it is a science, and using comps is part of the negotiating strategy (for both sides).

Consider two homes in the same neighborhood: Home A and Home B. Suppose Home B just sold for $300,000, but Home A has a brand new kitchen while Home B is stuck in the 1970s. In that case, the seller of Home A would argue that the right value for Home A is higher than $300,000, since Home A has a better kitchen. On the other hand, the potential buyer of Home A will be sure to note that Home A's driveway has a few cracks in it, while Home B's is freshly sealed. Let the negotiations begin!

One way to normalize comps across different buildings is to cite the *price per square foot*, which is calculated as (1) total price divided by (2) the size of the space (measured by number of square feet). Continuing the example above, if Home A is 1,000 square feet in size but Home B is 909 square feet, then the seller of Home A would argue that the true value of Home A should actually be more like $330,000 or above. Why so? Because Home B sold for $330 per square foot ($300,000/909 = $330), thus Home A should have at least the same price per square foot — that is, $330 × 1,000 = $330,000.

In leasing or renting transactions, the comp used would be the rental rate per square foot of a similar property, calculated as (1) annual rent (in dollars) divided by (2) size of space. These might be referred to as *comparable rents* or *market rents*. In the hotel industry, the pricing statistic usually cited is "revenue per available room" or "RevPAR." Whatever the specific data point used, the concept of a comparable transaction is the same—to anchor the negotiation around the prices that prevail for other, similar transactions in the market.

Real Estate Investment Strategies

"Hard" real estate investments are often segmented based on the operating strategies and investment plans of the owners of the real estate. *Core* real estate assets have stable, long-term cash flows that do not require a high degree of management focus, such as an office building that is 100 percent leased to a prestigious law firm for the next 15 years. Core real estate assets are like corporate bonds, since they generate a predictable stream of cash flows and their value derives in large part from the credit quality of the building's tenants. As such, core real estate assets usually generate lower, "bond-like" returns in comparison to other types of real estate.

Non-core assets require a higher level of proactive focus and work of some sort to improve or reposition the investment. In return for this higher level of risk, non-core assets are expected to generate higher levels of return than core assets. An example would be an old, rundown apartment complex. A non-core real estate investor would purchase the building, spend time and money to improve the facilities and attract new tenants, and then hope to sell the building at a tidy profit. The terms *value-added* and *opportunistic* are used to describe this type of strategy, with "opportunistic" usually denoting the highest level of risk.

Of course, many investors in the real estate market start from scratch and develop entirely new buildings. A *build-to-suit development* is one in which a building is developed with a tenant already in place (thus, the space is said to be *pre-leased*). Once the building is complete, the developer can rest assured that the building will start to generate income according to plan, since the tenant has already committed to rent the space. Build-to-suit development is less risky than the alternative—*speculative development*—just as core assets are less risky than non-core assets.

In a speculative development, a building is developed from scratch without any guarantee that anyone will ultimately pay for the space once it is complete. Speculative development is perhaps the riskiest of all real estate investment strategies because of the time and expense involved. Only at the end of a long and costly process will the real estate be sold or rented to generate income. A speculative development is thus a long-term bet on what the market will be like five years or more later.

Financial Projections and DCF Valuation

Fundamentally, investments in hard real estate assets can be valued using the same discounted cash flow techniques that are used to value investments in other assets (and are described elsewhere in this book). The expected net cash flows of the real estate are projected into the future in a format similar to the operating statement and development capital budget outlined previously. These projections are informed by the key drivers of value that we just reviewed. Finally, the resulting cash flows are discounted using the appropriate discount rate to arrive at the NPV of the real estate.

PROBLEM SET:
REAL ESTATE FUNDAMENTALS

Question 1

Which one of the following is NOT an operating expense in real estate?

A. Real estate taxes

B. Tenant improvements

C. Janitorial expenses

D. Utilities

Answer

B. Tenant improvements are non-recurring costs associated with the move-in of a new tenant. They are not included in operating expenses.

Question 2

Given the following information, calculate the property's NOI and CFBF:

Total Revenue $= \$50,000$

Operating Expenses $= \$35,000$

Capital Expenditures $= \$10,000$

Answer

NOI or Net Operating Income

$=$ Revenue $-$ Operating Expenses

$= \$50,000 - \$35,000$

$= \$15,000$

CFBF or Cash Flow Before Financing

$=$ NOI $-$ Capital Expenditures

$= \$15,000 - \$10,000$

$= \$5,000$

Question 3

True or False? You would like to determine the number of newly constructed homes that were built in your city last month. To find this information, you refer to last month's government release of housing permits issued.

Answer

False. Housing *permits* are required before construction begins; as such, they are a *leading* indicator of newly built homes. Housing *starts* are also a leading indicator, as they refer to units on which construction began (but was not necessarily completed) in the time period. To find the information you seek, you should refer to the government release of housing *completions.*

Question 4

A home (House A) measuring 1,600 square feet is listed for sale for $350,000. What is the price per square foot?

Answer

Price per square foot = $350,000 sale price/1,600 square feet = $218.75

Investing in Real Estate: Real Estate Loans

If the ownership of a hard real estate asset is the most direct means of investing in real estate, real estate loans are perhaps the first step removed from the hard asset. A real estate loan is directly backed (or secured) by the hard asset by means of a mortgage. An understanding of real estate loans lays the foundation for our next section covering mortgage-backed securities, which are yet another step removed from the hard asset.

What Is a Mortgage?

Let's first step back and answer the basic question "What is a mortgage?" A *mortgage* is defined as the right to a property (known as a *lien* against the property) that is granted by a borrower to a third party to secure a loan from the third party. The loan may be used by the borrower to purchase the property in question, or it might be used to refinance a property that the borrower already owns. The mortgage takes the form of a document that spells out all the specific legal technicalities and terms of the lender's lien against the property.

Often, the terms "mortgage" and "loan" are used interchangeably, but that is not technically accurate. Notice from the definition that a mortgage is a *right* to a property that is granted to *secure* a loan; it is not the loan itself. The homebuyer is the party that *grants* the mortgage (to the bank), not the other way around. The *mortgagor* is the party granting the mortgage (i.e., the home buyer/property owner) while the *mortgagee* is the party receiving the mortgage (i.e., the lender).

In return for the mortgage, the bank issues a loan to the borrower to buy or refinance the real estate. As part of the transaction, a *note* (or *bond*) is signed. This is the legal document that spells out the financial terms of the loan and the obligations of the borrower. Should the borrower fail in his or her responsibilities to pay back the loan under the terms of the note (a *default*), the mortgage is what gives the bank the right to ultimately *foreclose* on the property—that is, take ownership of the property to repay itself in place of the defaulted loan.

Financial Terms of Real Estate Loans

Whether the loan is used to buy a home, a hotel, an industrial warehouse, an office building, or any other type of real estate, the four key financial terms to be considered are:

1. Principal—The amount that is borrowed. Of the total purchase price, the portion that is not borrowed is the *equity*.
2. Interest Rate—The amount that is charged by the lender as compensation for lending the money to the borrower. The lender must take into account many different risk factors and opportunity costs to determine the interest rate that it will accept.
3. Term—The duration or period of time over which the loan must be repaid to the lender.
4. Closing Costs—The extra costs and fees associated with the loan. Some may be charged directly by the bank, while many others are charged by third parties.

Analyzing Real Estate Loan Cash Flows

The financial terms of the loan determine the structure of the series of cash flows associated with the loan, if all goes according to plan. To illustrate, we will use one of the most common examples of all: a fixed-rate, 30-year home loan with the terms outlined below. We are going to focus on the cash flows from the perspective of the *lender* (in other words, the bank granting the loan, not the borrower receiving the loan). This is the opposite of the typical perspective of a homebuyer (who is the borrower, not the lender), but this is the perspective from which investors analyze mortgage-backed securities, so we want to start adopting it ourselves.

Loan Terms

Purchase Price	= $300,000
Equity (aka Down Payment)	= $30,000
Principal	= $270,000
Interest Rate	= 6.0%
Term	= 30 years

Note: For simplicity, we'll assume that payments on the loan are due only one time per year, as opposed to the usual standard of one time per month. We'll also ignore closing costs.

Figure 7.1 shows the cash *inflows* associated with this loan, from the perspective of the lender. First, there is a large initial *outflow* of cash from the lender (the lending of the money to the borrower, not shown in the graph). Then, over the term of the loan, annual inflows of cash are received, as shown in the graph. Each payment that is received by the lender consists of two parts: (1) an interest payment, and (2) a partial repayment of the principal.

For a fixed-rate loan with a defined term, the sum of these two is known as the *mortgage constant.* The mortgage constant is, by definition, the constant regular amount that results in the orderly repayment of the

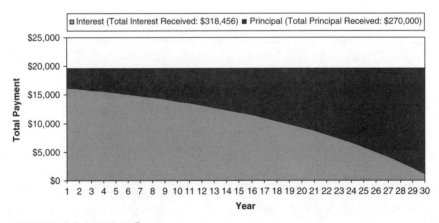

FIGURE 7.1 Cash Inflows.

loan with interest over the term specified, assuming all goes according to plan. In this case, it is just under $20,000 in total ($19,615 to be exact).

Here is the formula for calculating the mortgage constant, where i is the interest rate (6 percent, in our case) and n is the number of periods in the term of the loan (30 in our case).

$$\frac{\text{Principal Value}}{((1 - (1 + i)^{-n})/i)}$$

(In practice, computers or calculators are used as a shortcut for this formula, such as Excel or the HP12C calculator.)

While the mortgage constant remains the same over the entire term of the loan, the composition of the payment (the split between interest and principal) slowly changes over time. Each year, the interest payment is calculated by multiplying (1) the interest rate by (2) the then outstanding principal balance. The principal payment is then calculated as (1) mortgage constant less (2) interest payment. Thus, the payment is weighted more towards interest in the early years and towards principal in the later years.

As you can see in the example above, the "true" cost of buying a property with a loan is much more than just the purchase price. In this case, the total interest alone paid over the 30-year term of the loan is $318,456, slightly *more* than the initial purchase price of $300,000. And that is not to mention the repayment of the $270,000 of initial principal over time. Of course, from the perspective of the lender, this is exactly why they are in this business. The bank wouldn't lend money if it couldn't get compensated—in the form of interest payments—for the risk and opportunity cost of lending.

Sensitivity of Cash Flows   Lending (and borrowing) is a risky business because the cash flows are very sensitive to the financial terms. Very small changes in the principal, interest rate and loan term can have very large effects on the associated cash flows.

Consider the example above, with one change: an interest rate of 7.0 percent instead of 6.0 percent. As a result of this one seemingly minor change, the cumulative interest paid over the term is $382,750, a full $64,294 more than in the previous example. Similarly, a drop in the interest rate from 6 percent to 5 percent would decrease the cumulative interest by over $60,000. This is why public policy officials sometimes try to manipulate mortgage rates in the United States. Even small declines in mortgage rates have the potential to spur buying activity a great deal, since they have such a large impact on the total cost of borrowing over time.

Analyzing Real Estate Loans

As we reviewed in the previous chapter on Credit Analysis, real estate loans lend themselves to various statistics and ratios for analysis.

Loan-to-Value   This ratio, known by the shorthand *LTV*, is calculated as (1) principal value of loan divided by (2) total value of the property. This is a leverage ratio that answers the question "How much has been borrowed?"

The "value" of a property is not always apparent since real estate assets are not like stocks, which are priced in the market everyday. As a proxy for value, either the purchase price or an appraised value is usually used. A higher LTV means a higher degree of risk, and many lenders use LTV as a benchmark for the level of risk that they are willing to tolerate in a loan. A bank might say that it lends "up to a maximum LTV" of, say, 75 percent, meaning that for a purchase price of $100,000, the most the bank will lend is $75,000 ($100,000 × 75%).

The maximum allowable LTV offered by banks can have a huge impact on asset pricing. If an investor has $25,000 in equity to invest, then he or she can pay up to $100,000 with an LTV of 75 percent ($75,000 loan/$100,000 value), but up to $250,000 with an LTV of 90 percent ($225,000 loan/$250,000 value). Average LTVs vary across the real estate markets (home loans often allow for higher LTVs than commercial loans) and also across time (in more certain economic times, lenders are usually more comfortable with higher LTVs, and vice versa).

Debt Service Coverage Ratio   Known by the shorthand *DSCR*, this is the other key ratio in the evaluation of real estate loans, particularly commercial loans. It answers the question, "Can the company afford to service its debt?" and is calculated as (1) income generated during a time period divided by (2) debt service during that time. The "Income" value in the numerator is often the Net Operating Income (NOI) of the property. The DSCR captures how much flexibility or "margin of safety" a borrower has to meet its interest and principal payments. A higher DSCR implies more breathing room, and therefore less risk, while a lower DSCR implies less breathing room, and therefore more risk.

Other Borrower Characteristics The LTV and DSCR answer two important questions about a borrower, but other characteristics of the borrower may also be considered to analyze the quality of a loan. In residential loans, an important measure of a borrower's creditworthiness is the borrower's *credit score*, which is maintained by three credit tracking agencies in the United States. A lender might also consider things like a borrower's job and educational history, total assets, or other debt (such as student loans and auto loans). In commercial loans, a lender will often consider a borrower's track record in real estate investing (have they successfully owned or developed other buildings in the past?) and review the other properties in the borrower's current portfolio of real estate investments.

Legal Terms The legal terms of a loan can be heavily negotiated, in ways that are more or less favorable to the parties. For example, the definition of a "default" is negotiable—is the loan in default after the *first* missed payment or the *third* missed payment? Does the payment have to be 60 days late or only 30 days late? Once a loan is in default, can the lender seize other assets of the borrower (known as *full recourse*) or only the property backing the loan (known as *non-recourse*)?

Loan Covenants Loan covenants are periodic "tests" that assess the financial health of the loan and require corrective action (ultimately foreclosure) if deficient. Covenants often use the LTV and DSCR statistics as their basis. An example would be a quarterly calculation of the actual DSCR based on the latest operating results of the property. If the DSCR falls below a certain value (say 1.25x), then the covenant has been *breached*, and the legal terms will then spell out the remedy. Stronger covenants are more favorable to the lender, and weaker covenants are more favorable to the borrower. Some loans—called *covenant lite* loans—have few or no covenants at all. This gives borrowers greater leeway, to the obvious detriment of lenders.

Hard Asset Fundamentals Of course, lenders must also always look to the fundamentals of the hard real estate asset that secures the loan. This encompasses all the real estate valuation drivers that we reviewed earlier in this chapter—physical condition, demographics, economic conditions, supply and demand in the market, and so on.

Categories of Real Estate Loans

Residential loans are often categorized based on their perceived quality using the various criteria that we have just reviewed.

- ✔ Prime—Prime loans are the highest quality, safest loans. They charge the lowest interest rates and offer the greatest security that the financial obligations of the loan will be met by the borrower. Prime borrowers have excellent credit ratings, reasonable LTVs, and solid income to cover their debt service.
- ✔ Subprime—The subprime designation indicates that the borrower has been assessed a greater chance of defaulting on the loan, due to a poor credit score, high LTV, or the like.
- ✔ Alt-A—Alt-A loans are a relatively vague category that exists between prime and sub-prime. Loans on vacation homes or second homes are an example.

Exotic Real Estate Loans

Moving beyond the relatively simple fixed-rate, 30-year mortgage, financial innovation has brought about a host of newer, more complicated real estate loans. In these more complicated loans, some of the loan terms may change over time, and as a result, the cash flows may not be constant and/or the composition between interest and principal may vary in different ways (thus, the mortgage constant rule does not apply).

Adjustable Rate Loans   In these loans (also known as *variable rate* loans), the interest rate is not fixed over time. Changes in the rate are usually tied to changes in some recognized interest rate benchmark, like the 10-year U.S. Treasury Rate or the London Interbank Offered Rate (*LIBOR*). There may be a *cap* (a maximum interest rate allowed) or a *floor* (a minimum rate), and the rate may only adjust once (a *one-time rate reset*) or it may change on a regular basis throughout the loan (a *floating rate*). In the home loan business, adjustable rate loans are referred to by the shorthand *ARMs*, which stands for Adjustable Rate Mortgages. As we noted above, since loan cash flows are highly sensitive to the assumed interest rate, adjustable rate loans add a significant new risk factor to the loan.

Interest-Only Loans   To give borrowers greater flexibility in meeting their loan payments, some loans do not require the regular payment of principal; only interest is due each month. This may be for the life of the loan, or perhaps for only the first few years. Of course, the principal must be repaid eventually, so the added risk is that the borrower will ultimately be unable to pay the full principal whenever it does come due. In addition, interest-only loans result in a higher cumulative amount of interest paid over the term of the loan.

Payment-in-Kind   Like interest-only loans, a payment-in-kind option (known as a *PIK*) gives borrowers greater flexibility by lowering the cash payment that is due each month. In the case of a PIK loan, this financial magic is achieved by giving the borrower the right to borrow more, rather than paying whatever cash payment is due that month; the extra amount is then added to the current principal balance, resulting in a principal amount that goes *up* over time instead of going down, as in a more conventional loan.

Subordinated Loans   In a subordinated loan, a second lender receives a lien against the property that ranks below (or is *junior to*) another loan on the same property (which then may be known as the *senior loan* or *first mortgage*). For example, a buyer might borrow 80 percent of the purchase price using one loan (the first mortgage), then borrow an additional 10-20 percent of the purchase price using a second loan that is *subordinated to* the first loan. The subordinated lender has the right to repayment only after the financial obligations to the senior lender have been satisfied. As such, subordinated loans are subject to greater risk than senior loans and subordinated lenders charge higher interest rates than senior lenders. A *mezzanine loan* is another term for a type of subordinated loan.

Bridge Loans   A bridge loan is a short-term loan that is used as a temporary financing facility until a permanent, long-term loan can be put in place. This type of loan meets the needs of real estate investors seeking to move quickly, without having to wait to arrange a more complicated long-term loan. Ideally, the bridge loan is soon repaid with the proceeds of a new long-term financing facility. Needless to say, there is great risk inherent in doing business this way: What if the long-term loan hasn't been finalized by the time the bridge loan is due? Then the investor risks either a costly penalty to extend the term of the bridge loan or the prospect of losing the property to foreclosure or being forced to sell it at a fire sale price.

Investing in Real Estate: Mortgage-Backed Securities

In 2007–2008, the world became more familiar with a once-esoteric area of finance that was having a severe impact on economies throughout the world. Newspaper headlines screamed about "mortgage-backed securities," the "mortgage meltdown," and "toxic assets." What did these headlines mean? What went wrong? In this section, we will cover mortgage-backed securities and help answer these questions.

What Is a Mortgage-Backed Security?

Mortgage-backed securities (or *MBS*) are actually a subset of a larger category of securities known as *asset-backed securities* (or *ABS*). An asset-backed security is made up of a number of separate, distinct assets that have been aggregated together into a single security. In doing so, all the individual assets are used to "back" the cash flows of the resulting security. The security is then sold to investors in pieces known as *tranches*. This process of packaging several assets into a single security is also known as *securitization*, and the assets are said to have been *securitized*.

Over time, asset-backed securities markets have developed for all kinds of different assets. In the case of a mortgage-backed security, the individual assets in the package are individual loans. For example, a single mortgage-backed security might consist of 100 individual loans to homeowners throughout the country. All those loans are packaged together into one security and sold to investors. In that way, an investor with $300,000 in cash can buy a small piece of all 100 loans by buying the mortgage-backed security, rather than making only one loan of $300,000 to one homebuyer. In the case of home loans, the security is known as a *residential mortgage-backed security* (or *RMBS*). Similarly, individual office loans, shopping mall loans, apartment building loans, and other types of commercial real estate loans are also regularly aggregated into securities, known as *commercial mortgage-backed securities* (*CMBS*). In dollar terms, the RMBS market is much larger than the CMBS market, and in this section we will generally focus on the RMBS segment. Other examples of assets that have been securitized in the same way include credit card loans, auto loans, and student loans.

Creating a Mortgage-Backed Security

Mortgage-backed securities are complex financial instruments, so one of the best ways to understand them is by walking through the process of creating a mortgage-backed security. This will give insight as to the nature of mortgage-backed security cash flows as well as the potential risks and rewards inherent in owning a mortgage-backed security.

Step 1: Loan Origination   The borrowing of funds to finance a real estate purchase is the first step in the process, known as *loan origination*. This first step is no different than the real estate loan process that we covered in the preceding section, and can mean anything from borrowing $300,000 to purchase a modest single-family home to borrowing $500 million to purchase a downtown skyscraper. The term *loan originator* is used for the entity that has made the loan, which is traditionally simply a bank or insurance company. However, a group known as *mortgage brokers* has also increasingly inserted itself into this process over the years. Mortgage brokers are specialists who do not actually make loans, but instead maintain relationships with many lenders and help match borrowers with lenders (just like how a real estate broker helps match a buyer with a home to purchase).

In the real estate industry, a distinction is often made between *portfolio lenders* and *securitized lenders*. Portfolio lenders, including banks and insurance companies, make loans with the intention of keeping them for themselves. For portfolio lenders, the process basically ends right here. They make the loan to a borrower and keep the loan "on the books" until it is repaid in full with interest (subject to the risks of delinquency, default, foreclosure, etc.). Securitized lenders, on the other hand, make loans with the intention of selling them as mortgage-backed securities to investors. For securitized lenders, the loans move through the next steps as described below. Some large financial institutions may have different arms that act as both a portfolio lender and a securitized lender, depending on the details of the transaction and current market conditions.

Step 2: Creation of the Loan Pool　　Once it has been determined that a pool of loans is going to be securitized (i.e., made into a mortgage-backed security), some legal entity must buy all those loans to create the "pool." A legal entity commonly known as a *special purpose trust* or *Real Estate Mortgage Investment Conduit (REMIC)* is set up to do just that— it aggregates all the loans into one pool so that the mortgage-backed security can then be created. A trust structure is utilized that qualifies as a "pass-through entity" for tax purposes, meaning that it is not subject to tax at the trust level.

Step 3: Creation of the Mortgage-Backed Security Tranches　　Now that the pool of loans is in the custody of the trust, the mortgage-backed security can be created. This is where the fun begins—it means "slicing and dicing" the loans into various "tranches" that will appeal to investors. Unlike the common shares of stock, mortgage-backed securities are tranched (i.e., sliced) *disproportionately*, such that the legal rights, privileges, and claims to the cash flows accrue to different slices in different ways. An investment of $2,000,000 in one tranche of a mortgage-backed security can be very different from an investment of $2,000,000 in a different tranche of the *same* mortgage-backed security. Clearly, this is not like investing in regular common stock, in which one $2,000,000 slice is essentially the same as any other $2,000,000 slice.

The more appropriate analogy would be to think about the different tranches of a mortgage-backed security as you would think about the different ways you can invest in a company. If you wanted to invest $2,000,000 in Company A, you could invest $2,000,000 in its common stock, its preferred stock, or its bonds (among other options), and each investment would offer you something different—common stock would offer greater upside, bonds would offer greater protection under bankruptcy, and so on. In the same way, the different tranches of a mortgage-backed security also exhibit different characteristics.

Specifically, the tranches are created so as to spread out the risks and rewards differently. Creating the tranches is an exercise in *risk allocation*—the risks are tailored in each tranche so that investors can choose the level of risk that's right for them. The three primary levels of tranches are:

1. Investment-Grade—The investment-grade tranches of a mortgage-backed security have the lowest risk (and therefore the

lowest return) because they are legally given the first right of claim on the cash flows of the security. Since they are at the top of the chain, they are also known as *senior* tranches.

2. Mezzanine—The mezzanine tranches sit in the middle; they are riskier than investment-grade, but not as risky as high-yield.

3. High-Yield—Finally, high-yield tranches offer the highest risk, but also the highest return. They are sometimes known as the *B-Piece* of an MBS.

Yet another way to slice a mortgage-backed security is by separating out the two components of a borrower's regular mortgage payment: interest and principal. A *stripped mortgage-backed security* (*SMBS*) is one whose cash flows include only one or the other portion. An *interest-only* or *I/O* stripped mortgage-backed security consists of only the interest cash flows, and a *principal-only* or *P/O* mortgage-backed security consists of only the principal cash flows. Like the different bond tranches, these options give investors another way to tailor their investments to meet their specific cash flow needs.

Note that the risk levels of the tranches of a mortgage-backed security can be tailored *independently* from the risk levels of the underlying loans. In other words, there can be a *low-risk* investment-grade tranche of a mortgage-backed security consisting of *high-risk* subprime loans. Along the same lines, buying a B-Piece tranche of a mortgage-backed security consisting of *prime loans* could be even riskier than buying an investment-grade tranche of a mortgage-backed security consisting of *subprime loans*. When all goes according to plan, this is one of the true feats of financial "magic" in the mortgage-backed security industry. In theory, it can increase the "appetite" for riskier loans by giving investors a way to purchase them in a less risky way.

Investment banks play a key role in this process, bringing their financial expertise and understanding of the markets to create the tranches correctly. Rating agencies and credit enhancers also enter into the picture at this stage. *Rating agencies* are financial experts who analyze mortgage-backed securities and assign the tranches letter ratings based on their quality, with AAA being the highest rating. This gives investors an added level of comfort about the true quality of the security, thereby making them more likely to invest. (The main rating agencies we discussed in the Credit Analysis chapter—Standard & Poor's, Moody's, and Fitch—are also prominent in rating MBSs.)

Credit enhancers are means employed to boost the rating of a security to a higher level than it would otherwise be. Suppose a mortgage-backed security does not receive an "investment grade" rating because the risk of loss appears too great. The investment bank may then *over-collateralize* the security, meaning that an extra level of guarantee is added to the security in some way. One example would be to set up a *reserve account*—cash to be held on the sidelines and used to offset losses if necessary. The credit rating can also be enhanced through *bond insurance*, which is provided by financial institutions that agree to absorb some of the potential losses on the bond in exchange for a fee (the insurance premium). Whatever method is employed, the goal is the same: to boost the rating of the security by providing an extra cushion of support against losses.

Step 4: Sale of the Mortgage-Backed Security Tranches to Investors
Once created, the tranches of the mortgage-backed security are sold to investors. This process is led by the *underwriter*, which is often the investment bank involved in the purchase of the loans and/or creation of the security. The underwriter must price the securities correctly and market them for sale. Hedge funds, mutual funds, pension funds, and many others are generally active buyers in this market. Beyond this *initial offer*, there is also an active *secondary market* for mortgage-backed securities, just as there is trading in stocks after an IPO.

Step 5: Loan Servicing and Resolving Troubled Loans
The process does not end once the preceding four steps have been completed and the mortgage-backed security tranches have been successfully sold to investors. There still exist hundreds of underlying loans with borrowers who must remit regular interest, principal, and other debt service payments over time. All these cash flows must be collected, pooled, and distributed accurately to the many holders of the mortgage-backed security. In addition, someone must have responsibility for mundane functions like updating borrowers' phone numbers or e-mail addresses when necessary.

This process, known as *loan servicing*, is governed by the Pooling & Service Agreement (PSA). The PSA is a legal document that spells out the exact methods by which all the administrative functions of loan servicing are undertaken—that is, *who* is responsible for *what*. Under normal circumstances, an entity known as the *primary servicer* has the responsibility for overseeing all the administrative functions of the mortgage-backed security. This is a relatively seamless process when all goes according to plan.

Unfortunately, that is not always the case. When borrowers under securitized loans default on their loans, the servicing of the loan(s) is transferred from the primary servicer to the *special servicer.* The special servicer is responsible for resolving troubled (or *non-performing*) loans. The best way to "resolve" a non-performing loan is not always clear in practice, however. What the world learned during the financial crisis that began in 2007 was that when trouble brews, mortgage-backed securities can become overwhelmingly complex and contentious. Mortgage-backed securities can have hundreds of investors, each with their own unique financial objectives, ownership of various complicated tranches, and teams of lawyers working to exploit any legal ambiguity.

This is often further complicated by the fact that the special servicer is sometimes also an investor in the B-piece of the mortgage-backed security. To cite one example of the type of conflict that can arise: Suppose that cash flow is sufficient only to pay the amounts owed to the most senior tranches of a mortgage-backed security following a number of loan defaults. Now, the financial incentives of the senior tranches and the B-piece tranches are in conflict. Senior tranche holders might prefer to continue to *hold* on to the non-performing loans, since they are still collecting all their cash, while B-piece tranche holders might prefer to *foreclose* on the non-performing loans, in the hopes that they can achieve some residual value by taking ownership of the underlying property.

The situation is also ambiguous and complicated from the perspective of the borrower. In the "good old days," when a homeowner simply borrowed money from the local neighborhood bank and the bank held the loan in its portfolio, there was a clear line of communication between the two parties and often a personal relationship. If the borrower encountered financial difficulties, he or she could easily reach out to the local bank, discuss the situation, and perhaps even have a face-to-face meeting and work out a friendly resolution acceptable to both parties. In the age of securitization, however, the process is not so straightforward. Often, it is not known who to call or what can be negotiated—for example, does the special servicer have the right to offer forgiveness of some principal and a lower interest rate to accommodate the borrower? The answer is rarely clear.

Government Entities   Before ending this section, we must not overlook the Federal National Mortgage Association (aka *Fannie Mae*), the Federal Home Loan Mortgage Corporation (aka *Freddie Mac*), and the Government National Mortgage Association (aka *Ginnie Mae*). These are the three government entities that are responsible for the vast majority of residential mortgage securitizations in the U.S. In fact, some investment funds specialize solely in the purchase of mortgage-backed securities associated with these entities. These securities are known as *agency mortgage-backed securities* (*AMBS*).

Mortgage-backed securities have existed in the U.S. for over 70 years. It was in 1938—in the throes of the Great Depression—that the U.S. government chartered the first government agency (the predecessor to Fannie Mae) to create and sell mortgage-backed securities. Ginnie Mae came about in 1968 (as an offshoot of Fannie Mae), and Freddie Mac followed in 1970.

Today, these three agencies are still the dominant players in the industry, though their role has been the subject of heated debate for some time, and this debate has been brought to a head by the financial crisis beginning in 2007. One issue is the role that government should play in the mortgage market. Specifically, how much intervention is appropriate? Should the government provide direct guarantees to these agencies, implied guarantees, or perhaps no guarantees at all?

Another hot topic is the concept of "keeping some skin in the game." This means requiring agencies to retain some ownership interest in the security itself after it has been created. Without any "skin in the game," an issuer has little incentive to thoroughly review the quality of the loans that are securitized. They make their money through fees earned during the securitization process, and thus they are incentivized to simply package and sell as many loans as possible, regardless of their quality. (The same concept applies to any loan originator or issuer of mortgage-backed securities who ultimately relinquishes the ownership of the underlying loan.) Going forward, many regulatory changes may be in store for this complex industry, but almost all agree that the securitization market is here to stay in some form.

Analyzing Mortgage-Backed Securities

As we now know, mortgage-backed securities are bonds backed by individual real estate loans; those loans are in turn backed by individual pieces of real estate. Thus, mortgage-backed securities are analyzed on three levels: (1) the underlying properties, (2) the underlying loans, and (3) the mortgage-backed security bond.

Level One: The Underlying Property   We discussed earlier the various factors that help determine the value of a particular piece of hard real estate. These include physical condition, demographics, economic performance, area amenities, infrastructure, political factors, and supply and demand statistics. A property-level analysis of a mortgage-backed security would consider these factors for all the individual pieces of real estate that are securing all the individual loans that back the security. Needless to say, it is a complicated and time-consuming endeavor—and one that was not always carried out to the fullest extent preceding the mortgage meltdown.

Level Two: The Underlying Loans   The next step in analyzing a mortgage-backed security is the analysis of the individual loans that have been packaged together to create the mortgage-backed security. In the previous section we reviewed real estate loans and their analysis, highlighting factors such as LTV, DSCR, borrower characteristics, legal terms, and loan covenants. Again, these factors must be considered for all the individual loans that are in the pool, just as the property-level analysis must focus on all the individual pieces of underlying property.

Level Three: The Mortgage-Backed Security Bond   Finally, we proceed to analyze the mortgage-backed security bond itself.

Prepayment Risk   A *prepayment* is the payment of the principal balance of a loan at an earlier date than that specified under the original loan term. If a homeowner buys a home with a 30-year loan, but then sells the home after five years and repays the loan at that time, the loan is said to have been *prepaid. Prepayment risk* is thus the risk that a loan will be repaid early.

Why is prepayment a "risk"? Because mortgage-backed security bonds are structured to produce specific cash flow streams over time, and prepayments significantly disrupt those streams. In theory, a bank issues a 30-year loan because it wants to put its money "to work" for 30 years and collect a periodic interest charge over that time; it doesn't want its money back after only five years because it then loses the remaining interest payments and must find another way to put its money back to work.

Significantly, prepayment risk is highest when interest rates are lowest, since that is when borrowers are most likely to refinance their current loans into new loans with lower rates. But from the perspective of the investor/lender, this is the worst possible time for prepayments, since the low interest rates mean that they will earn lower returns wherever they choose to put their money back to work. So prepayments can be a real double-whammy: they become more common just when it hurts the most.

Residential loans are particularly subject to this risk because they usually have no restrictions against prepayment, while many commercial loans impose stiff penalties or prohibitions against repaying early. Therefore, in the world of CMBS, prepayment risk is mitigated. Some specific terms that limit the level of commercial loan prepayments include: (1) a "lock-out period" during which the loan cannot legally be repaid, such as the first 12 or 24 months of the loan, (2) a "prepayment fee," such as 1 percent or 2 percent of the loan balance, and (3) a "yield-maintenance fee," which requires the borrower to compensate the lender for the lost yield due to prepayment (as calculated via a complicated financial formula).

Since prepayments of home loans are so common, RMBS investors automatically factor in certain levels of prepayments when they project the cash flow streams of residential mortgage-backed securities. The industry standard for doing this is the Public Securities Association Standard Prepayment Model, which is an assumed monthly rate of prepayment based on historical data. Investors can then tailor their own projections relative to the PSA. To use the PSA standard model without any adjustments, the assumption would be 100 percent of the PSA or "100% PSA" for short. But if investors believe that prepayments will occur even faster than the PSA standard, they might model the prepayments at a "speed" of 140% or 160% PSA. Thus, the true "risk" is not that prepayments will occur at all (which they surely will), but that the speed of prepayments will diverge from the original assumption.

Default/Delinquency Risk   Bondholders also face the risk that borrowers will fail to meet the financial obligations of their loans, known as a *default*. The exact legal definition of a "default" can be the subject of some negotiation under the loan, but all loans have default provisions of some sort. One possible cause of a default is a delinquency, which occurs when a borrower fails to pay his or her periodic payment of interest and/or principal (the borrower is then said to be *delinquent*).

Both defaults and delinquencies are tracked to assess the overall health of a bond. The *default rate* is the proportion of all the loans in a pool that are in default, and the *delinquency rate* is the proportion of all the loans in a pool that are delinquent. They are calculated as (1) the number of loans in default or delinquent divided by (2) the number of loans in the pool. Needless to say, defaults and delinquencies directly impact the cash flow streams of the bonds. When these rates are high or trending up, it is indicative of cash flow streams that are less certain and therefore riskier.

Weighted-Average Maturity and Weighted-Average Coupon The maturity of a bond is another way of describing its term. A loan with a term of 10 years could also be said to mature in 10 years or have a 10-year maturity. This concept becomes more complicated in mortgage-backed securities since they are backed by many different loans with different maturities. This is why *weighted-average maturity (WAM)* is used. It is calculated by assigning a weighting to each loan based on its size, and then averaging the maturities across the pool of loans in proportion to their weighting. Consider the three loans below. Table 7.1 shows their assigned weighting and the calculation of WAM. As you can see, even though one of the loans has a maturity of only 15 years, the WAM is close to 30 (27.4 to be exact), since the two 30-year loans are much larger than the 15-year loan, and therefore have a higher weighting.

TABLE 7.1 Calculating Weighted-Average Maturity

	Loan 1		Loan 2		Loan 3		Total Pool
Principal	$350,000	+	$350,000	+	$150,000	=	$850,000
Maturity (years)	30		30		15		
Weighting (Loan Principal/ Total Pool Principal)	41.2%		41.2%		17.6%		100.0%
WAM (years) (Loan Weighting × Loan Maturity)	12.4	+	12.4	+	2.6	=	27.4

TABLE 7.2 Calculating Weighted-Average Coupon

	Loan 1		Loan 2		Loan 3		Total Pool
Principal	$150,000	+	$150,000	+	$300,000	=	$600,000
Coupon	6.0%		6.0%		3.0%		
Weighting (Loan Principal/ Total Pool Principal)	25.0%		25.0%		50.0%		100.0%
WAC (%) (Loan Weighting × Loan Coupon)	1.5%	+	1.5%	+	1.5%	=	4.5%

The *weighted-average coupon (WAC)* applies the same weighting concept to the coupon rates of the individual loans in a pool. In Table 7.2, there are two smaller loans, but taken together, they have as much weighting as the one larger loan. As a result, the WAC is 4.5 percent, right in the middle between the 6.0 percent coupon of the two smaller loans and the 3.0 percent coupon of the one larger loan.

The WAM and WAC values for a mortgage-backed security are not necessarily "good" or "bad" per se. It isn't always fair to say, for example, that a lower WAM is *better* than a higher WAM, or vice versa. It depends on the individual needs and risk profile of the buyer of the bond. One buyer might prefer a WAM of 15 so as to offset a certain liability that also has a WAM of 15, while another buyer might prefer a WAM of 30 so as to offset a liability that has a WAM of 30.

Yields and Spreads We defined the *yield* of a bond earlier in this book, and the concept of yield for a mortgage-backed security bond is the same—it is the annual cash flow generated, divided by the price paid for the bond. As a result, there is an inverse relationship between the yield and the price of a bond—if prices go up, yields go down, and vice versa. Note that a bond's yield and its WAC are both measures of the bond's cash flow generation, but the two do not have to be the same, or even anywhere near each other, for that matter. If a bond with a WAC of 6 percent is purchased at a large discount to its principal (or *par*) value, then the yield would be much higher than 6 percent, while if the bond is purchased at a large premium to its principal value, then the yield would be much lower than 6 percent. Thus, yield is the more informative measure of the return to an investor, since it incorporates the price paid for the cash flows of the bond.

So how do we know the "right" yield for a given mortgage-backed security bond? Of course, the bond must first be analyzed and assessed by judging all the criteria we have just reviewed in this section—underlying property and loan quality, prepayment risk, default rates, and so on. But once these factors are all understood, the question remains: Is this yield adequate to compensate me for the specific risks of this particular bond? This is where the concept of spread can be utilized.

As we discussed in the Credit Analysis chapter, the *spread* is the differential in yield between two securities. In this case, one security is the mortgage-backed security bond, and the other security is usually the yield on a U.S. Treasury bond. U.S. Treasury bonds are used because they are assumed to be "risk-free" investments. As such, the spread shows how much extra return (in the form of yield) the mortgage-backed security bond is expected to generate as compensation for the extra risk versus a risk-free U.S. Treasury bond. For example, if a mortgage-backed security yields 10 percent and a U.S. Treasury bond yields 3 percent, the spread is $10\% - 3\% = 7\%$.

Now we have a means of judging whether or not a yield seems right. Suppose you predict an upcoming "mortgage meltdown." You think that the underlying properties of a mortgage-backed security bond are not as valuable as they seem, that the underlying loans are suspect due to low-quality borrowers, and that subsequently default risk on the bonds is very high. This would cause you to judge the bonds as *extremely risky*. But when you look at the market, you find very *low* spreads between the mortgage-backed security bonds and U.S. Treasuries, implying *low risk* for the bonds. This would be your time to act—you could sell short the mortgage-backed security bonds, betting that their prices will fall and their yields rise to become more realistic in relation to the true riskiness of the bonds. At other times, the opposite strategy can be utilized. If investors are fearful and spreads are very high, but you think the bonds are actually *not* as risky as they seem, then you could buy the bonds and make a profit as the price rises (and yields fall) so that the spread is more reflective of reality.

In practice, spreads are tracked very closely as a key indicator of the health of the mortgage-backed security market. An analyst or newspaper might say "spreads are widening"—this would indicate that there is trouble in the market, because it means that prices are falling and investors are demanding higher yields to compensate them for the (presumably) higher risk of holding the bonds. On the other hand, if "spreads are narrowing" this indicates that prices are on the rise and the perceived risk of holding the bonds is declining.

PROBLEM SET:
MORTGAGES AND MBSs

Question 1

Calculate the annual mortgage constant for a loan with the following characteristics:

Purchase Price   = \$400,000
Down Payment   = \$80,000
Fixed Interest Rate = 6.5%
Term   = 30 years

Answer

First we calculate the principal value of the loan: Purchase Price – Down Payment.

$$\text{Principal Value} = \$400,000 - \$80,000 = \$320,000$$

Next, we use the mortgage constant formula:

$$\frac{\text{Principal Value}}{\dfrac{1 - (1+i)^{-n}}{i}}$$

where:

i = Fixed Interest Rate = 6.5%
n = Term = 30
Mortgage constant = \$24,505

Question 2

True or False? The annual mortgage constant for a 5-year ARM with an interest rate of 5.5 percent, a term of 30 years, and a principal value of \$350,000 is \$24,082.

Answer

False. \$24,082 is indeed the value that results from the mortgage constant formula using an interest rate of 5.5 percent, a principal value of \$350,000 and a term of 30 years. However, an ARM is an adjustable rate mortgage, meaning that the interest rate (i) is not fixed for the entire term of the loan. Therefore, the mortgage constant might change over time and the formula is not applicable.

Question 3

Calculate the WAM for an MBS comprised of the following three loans:

	Loan 1	Loan 2	Loan 3
Principal	$400,000 +	$500,000 +	$250,000
Maturity (years)	30	30	20
Coupon	6.0%	8.0%	5.0%

Answer

The WAM is the *weighted average maturity* of a pool of loans.

Step 1: Calculate the total loan pool = 400,000 + $500,000 + $250,000 = $1,150,000

Step 2: Calculate the weighting of each loan = Loan Principal/ Total Pool

Loan 1 = $400,000/$1,150,000 = 34.8%

Loan 2 = $500,000/$1,150,000 = 43.5%

Loan 3 = $250,000/$1,150,000 = 21.7%

Step 3: Multiply each loan's maturity by its weighting:

Loan 1 = 30 years × 34.8% = 10.4 years

Loan 2 = 30 years × 43.5% = 13.0 years

Loan 3 = 20 years × 21.7% = 4.3 years

Step 4: Add the results from Step 3 = 10.4 + 13.0 + 4.3 = 27.8 years = WAM

Question 4

Calculate the WAC for the same pool of loans.

Answer

The WAC is the *weighted average coupon* of the pool of loans.

Steps 1 and 2 are the same as in Question 3. Now Step 3 is to multiply each loan's coupon by its weighting:

Loan 1 = 6.0% × 34.8% = 2.1%

Loan 2 = 8.0% × 43.5% = 3.5%

Loan 3 = 5.0% × 21.7% = 1.1%

Step 4: Add the results from Step 3 = 2.1% + 3.5% + 1.1% = 6.7%

Question 5

Which of the following is not applicable to the analysis of a mortgage-backed security bond?

    A. Prepayment risk

    B. Physical condition of properties

    C. Delinquency rate

    D. LTV

    E. None of the above

Answer

E. None of the above. All are applicable to an MBS bond, but they represent different *levels* of the analysis. Physical condition is relevant to the underlying properties (Level One), LTV is relevant to the underlying loans (Level Two) and prepayment risk and delinquency rate are relevant to the bond (Level Three).

Investing in Real Estate: Real Estate Investment Trusts

What Is a Real Estate Investment Trust?

A *real estate investment trust,* or *REIT,* is a company that owns and operates income-producing real estate. Note that the definition specifies *income-producing* real estate. This means that REITs cover the commercial real estate sector—office buildings, apartment complexes, retail stores, shopping malls, industrial warehouses, hotels, healthcare facilities, and the like (including core, non-core, and/or development strategies). REITs can also lend money directly or indirectly to other companies to finance the acquisition of real estate; this is not direct ownership per se, but it is still a means of producing income through real estate, and thus qualifies as a REIT. REITs issue common stock for purchase by investors, but they may also issue debt, preferred stock, or other types of securities. The most significant distinction of a company that qualifies as a REIT is that it is *exempt from corporate income taxes at the federal (and usually the state) level.* This is known as being a "pass-through entity" in taxation terminology, because the tax burden is eliminated at the corporate level and passes to the individual stockholder who owns shares in the REIT.

REITs were created by an act of Congress in 1960 to give the average investor the opportunity to invest in commercial real estate. Through REITs, investors can purchase a stake in a portfolio of commercial real estate projects that they would not otherwise be able to purchase on their own, just like the stock of Coca-Cola gives average investors the opportunity to purchase a small stake in a worldwide beverage production and distribution company that they would not be able to create on their own. From the perspective of real estate owners, the benefit of the REIT structure (in addition to the obvious tax exemption) is that it gives them access to an additional source of capital—that is, raising money through a sale of common stock or debt to investors—to finance their operations.

However, to qualify as a REIT, a company must meet certain very strict guidelines as established by the IRS. Most significantly, a REIT must pay out at least 90 percent of its annual taxable income as a dividend to shareholders. This makes REIT stocks a greater source of *current cash flow* than many other types of stock investments, which may pay little or no dividend. Other IRS requirements are that REITs must invest at least 75 percent of their assets in real estate, must meet certain ownership conditions (e.g., have a minimum of 100 shareholders), and must derive at least 75 percent of their income from rents or mortgage interest.

Publicly-traded REITs are stocks and bonds like any others, so some of the analysis techniques that we have reviewed elsewhere in this book are also applicable to REITs. That being said, REITs are specialized investment vehicles with their own unique statistics and data points. Rather than being repetitive with the general analysis techniques already covered, our focus here will be on the unique aspects of analyzing REITs. In addition, our primary focus will be on the analysis of equity REITs, which constitute the vast majority of the REIT market. Mortgage and hybrid REITs are highly specialized financial vehicles with many complex valuation criteria and metrics that are beyond the scope of this book.

Types of REITs

The major classifications of REITs are based on what they do and how they are bought and sold by investors.

✔ Equity—Equity REITs mostly own and operate real estate. They might also undertake other real estate activities that are associated with real estate ownership, such as leasing and property maintenance. About 91 percent of all REITs are equity REITs.

✔ Mortgage—Mortgage REITs mostly lend money to finance real estate acquisitions, either directly or indirectly. By *directly*, we mean loans that are made directly to real estate owners, while *indirectly* means the purchase of loans that others have made (such as the purchase of mortgage-backed securities). About 7 percent of REITs are mortgage REITs.

✔ Hybrid—Hybrid REITs conduct the activities of both equity and mortgage REITs. They comprise only a small portion of the REIT universe (about 2 percent).

✔ Publicly Traded REITs—Publicly traded REITs have shares that openly trade on a stock exchange every day. They have ticker symbols just like any other stock and can be purchased in the same way, from one share to 1,000,000 shares. This makes them the easiest type of REIT to purchase by the average investor.

✔ Non–Exchange-Traded REITs—These REITs are registered with the SEC (meaning that they must file regulatory paperwork, routine financial statements, etc.), but they do not trade on the stock market. Instead, they must be purchased through specialized broker-dealer channels, usually subject to minimum investment amounts and/or investor qualifications (like minimum net worth of the investor).

✔ Private REITs—Private REITs are not registered with the SEC and do not trade on the stock market. These are the least "transparent" of REITs, since they are not even required to file regular financial statements. Not coincidentally, they are also the most difficult to purchase, since they have the highest standards that must be met by the investor.

✔ Other REIT Investment Vehicles—Instead of taking direct ownership of individual REITs, investors may also choose to invest in diversified baskets of REITs through a variety of vehicles. These include (1) REIT mutual funds, which many of the larger fund families offer, (2) Exchange-Traded Funds, which are traded just like stocks but are set up to represent all the shares of a certain index (in this case, REITs), and (3) Unit Investment

Trusts, which are like mutual funds but with a "passive management structure" that does not involve active trading of stocks after its initial set up.

Analyzing REITs: Stability and Timing

As an asset class, REITs are generally viewed as more *stable* than other investment types. Part of this is explained by the dividend requirement—the high dividend payout of REITs means more cash back in the hands of stockholders on a regular basis, thus stabilizing returns. It is also explained by the nature of real estate operations. The real estate properties that back REITs are hard, tangible assets that generally do not fluctuate in value as quickly as other assets, and contracts in the commercial real estate industry tend to be long-term in nature. For example, most tenants in office buildings, industrial warehouses, and shopping malls sign leases for five years or more. This decreases the volatility of their cash flows in relation to the rest of the business cycle. (Note that apartments and especially hotels have shorter lease periods. For apartments, the typical lease is six to 12 months, while for hotels the typical "lease" is only a few nights. Thus, apartment and hotel cash flows are relatively more volatile and more exposed to the economic cycle.)

Note that this often results in a lag between a REIT's performance and the rest of the economy—that is, when the economy declines, there can be a lag in the decline of a REIT's operations, since tenants are locked into long-term leases at previously agreed upon rents. Of course, the reverse is true as the market is rising—that is, it won't be possible to raise the rents of tenants who are locked into low rents until their leases expire. This is vital to remember when analyzing the financial performance of a REIT during the ups and downs of the economic cycle. It probably isn't accurate to conclude that a REIT with strong financial performance during the start of a recession is somehow "recession proof"—it may just reflect the inherent lag due to the long-term contracts in place and the less volatile nature of changes in the value of real estate assets.

Analyzing REITs: Operations

Investment Strategy Perhaps the most basic question of all is, "What does this REIT do?" We know that it must generate income through commercial real estate in some way, but as we have seen earlier, there are several different asset classes and investment strategies that can be pursued. Most REITs tend to specialize in one or another, so the first step is to determine the specialization of the REIT you are analyzing. Is it an equity REIT, a mortgage REIT, or a hybrid REIT? Does it focus on hotels, office buildings, apartment complexes, healthcare, self-storage, and so on? Does it pursue a core or value-added strategy? Does it develop new buildings from the ground up or purchase existing buildings?

Portfolio Composition   An investment in a REIT is an investment in a portfolio of real estate assets, so next we look at the current composition of a REIT's portfolio. We must consider things like:

- ✔ Size—How large is the portfolio? This is measured by the *number of buildings* and the *number of square feet*. The larger the portfolio, the greater the diversification potential, but the greater the complexity in managing the portfolio and driving growth.
- ✔ Geographic Distribution—Many REITs specialize in certain areas of the country (Northeast, Southwest, etc.) and/or certain market sizes (larger or smaller cities, CBD or non-CBD areas). If there is a heavy focus on certain markets, the relative strengths and weaknesses of this strategy must be assessed.
- ✔ Quality—What is the quality distribution of a REIT's holdings? Does the REIT hold mostly high-quality Class A properties, low-quality Class C properties, or a mix of all types? It is not necessarily "bad" to hold low-quality properties—the REIT's strategy might be to buy low-quality assets at a low price and redevelop them into higher quality assets.
- ✔ State of Service—By *state of service* we mean the breakdown of a portfolio between buildings that are existing and in-service (i.e., a hotel that is open for business and taking reservations) versus buildings that are in development (being designed, permitted, constructed, etc.).

Other Business Lines   There is leeway for REITs to generate some revenue through means other than rents and/or mortgage interest. REITs often take advantage of this flexibility to operate other real estate related businesses to enhance their value, sometimes known as a "Taxable REIT Subsidiary" (or "TRS"). Most commonly, many REITs offer real estate services to other owners/operators in the real estate industry, such as third-party property management services or development consulting services. As such, in considering the valuation of a REIT, it is important to understand the merits of these separate business lines and their impact on the value of the REIT as a whole. In some cases, a REIT might not seem like a good investment based on the value of its real estate assets alone, but when the value of its other real estate service businesses are factored in, the stock price may appear more attractive.

Operating Metrics A number of key metrics are used to assess a real estate portfolio's operating performance and potential for growth or decline.

- ✔ Occupancy/Vacancy—Occupancy and vacancy say the same thing (one is the inverse of the other). *Vacancy* is calculated as the number of *unoccupied* square feet across a portfolio divided by the total square feet in the portfolio, while *occupancy* is the number of *occupied* square feet divided by the total portfolio. Both are expressed as percentages. If a portfolio's vacancy rate is 5 percent, then the occupancy rate is 95 percent (the two will always sum to 100 percent). Vacancy is a double-edged sword: It may signify a poor asset with little hope for the future, or it may offer the opportunity to increase operating income significantly by renting the vacant space to tenants.

- ✔ Trends in Occupancy/Vacancy—It is important to monitor trends in vacancy over time—namely, is vacancy trending higher or lower? A distinction is often made to isolate "same-property" vacancy statistics, by which is meant vacancy for real estate that was owned at both the *beginning* and *end* of the time period in question. For example, if a REIT purchased a nearly vacant building towards the end of the time period, that could distort the apparent trend in vacancy for the other buildings in the portfolio. To adjust for this, the new building would be excluded from the portfolio's overall vacancy calculation to arrive at a more apples-to-apples comparison of vacancy over time. (Note that the same concept is also applicable to the other metrics discussed here.)

✔ In-Place Rents and Market Rents—In-place rents refer to the rents that current tenants are paying for space in a building (under leases that may been signed many years ago). In-place rents can then be compared to *market rents*—that is, the rent that a tenant would be expected to pay for a new lease in the building. Are in-place rents higher or lower than market rents? Again, the answer to this question can be ambiguous. If in-place rents and market rents are close, it means that the building owner has done an excellent job of negotiating leases to achieve the best possible rents. However, it leaves little room for upside. On the other, hand, if in-place rents are much lower than market rents, it means that higher income can be achieved by charging higher rents to tenants in the future.

✔ Lease Expiration Schedule—The *lease expiration schedule* (also known as *rollover schedule*) indicates the percentage of tenant leases that are expiring over a given period of time. For example, if a building with 100,000 SF of space has a 20,000 SF tenant whose lease expires in Year 1, the Year 1 lease expiration would be 20,000 SF/100,000 SF = 20%. Once again, this bodes the potential for gain or loss. If the market is robust and rents are high, the REIT might be very happy to have many lease expirations in a given year, because it will be able to easily re-lease the space at higher rents. But if the market is in bad shape and rents are low, the REIT would probably hope for low expirations so as to keep the income that it already has. Analysts sometimes use the term "gain on rollover" to refer to the potential upside of increasing rent when a given lease expires.

✔ Leasing Activity—Leasing activity captures how well the REIT is leasing its vacant or expiring space (and thus generating additional income from its asset). It is usually measured by the *number of leases* signed, the *number of square feet or units* leased, and the *average rental rates* achieved.

✔ Tenant Financial Strength and Diversification—This speaks to the ability of a REIT's tenants to pay their financial obligations. For example, an industrial warehouse might be leased to a single company that distributes computer chips. But if that type of computer chip has become obsolete and demand is plummeting, there might be a risk of the company going bankrupt and becoming unable to fulfill the obligations under its lease. Most REITs disclose the percentage of their revenue that is derived from their top 10 or 20 tenants so that the analyst can ascertain the concentration and quality of the REIT's tenant roster.

Pipeline   What about the future of a portfolio? What is the REIT expected to own next year, or 10 years from now? By *pipeline*, we are referring to the acquisitions, dispositions and new developments that the REIT is expected to undertake in the future. The ability of a REIT's management team to act efficiently and consistently deliver acquisitions, dispositions, and developments *on time* and *on budget* is a key driver of success.

- ✔ Developments—It is important to consider the number of projects under development, the total square feet of those projects, their locations, and the expected project costs. Just as importantly, what is the timing of the projects in the pipeline? Are they expected to open for business soon, or are they years away due to complicated permitting and construction challenges?

- ✔ Acquisitions and Dispositions—Pricing is the name of the game for a REIT's acquisitions and dispositions pipeline. What price is the REIT paying for buildings that it has acquired, and what price is it expected to garner for buildings that it is selling? As we discussed previously, the absolute price for a piece of real estate is usually expressed in terms of *price per square foot*, and it is essential to consider price in relation to *comparable sales*. Of course, questions must also be asked about the expected timing of future acquisitions and dispositions, as well as the expected volume (how many buildings and how many total square feet?).

- ✔ Accretive/Dilutive—The terms accretive and dilutive are often used to assess an acquisition. Wall Street analysts will clamor to know: "Is this acquisition accretive or dilutive?" An acquisition is *accretive* if earnings per share are higher after the acquisition than before; it is *dilutive* if earnings per share are lower after the acquisition than before. This takes into account all factors of the acquisition, including financing arrangements, purchase price, and the earning potential of the target acquisition (for example, if new stock is issued to finance the purchase, the new shares have an impact on any "per share" calculation). This is considered a shorthand scorecard for the success or failure of an acquisition.

Growth Strategy As we know for any equity investment, growth in financial performance is a key driver of value. Based on all the preceding factors, the REIT's growth strategy should be evident. Is it growing primarily through acquisitions or development of new properties? Redevelopment of its existing properties, so as to raise rents? Upgrades to the tenant base, from lower-paying tenants to higher-paying tenants? Leasing up vacant space? Rental rate gains on lease rollovers? The list goes on. Most likely, it is a combination of many different factors. The analyst must understand each factor and its likelihood for success or failure.

Analyzing REITs: Financial Metrics

Now that we understand a REIT's operational performance, we must measure how this performance has translated into financial results.

Funds from Operations *Funds from Operations* (or *FFO*) is commonly used as the key measure of the "bottom line" financial performance of a REIT, similar to how earnings or net income is the bottom line result for other stocks. FFO is calculated as Net Income (as measured by GAAP) *excluding* (1) gains or losses from sales of most property and (2) depreciation of real estate. These items are excluded in an attempt to capture the recurring performance of the underlying real estate portfolio without being swayed by non-recurring, one-time events (sales) or by significant non-cash expenses (depreciation).

FFO and its derivatives are used in a variety of ratios to analyze the financial performance and valuation of a REIT stock relative to others.

- ✔ FFO per Share—Calculated as (1) FFO divided by (2) the number of shares outstanding. This is like the earnings per share or EPS measure for other stocks.
- ✔ FFO Yield—Calculated as (1) FFO per share divided by (2) the REIT stock price per share. So if FFO per share is $2.00 and the stock price today is $25 per share, the FFO yield would be 8 percent. This is like the yield on a bond—it indicates how much return is generated per dollar of investment.

✔ Price–FFO Multiple—This is the inverse of FFO yield, calculated as (1) REIT stock price per share divided by (2) FFO per share. This is equivalent to the P/E multiple of other stocks and can be used in the same way for relative valuation purposes.

✔ AFFO—Many analysts customize FFO by adding or subtracting other items to arrive at *Adjusted Funds from Operations* (*AFFO*). A common example is subtracting an estimate for recurring capital costs that are required to keep the real estate in acceptable condition. If FFO is $10,000,000, but estimated recurring capital costs are $2,000,000, then AFFO would be $10,000,000 − $2,000,000 = $8,000,000.

✔ CAD—Finally, AFFO can be even further refined by subtracting certain non-recurring expenditures to arrive at a measure known as *Cash Available for Distribution* (*CAD*)—in other words, the amount of cold, hard cash that can be paid out to shareholders.

As noted above, the exact calculation of FFO, AFFO, and CAD is somewhat subjective and may vary across different sources. One analyst might choose to exclude a certain item in the calculation of CAD, while another analyst might choose to include the same item. It is important to note the specific calculation methodology and ensure that they are consistent (and thus truly comparable) for different REITs.

Dividends By definition, dividends are a key focus in the REIT industry since they are required to be high for a REIT to even exist, and stable cash dividend payments are a great part of a REIT's appeal to investors.

✔ Dividend per Share—Calculated as (1) dividends paid divided by (2) number of shares outstanding. While past performance is no guarantee of future success, a solid history of consistent and growing dividends per share is a good sign.

✔ Dividend Yield—Calculated as (1) dividend per share divided by (2) REIT stock price per share. Like FFO yield or bond yield, this shows how much return (in this case, in the form of dividends) is generated by the investment. The average dividend yield of REIT stocks is usually much higher than the average dividend yield of other types of stocks. As such, when evaluating a REIT investment, it is essential to remember to include the dividend yield as an element of the total return on your investment. (Capital appreciation—the increase in the stock price over the period of ownership—is the other component of total return.)

✔ Payout Ratio—The payout ratio is used to assess the ability of a company to pay *future* dividends. It is calculated as (1) a REIT's dividend per share divided by (2) FFO per share, thereby showing how much FFO cushion the REIT has to "cover" its dividend payment.

✔ Ex-Dividend Date—All companies that pay dividends have an *ex-dividend date*, which is the date by which the stock must be owned in order for the stockholder to be entitled to receive an upcoming dividend. For example, if a dividend payment is scheduled for September 30th and the ex-dividend date is September 1st, then the stock must be purchased by September 1st in order to receive the dividend payment on the 30th. Thus, it is important to know not only the amount of the dividend, but also the ex-dividend date.

Operating Leverage   An important notion to consider in evaluating a REIT's FFO or NOI is the concept of *operating leverage*. This refers to the breakdown between variable expenses (costs that can easily be adjusted upwards or downwards in the short-run based on sales volumes) and fixed expenses (costs that are difficult to change in the short-run). If a company has a high percentage of fixed expenses, it is said to have *high* operating leverage, and vice versa.

In general, the real estate industry operates with a relatively high fixed-cost base, meaning it has high operating leverage. (After all, even if a building is only 50 percent occupied, it must still pay all its real estate taxes and mortgage payments.) This is important to keep in mind when projecting past trends into the future. In good times, profits will grow rather quickly, since expenses are fixed and the higher revenues will fall straight to the bottom line. But when revenues fall, profits can plummet just as quickly, since there is less flexibility to cut operating expenses in response to the lower revenues. This also explains why vacancy rates are so closely watched in real estate circles—the revenue lost due to vacancy is difficult to offset by cutting expenses since fixed costs are relatively high.

Capitalization Rate   Another all-important statistic in the real estate world is the *capitalization rate* (or *cap rate* for short). The cap rate is calculated as (1) NOI divided by (2) asset value, resulting in a percentage. For example, if a building generates NOI of $1,000,000 and just sold for $10,000,000, the cap rate would be 10 percent ($1,000,000/$10,000,000). Cap rates are most commonly cited upon the purchase or sale of an investment. This is because the cap rate is essentially another measure of yield on the investment, showing how much NOI is generated per dollar invested. High cap rates imply that buyers are demanding a high yield on their investment, while low cap rates imply a low required yield. For this reason, they are an important gauge of investor sentiment (i.e., How much incentive, in the form of yield, are investors requiring to execute a purchase?) and cap rates are closely monitored in real estate circles. In addition, market cap rates can be compared to a REIT's FFO yield. If there is a wide divergence between the two, it may point to a distinctive element of the REIT's portfolio that is worth investigating further.

Net Asset Value   *Net Asset Value* (or *NAV*) is the theoretical value that would be received if *all* of a REIT's real estate assets were sold today at market price, net of all liabilities. This value must be approximated, since there is no way of truly knowing it exactly. As such, a popular method of approximating NAV is by using the cap rate in reverse. Since we know (or can approximate) NOI, we can *assume* a cap rate, and then rearrange the cap rate formula to back into the asset value. Namely: (1) NOI divided by (2) cap rate = asset value. Suppose we have NOI of $1,000,000 and assume a cap rate of 10 percent. We could then back into an asset value of $1,000,000/10% = $10,000,000. The appropriate cap rate is assumed based on comparable sales, industry averages, and the like. It is then applied to the NOI of the REIT in question to arrive at an NAV.

Once approximated, the NAV per share is compared to the current stock price per share and considered as a valuation metric. Suppose estimated NAV per share is $25 and the stock price is $30. This would be said to be a *premium* of 20 percent over NAV ($30/$25 −1 = 20%). Such a premium means that some degree of optimism about the future growth of the REIT has been incorporated into the stock price. Is this optimism justified based on a review of the REIT's operating metrics, pipeline, FFO yield, and so on? If so, the stock may be fairly valued; if not, it would be a stock to avoid (or to short). Conversely, a REIT might trade at a *discount* to its NAV, meaning that something has led investors to question the potential of the REIT.

Another estimate of the value of all the real estate holdings of a REIT is known as *replacement cost*. This is the cost of completely rebuilding the entire REIT's portfolio from scratch. Recall all the elements of the Development Capital Budget that we reviewed earlier in this chapter—land acquisition, demolition, construction, A&E, carrying costs, and so on. All these are taken into account in estimating the replacement cost. Like NAV, replacement cost is a theoretical value that cannot be truly known; it must be estimated based on expertise and knowledge of the development industry.

Our discussion of asset values also leads to a particular accounting nuance of REITs. A REIT's real estate assets are illiquid and therefore difficult to value on a day-to-day basis (unlike the price of a stock or the price of a barrel of oil, for example). Under U.S. GAAP, "mark-to-market" accounting principles are the rules that determine how to recognize the value of illiquid assets on a company's balance sheet. Unfortunately, mark-to-market rules can be vague and subjective in practice. Therefore, the asset values stated on a REIT's balance sheet may differ widely from their actual market values. Bear this in whenever reviewing a REIT's balance sheet—the stated asset values may not be what they appear.

Analyzing REITs: Leverage

A final critical aspect in the evaluation of a REIT is its leverage or *capital structure*, which is to say, the various financing arrangements that a REIT has used to carry out its operations.

Why Use Leverage?   Leverage is widely used in the REIT industry for a simple reason—it has the potential to greatly enhance the upside returns to shareholders. Unfortunately, the downside of leverage is that just as it enhances gains when things go well, it significantly magnifies *losses* when things go poorly. Because the fixed principal amount of debt must be repaid no matter what, even a small decrease in the selling price could translate into a disastrous decline in equity value.

Given the magnifying effect of leverage—on both the upside and downside—its use must be carefully assessed. As we saw in the Credit Analysis chapter and earlier in this chapter, when it comes to debt, three of the key questions that must be answered include: (1) How much leverage does the REIT use? (2) How comfortably can the REIT afford its debt payments? and (3) What is the REIT's liquidity position?

How Much Leverage? A REIT's SEC filings must indicate the amount of borrowings outstanding. These are found on the balance sheet, along with additional details in the footnotes to the financial statements. Be sure to consider both short-term debt and long-term debt in your review of these statements. As we have seen elsewhere in this book, there are various ratios for evaluating the amount of leverage. The National Association of Real Estate Investment Trusts ("NAREIT") uses the following leverage ratio in its monthly "REITWatch" publication:

$$\frac{\text{Total Debt}}{\text{Total Market Capitalization}}$$

where Total Market Capitalization = Total Debt + Common Stock Outstanding + Operating Partnership Units

How Comfortably Can the REIT Afford Its Debt Payments? Throughout this book we have also seen a variety of debt service coverage ratios, which indicate how much "breathing room" a company has to meets its debt service payments. The higher it is above 1.0x, the more flexibility there is for the company's performance to deteriorate but still meet its debt service. NAREIT uses the following DSCR in its REITWatch publication:

$$\frac{\text{EBITDA}}{\text{Interest Expense} + \text{Preferred Dividends}}$$

An alternative DSCR can be calculated by subtracting recurring non-operating expenses from NOI, such as:

$$\frac{\text{Net Operating Income} - \text{Replacement Reserve}}{\text{Debt Service}} = \text{Adjusted DSCR}$$

The *replacement reserve* is an estimate of the amount of capital that must be expended to maintain a piece of real estate. The replacement reserve is subtracted from NOI to account for the fact that not all of a company's NOI can always be used to meet debt service. Maintenance might be deferred for the short-term, but the longer it is avoided, the more difficult and expensive it eventually becomes. Similarly, the DSCR might also be adjusted for tenant improvements or leasing commissions, costs that also cannot be avoided forever.

What Is the REIT's Liquidity Position? We discussed earlier one of the golden rules of real estate: "Location, Location, Location." To this we would add another golden rule for REITs: "Liquidity, Liquidity, Liquidity." Liquidity is so important because the real estate that REITs buy and sell is, by definition, *illiquid*—meaning that it cannot quickly and easily be exchanged for cash. Hard real estate assets do not trade on a stock exchange. A REIT manager cannot wake up one morning and simply decide to sell or buy an asset without undergoing a long, cumbersome, and costly process. A purchaser cannot secure a loan overnight. A developer cannot snap his fingers and create an apartment complex in a week. Rental income and expenses may be somewhat smooth (due to long-term contracts and fixed expenses), but the buying, selling, and developing of real estate tends to result in large, sporadic bursts of cash inflows or outflows.

What this means for the analysis of a REIT is that careful attention must be paid to the *alignment of cash flows*—in other words, is the REIT being managed in such a way that enough cash is available when it is needed? One item to study is a REIT's *schedule of debt maturities*, which can be found in its SEC filings. Suppose the schedule shows that $50,000,000 in debt must be repaid next year. The REIT must start planning well in advance to account for this repayment, and you should understand the REIT's strategy as part of your analysis. Will the debt be refinanced (that is, a new loan used to repay the loan that is coming due)? If so, what will be the terms of the new loan? Is the sale of a property in the portfolio expected to generate enough cash before the debt comes due? Or perhaps the REIT simply has enough cash on its balance sheet already? Similarly, if a REIT is planning to acquire an asset next year, or start a new development, you must ask how this will be funded—through additional borrowing, a stock offering, and so on?

An assessment of a company's *access to liquidity* will help determine its ability to meet cash funding needs. Nothing is more liquid than *cash on hand*, but too much cash can harm investment returns as it sits unused on the balance sheet. Another source of liquidity is a *line of credit* or *revolving credit facility*. This is like a gigantic credit card that can be tapped for short-term funding when needed, but of course it must be repaid sooner or later. The *sale of assets* can also generate cash, but this is much harder to arrange in the short run—it is a timely, costly, and uncertain process. Finally, *new equity or debt* may be issued, but this is another long and uncertain process.

The key is to understand both short-term and long-term funding needs and make sure that management has credible strategies in mind given the non-liquid nature of real estate assets. Being *forced* to sell an asset or issue new debt or equity to meet a liquidity crisis can be extremely disadvantageous. If you see a REIT that makes use of complicated, short-term financing arrangements—under the assumption that asset sales or new long-term borrowing will be available whenever it is needed—this should serve as a red flag of warning. If all does not go exactly according to plan, foreclosure or bankruptcy could be the result.

Analyzing REITs: Market Indices

A number of indices have been created to specifically track the performance of REITs and real estate, just as the S&P 500 and Dow Jones Industrial Average track the performance of the wider universe of stocks. Specific real estate indices include:

- ✔ Dow Jones REIT Composite Index—Includes all publicly traded U.S. REITs. Also broken into equity, mortgage, and hybrid subcategories.
- ✔ FTSE NAREIT U.S. Real Estate Index Series—This is a comprehensive series of indices whose subcategories include equity, mortgage, and hybrid, as well as property-type distinctions (office, residential, etc.).
- ✔ NCREIF Property Index—This is not an index of REITs, but an index of the returns on individual real estate properties acquired in the private investment market. As such, it is a benchmark of the *underlying* real estate assets that REITs buy and sell.

The value of these specialized indices is that they can be used to benchmark the performance of an individual REIT against the rest of the real estate industry. This can be a more informative "scorecard" than comparing a REIT to the S&P 500, for example, which is composed of hundreds of companies that have nothing to do with real estate.

PROBLEM SET: REITs

Question 1

- A. What is the difference between an equity REIT and a mortgage REIT?
- B. For a mortgage REIT, what is the difference between direct and indirect lending?

Answer

A. Equity REITs mostly own and operate real estate themselves, while mortgage REITs mostly lend money to finance the real estate acquisitions of others.

B. Direct lending is when loans are made directly to real estate owners, while indirect lending means the purchase of loans that others have made (such as the purchase of a mortgage-backed security).

Question 2

Below are the statistics for a portfolio of real estate assets owned by an equity REIT that specializes in office properties.

Portfolio Composition		Leases signed during year	
Number of buildings owned	25	Number of leases	30
		Number of SF	15,000
Average building size (SF)	250,000	Average rental rate/SF	$22/SF
Occupied SF	5,312,500		

Financial Statistics		Market Statistics	
Rental Revenue	$159,375,000	Number of shares outstanding	17,800,000
Other Revenue	$22,125,000		
Operating Expenses	$112,500,000	Stock price	$42.00
FFO	$48,300,000.0	Dividends per share	$2.94

A. Using these statistics, calculate the portfolio's overall vacancy rate, in-place rents per square foot, and NAV using a cap rate of 7.0 percent.

B. Based on the given information and your answers in part (A), what questions are you prompted to ask management about the REIT's leasing activity?

Answer

A. Vacancy Rate: First, we calculate the total portfolio square footage by multiplying 25 buildings by the average building size of 250,000 SF, for a total of 6,250,000 SF. Now we calculate the amount of vacancy as 6,250,000 − 5,312,500 = 937,500 SF. Finally, we calculate the vacancy rate as 937,000 SF/6,250,000 SF = 15.0 percent. Conversely, we could say that the occupancy rate is 85.0 percent (5,312,500 SF/6,250,000 SF). The vacancy rate is always 1 minus the occupancy rate.

In-Place Rents: Rental Revenue/Occupied SF = $159,375,000/ 5,312,500 = $30.00/SF.

NAV: We start by calculating the REIT's total NOI. This consists of rental revenue plus other revenue less operating expenses, or $69,000,000. Now we apply the cap rate of 7.0 percent to this NOI, meaning that we divide $69,000,000 by 7.0 percent, for a total NAV of $985,714,286.

    B. We are given the information that the average rental rate for leases signed during the year was $22/SF. However, in part (A), we calculated average in-place rents of $30/SF. As a result, we must ask management for an explanation of this discrepancy. Why are recent lease transactions so much lower than in-place rents ($30 vs. $22)? Is the market "soft" (i.e., weakening demand or oversupply)? Is management competing on price (i.e., offering cheap rents to lure tenants and boost occupancy)? What rents are competitors charging?

Question 3

    A. Using the same information from Question 2, calculate the REIT's dividend yield, FFO yield, price-to-FFO multiple and payout ratio.

    B. Of the four statistics calculated above, which is the most troubling to you and why?

    C. How does this REIT's stock price compare to its NAV? Does this mean that the stock is a "buy" or a "sell"?

Answer

    A. Dividend Yield = Dividends per share/Stock price = $2.94/$42.00 = 7.0%.

FFO Yield: Recall that FFO is Funds from Operations, a key measure of a REIT's "bottom line." FFO yield is FFO per share divided by stock price per share. First, we must calculate FFO per share, which is $48,300,000 divided by 17,800,000 = $2.71 per share. Now we can divide $2.71 by $42.00 to arrive at an FFO yield of 6.5 percent.

Price-to-FFO multiple: For REITs, this ratio is parallel to the standard PE ratio for other types of stock. It is calculated as stock price divided by FFO per share, or $42.00/$2.71 = 15.5. It can also be calculated as the inverse of FFO yield (1/6.5% = 15.5).

Payout ratio = Dividends/FFO (or dividends per share/ FFO per share) = $52,332,000/$48,300,000 = 108.3%.

B. The REIT's payout ratio should raise a red flag. The payout ratio is over 100 percent, meaning that the REIT is actually paying *more* in dividends than it has generated through its operations. We do not have enough information to pinpoint the exact cause. Perhaps the REIT is using leverage, selling non-core assets, or using an accounting trick to accomplish this. Whatever the cause, the problem is that this calls into question the *stability* of the REIT's dividends. No firm can continue to distribute more money than it collects forever. As such, there is a risk that this REIT's shareholders may be in for a negative surprise in the future when dividends are cut to match the actual cash flow generated.

C. The NAV per share of $55.38 ($985,714,285.71/17,800,000) is higher than the stock price of $42.00. This stock would be described as trading "at a discount to its NAV." However, this fact alone does not give us a decisive "buy" or "sell" signal. The discount may be justified because of a fundamental flaw in the REIT's strategy or future prospects. Like many of the financial indicators we have covered in this book, this one requires further research before any conclusions can be drawn.

Question 4

Name at least three sources of liquidity for a REIT that must make an upcoming loan repayment.

Answer

Quick sources of liquidity are (1) cash on hand and (2) borrowing under a line of credit. Given more time, a REIT may be able to (3) issue new debt or borrow, (4) issue new stock/IPO, or (5) sell one or more assets. These are more expensive and time-consuming sources of liquidity that CANNOT be relied upon for a short-term funding need.

Part

Portfolio Management

We have gone through the maze of financial analysis that is taught in most business schools. While business schools are more in-depth than our discussion, the basics are the same. We have learned, used, and understood, in a format that is both practical and realistic, the tenets of financial analysis. These tenets are clearly applicable to the task of valuing a financial security. But what about developing a portfolio? Can financial analysis provide today's investor with the all-important fundamentals of portfolio management? An analogy that would probably suffice is something along the lines of the following: Financial analysis is the laboratory work of a biotechnology enterprise, while portfolio management is the corporate presentation that seeks venture capital backing.

In Chapter 8, "The Investment Management Process," we uncover many important issues that plague even the savviest investor. The importance of a developed investment policy statement and asset allocation model, the emotions involved in the investment management process, and the ethical issues encompassing the financial services industry. Where the first two parts provide the framework for the evaluation of a security, this last part discusses how a given security is placed in a portfolio. What is the incremental expected return or risk of this additional security? Are there some diversification benefits to the addition of this security? What is the optimal asset allocation strategy given this investor's investment policy?

Although the topics that comprise this section are less focused on the quantitative, empirical constructs of the previous chapters, the tenets of portfolio management are clearly critical to the final success of the investor. The investment management process is the four-step process that each investor should muddle through in order to attain a better understanding of the basic construction of any given portfolio. It is this four-step process that any proactive investor is subjected to in order to attempt the fulfillment of any stated investment goal. There are many quantitative formats that also permit a full understanding of the background that goes into the process—correlations between assets, the Modern Portfolio Theory and the security market line—each of which are discussed in Chapter 8.

Lastly, several appendices are offered to further the education of the practitioner in the tenets of portfolio management. The ethical issues of the financial services industry are discussed so that an investor may better understand the playing field that regulates today's investment services industry. It is the basics of these ethical issues that make today's investor more empowered than ever before; for the underlying fundamental of ethical behavior in the financial services industry is the creation of a level playing field. With this level playing field today's investor can compete in markets where they could never before—herein lays the mantra of this new era of investing: Become proactive and stay empowered.

Chapter

The Investment Management Process

n this chapter, you will learn:

- ✔ The importance of diversification—Modern Portfolio Theory and the science of portfolio management.
- ✔ Investment management—a four-step process.
- ✔ Ethical issues in the investment services industry.

Modern Portfolio Theory

A caveat is in order before presenting this information: Much of this work is theory and therefore may not be perfectly applicable in the practical sense. As a matter of fact, much of this work is based on the assumption that investors are rational beings seeking the highest return with the least risk. But we know better, right? We know that investors are riddled with emotions—after all we are humans—and that fact makes the assumption essentially null and void. With emotions entering the equation, all bets for rationality are off. However, if we could move toward that financial utopia where investors are unemotional and rational, then we can clearly value these tenets. Perhaps investors are gravitating in that direction already, given that the work of unemotional (it is not their capital at risk) intermediaries on behalf of the investing public may move us there after all. Perhaps this utopia looks like a cadre of well-informed, financially viable (low leverage), rational-seeking "investor-robots" that utilize this quantitative data effectively and efficiently for outsized gains. It could happen, and even if it is not around the corner, much can be learned from these academic works that are clearly critical in the investment paradigm.

We start with a graph of all the risky assets, as depicted in Figure 8.1 (top), with their return and risk coordinates illustrated. The question is

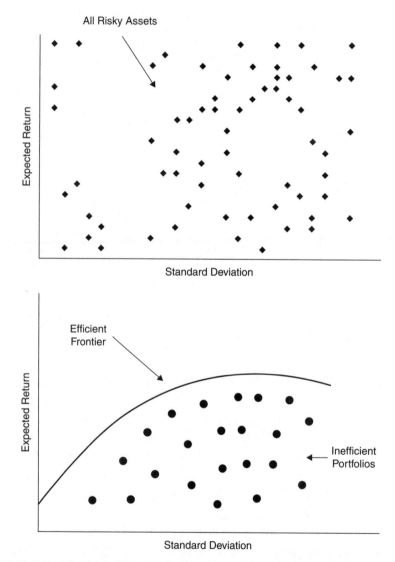

FIGURE 8.1 The Risk/Return of All Risky Assets and the Efficient Frontier.

then posed: Can we somehow combine these risky assets so as to optimize the return and minimize the risk to a portfolio? This is where Dr. Harry Markowitz and covariance come in. As illustrated in Figure 8.1 (bottom), Markowitz combined, the risky assets in a way which produced portfolios that are considered "mean-variance portfolios" or, in other words, the best return with the lowest risk. Markowitz's portfolios combined to make a line known as the "efficient frontier"—those portfolios that have the highest return for a stated level of risk. The efficient frontier provides an investor with the best set of investment combinations, based on historical average returns and standard deviations.

The concept of asset allocation between the risky assets and the risk-free assets is illustrated in Figure 8.2; the capital allocation line (CAL) is drawn from the risk-free asset, and the point of tangency with the efficient frontier is the CAL whose slope (also known as the Sharpe Ratio) is maximized. The Sharpe Ratio is the amount of return a portfolio achieves at a given level of risk; in its broadest sense the Sharpe Ratio is a measure of portfolio efficiency. Depending on the individual investor's tolerance for risk, his position along the CAL is demonstrated using utility curves (those closer to the y- or vertical axis are more risk-averse than those further out on the line).

With the introduction of the market portfolio, the Capital Asset Pricing Model and the fact that all investors follow Markowitz's tenets would mean that investors would choose the portfolio that is tangent

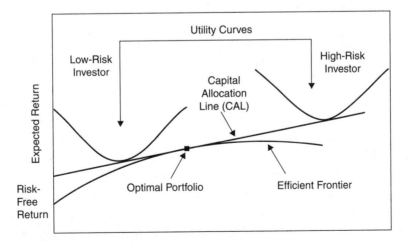

FIGURE 8.2 Asset Allocation between Risky Assets and Risk-Free Assets—The Capital Allocation Line.

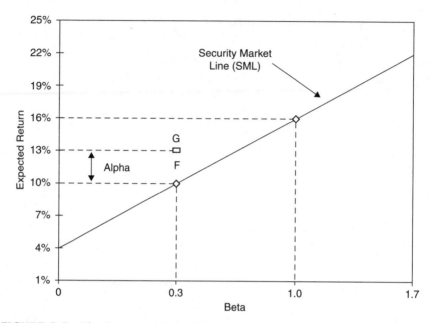

FIGURE 8.3 The Security Market Line.

to the efficient frontier, therefore making that portfolio the market portfolio. So with the assumptions imbedded in the Capital Asset Pricing Model, the CAL graph now becomes the security market line (SML), as illustrated in Figure 8.3. Notice the changing risk measure from standard deviation to beta—the covariance measure between the market and a security.

In Figure 8.3, the distance identified between points F and G is known as alpha—the amount of positive return above the expected return given a stated risk measure. Typically, one would associate this positive alpha with active management; that is, an asset allocation model may have an expected return of, say, 10 percent, but due to the abilities of the individual managers of these asset portfolios, a return of 13 percent or a 3-percent positive alpha may be possible.

Additionally, if we were to take Figure 8.3 one step further and develop four quadrants (separated by the market portfolio's risk and return), a very useful risk-to-reward graph emerges—see Figure 8.4. The managers that are located in quadrant 1 are, hands down, the very best at their craft—that is, achieving a higher (or equal) return compared to the market with less risk. Where it may be difficult to consistently find managers in this quadrant, an investor may, through portfolio optimization

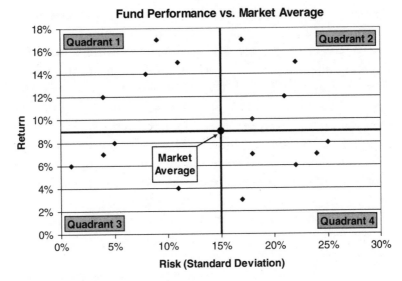

FIGURE 8.4   Risk/Return Quadrants.

programs, combine managers in such a fashion (asset allocation) that the resulting portfolio resides in the enviable northwest.

Markowitz and the Portfolio Selection Theory

Harry Markowitz, PhD (Baruch College, New York City), is the undisputed father of portfolio theory. He showed quantitatively how diversification works to reduce risk. The key to his seminal work is the covariance relationships between security returns. Markowitz demonstrated how the risk of the portfolio is less than the weighted average of the standard deviations of the individual securities; he developed the concept of efficient portfolios. An efficient portfolio is one with the largest expected return for a given level of risk, or the smallest risk for a given level of return.

Efficient portfolios can be calculated using quantitative techniques. When calculating the risk of a portfolio of securities, it is important to realize that the risk is *not* the simple weighted average of the individual securities' standard deviations; it is critical to take into account the covariance between the securities. Consider the following simple example:

Assume we have data for two companies, ABC and XYZ, with standard deviations (measure of risk) of 37.3 percent and 23.3 percent, respectively. The correlation coefficient between their returns is +.15.

Note. As mentioned in the statistics chapter, the correlation coefficient is a relative measure of the relationships between security returns. If positive, the security returns move together and the higher the positive correlation, the more the movements are directly related. If negative, security returns are inversely related—they move opposite each other, and therefore some bad returns can be offset with good returns. A perfectly negative correlation is a theoretical premise only; it does not exist in the real world. If correlation is zero, security returns are independent of each other; that is, they are not related.

Assume the weightings of each security in the portfolio are equal (50 percent each). With this data, the standard deviation (risk) of the portfolio would be calculated as follows:

$$\text{SD port} = [(wt1)^2 (sd1)^2 + (wt2)^2 (sd2)^2 + 2(wt1)(wt2)(sd1)(sd2) \text{ Corr } 1,2]^{.5}$$

$$\text{SD port} = [(0.5)^2 (0.373)^2 + (0.5)^2 (0.233)^2 + 2(.5)(.5)(.373)(.233) \text{ Corr ABC,XYZ}]^{.5}$$

$$= [0.0348 + 0.0136 + 0.0435(0.15)]^{.5}$$

$$= 23.4\%$$

where:

SD port = the total standard deviation of the entire portfolio

wt = the percentage weight of the security (either 1 or 2, in this case) in the total portfolio

sd = the standard deviation of the respective security

Corr 1,2 = the correlation measure, as defined above, between the two securities

It is important to discuss the effect of changes in the correlation between the two securities on the standard deviation of the entire portfolio. Consider the following correlation coefficients for ABC and XYZ:

$$\text{Corr} = +1.0: \text{SD port} = [0.0348 + 0.0136 + .0435(1)]^{.5} = 30.3\%$$

$$\text{Corr} = +.5: \text{SD port} = [0.0348 + 0.0136 + .0435(.5)]^{.5} = 26.5\%$$

$$\text{Corr} = +.15 \text{ SD port} = 23.4\% \text{ (see earlier calculation)}$$

Corr = 0.0: SD port = $[0.0348 + 0.0136 + .0435(0]^5 = 22.0\%$

Corr = −0.5 SD port = $[0.0348 + 0.0136 + .0435(−0.5)]^5 = 16.0\%$

Corr = −1.0: SD port = $[0.0348 + 0.0136 + .0435(−0.1)]^5 = 7.0\%$

Given the evidence from these calculations, the smaller the correlation between assets (or greater negative correlation) the less the portfolio standard deviation or risk. This indicates that diversification pays. The more diversified a portfolio is, the lower the correlation among assets will be except when, in times of market stress, where all assets seem to move together, that is, have high correlation.

Figure 8.5 shows the effect of adding securities to a portfolio. Graphically, this represents what the preceding calculations show quantitatively—the more issues in a portfolio, the more likely the correlation between issues will be less and therefore the portfolio risk is decreased. There are two broad measures of risk—systematic risk and unsystematic risk. Systematic risk (market risk or nondiversifiable risk) is the amount of risk that cannot be diversified away. Systematic risk is important to investors because they need to be compensated for this risk. It is the result of common sources, such as changing economic conditions, which affect all stocks. Unsystematic risk (firm-specific risk, diversifiable risk) can be decreased as the portfolio begins to diversify. As the number of issues increases, the total risk declines as the diversifiable risk declines. It is possible to diversify away most of the unsystematic risk by adding securities to a portfolio (about 22–30 securities from different industries is optimal

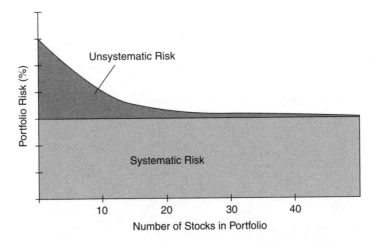

FIGURE 8.5 Reducing Risk by Adding Securities to the Portfolio.

for a diversified portfolio). For the individual investor, however, the growth in the number of mutual funds provides solid footing to achieve this all-important diversification benefit.

The Sharpe Ratio

William Sharpe, Nobel laureate, developed a mathematical construct to calculate the amount of return an investor can expect to receive from each unit of risk that he is taking with y by investing in that specific security. The Sharpe Ratio is therefore considered an "efficiency measure"—sort of the finance equivalent of the torque measurement in physics.

The mathematical equation used:

$$S = \frac{R - R_f}{\sigma} = \frac{E[R - R_f]}{\sqrt{\mathrm{var}[R - R_f]}},$$

Where the expected return is the return an investor can expect given the security's correlation with the market (beta) via CAPM equation (see below) minus the risk free rate divided by the standard deviation (of that security's returns over time).

Compare the two different securities:

ABC has an expected return of 12 percent and a standard deviation of 15 percent. The risk-free rate is 4 percent (10-year Treasury bond yield)—the Sharpe Ratio is:

$$12\% - 4\%/15\% = .53$$

So that is a Sharpe Ratio of .53.

Now let's compare that to another security, XYZ, which has an expected return (over a series of years) of, say, 16 percent, and a standard deviation of 10 percent. Again, the risk-free rate is 4 percent—the Sharpe Ratio is:

$$16\% - 4\%/10\% = 1.2$$

So we can see that XYZ is bringing more to the "return for unit of risk" table (that is, its risk-adjusted return is higher) than ABC—that is clear, quantatively as well as intuitively for XYZ has a larger expected return with less risk.

The Capital Asset Pricing Model

As discussed in the equity chapter, investors use the Capital Asset Pricing Model (CAPM) equation to ascertain a risk-adjusted capitalization rate that would allow further explanation toward the discounted value of future cash flows. The CAPM is derived on the basis of a set of assumptions such as perfect capital markets (all players have same information; there are no taxes or other fees), homogeneous expectations by all participants, and market players who are all Markowitz (mean-variance) diversifiers.

$$\text{The CAPM equation: } E(R_i) = R_f + [E(R_m) - R_f]\beta$$

where:

$E(R_i)$ = The expected return for a given security

R_f = The risk-free rate of return

$E(R_m)$ = The expected rate of return for the market portfolio (the index portfolio)

β = Beta, the covariance measure between the return of a security and the market

The CAPM equation states: "The expected return of a security (i) is equal to the risk-free rate (usually the Treasury 10-year bond's yield) plus beta (the covariance of that security's return with the market's) times the difference between the return on the market (usually the S&P 500) and the risk-free rate (this difference is known as the risk premium)."

Consider the following simple example: ABC Company has a beta of .8, the market's rate of return is 12 percent, and the Treasury bond is yielding 5 percent. The expected rate of return for this security (according to CAPM) is as follows:

$$E(R_{ABC}) = 5\% + [12\% - 5\%]\,(.8)$$
$$= 10.6\%$$

This rate would be useful in determining if the shares were undervalued or overvalued by comparing the expected rates of return with this "calculated" or "theoretical" rate of return. Also, this rate could be used as a discount rate in the valuation process of the particular security.

CAPM is used to estimate the required or expected rate of return for a security or portfolio and is based on systematic risk, which is proxied by beta. Investors should expect to be rewarded for taking risk, but only systematic risk because it cannot be diversified away—the beta in the CAPM equation captures this risk. Although the CAPM model is widely used in finance, it has never been fully supported in empirical tests; furthermore, beta itself has been subject to criticism.

Investment Management

Investment management was first practiced in the 1920s, when it was considered a service of bank trust departments and a few specialty firms. At that time, investment management was the province of the very rich. Not only did the Carnegies, Mellons, and Rockefellers go to banks to have their money managed, they established their own banks.

After World War II, corporations and the public sector began to create pension funds for their employees. These funds soon accumulated millions of dollars of assets and began to use full-time professionals both to keep the fund safe and provide for a modicum of growth. As the need for professional investment management grew, an industry of advisory firms emerged.

Since the mid-1970s, investment management has grown to address the needs of individual investors as well. The expansion of the managed money business has caused a proliferation of firms specializing in investment management, employing well over 22,000 registered investment advisers. Choosing the right investment adviser is a crucial decision.

Please see Figure 8.6.

This chapter introduces the investment management methodology practiced by many financial advisers. As Figure 8.6 illustrates, four distinct steps make up the investment management process:

1. Ascertainment of the investor's needs and constraints.

2. Understanding of capital markets.

3. Portfolio construction and implementation.

4. Account and manager monitoring.

Although the steps are distinct (with their individual functions and expertise), together they form a process and by definition need to be viewed and operated as such.

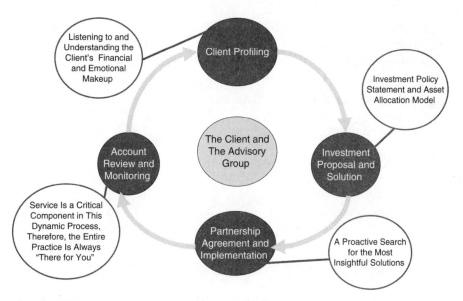

FIGURE 8.6 The Investment Management Process.

Step 1. Investor Diagnosis—Ascertaining One's Needs and Constraints

The primary step for the investor is to determine the specific needs and constraints in his investment goals. Questions asked in a medical practice such as "Where does it hurt?" "How long have you been feeling this way?" and "Are you allergic to any medications?" provide a useful model for the investor's self-assessment of his investment posture. It is easy to see just how critical the interview can be.

In the investment management practice, the client diagnosis, or interview, is also crucial; for only with clearly defined investment objectives and constraints can the professional perform his task effectively. So it is with the individual investor. For example, if Mr. and Mrs. Jones were to open an account with broker Bob Smith without first identifying their requirements, it could lead to disaster: Smith might invest the funds for growth and later learn that the Joneses are retired and require a monthly income to subsidize their living expenses. This exaggerated example highlights the critical need for both professional and client to be proactive in the investment management process. If the professional does not know enough to ascertain his client's needs and constraints, then the client should make them known and then probably seek further counsel.

The *Investment Policy Statement*, as shown in the box "Write Your Investment Policy Statement," enhances the ability of the financial services professional to recognize and better manage a client's expectations. These written guidelines will foster a longer, more productive relationship between financial advisor and client. Although the structure illustrated in this box is the most common form of the policy statement, it is not the only one. These statements can be written in almost any manner one chooses; however, the information described in the skeleton form provided here (objectives, risk and liquidity constraints, tax and legal issues, time horizon, unique issues) is typically required by the investment management community.

Write Your Investment Policy Statement

Objectives

Return. In general, total return objective should be aligned to some recognizable benchmark. Typically, this benchmark ranges from the total return of the S&P index (Standard & Poor's broad index of 500 actively traded stocks) for those portfolios mostly geared toward a growth objective; to Lehman Brothers' Bond Indices for those portfolios focused more on income; or lastly, the CPI (Consumer Price Index) for those portfolios with the aim of mostly preserving purchasing power.

Risk. In investment finance, risk is measured as the volatility around the mean of not simply one asset in a portfolio, but of the entire portfolio's assets working together (modern portfolio theory). An investor should expect compensation, by means of a greater return, for any additional risk above the risk-free rate (assumed to be the Treasury bill rate) that he takes on in an investment. An investor needs to be aware of the critical trade-off between return and risk in the investment paradigm. Furthermore, time horizon (discussed next) also takes an important role in defining risk.

To measure accurately an investor's tolerance for risk, the investor must identify his level of comfort with negative market movements. Could the investor withstand negative account performance spanning more than two quarters? More than four quarters? For an extended period of time, given that this is often a trade-off for upside appreciation?

Write Your Investment Policy Statement *(Continued)*

Constraints

Time Horizon. An investor's time horizon can range from one year to as many as several years, even (as in the case of many retirement plans) several decades. For the investor who is focused more on growth, it is recommended that a commitment (to a stated policy program) be made for at least one full market cycle (four to six years). Investors whose time horizon may be less than that of a full market cycle could cushion any typical market declines by maintaining a high cash position.

Taxes. Taxes and legal issues are certainly categories that warrant professional advice. Each investor needs to examine tax issues carefully, for as the old adage goes, "It is not what you make but what you keep." There are, of course, portfolios such as tax-deferred pension accounts and IRAs, where tax issues are not a major consideration. The investment professional is expected to be aware of tax issues to maximize the after-tax efficiency of the portfolio. For example, in an IRA account the investments would typically be of the high portfolio turnover type that would maximize the tax-deferred growth.

Legal Issues. Covered in this constraint are all statutes pertaining to the Employee Retirement Income Safety Act of 1974 (ERISA), which applies to pension and retirement accounts. In addition, the standards of prudence in investment management of all portfolios are fundamental to this constraint. Also covered are any outstanding legal issues (divorce, estate planning, lawsuits, etc.) that may affect the cash flows of the portfolio in question.

Liquidity. The immediate need for cash is always a constraint in the investment management process. Does the investor have other sources of emergency capital at his disposal to withstand any short-term necessities or would the portfolio be subjected to such withdrawals? Liquidity also pertains to the cash-flow generation that may be required by a particular policy statement.

Unique Issues. This catchall category becomes very important when dealing with circumstances that may be specifically sensitive to the investor (children's educational needs, long-term care insurance concerns, etc.). In addition, certain investment restrictions are also carried in this constraint—such as socially conscious investing (no "sin" stocks, or only environmentally sensitive companies), or American-only (non-international) investments.

Different Versions of the IPS

Individual Small Business Owner with Two Accounts

- ✔ **Objective:** Account #1: Capital Appreciation—portfolio managed to provide returns that exceed the long-term inflation-adjusted return. In Account #2, the policy directive shifts strictly to capital preservation with a secondary objective of income generation.

- ✔ **Risk Tolerance:** "Conservatively Opportunistic"—negative (vs. benchmarks) performance not to exceed two to three quarters. The portfolio is subject to principal volatility, which is accepted in the pursuit of greater long-term returns. However, in Account #2, we are directed to be ultra-conservative in our deployment of capital.

- ✔ **Liquidity Constraints:** The entire portfolio is invested in securities that can be liquidated (into cash) within three trading days. There may be significant liquidity requirements from the portfolio due to business activities and expansion projects.

- ✔ **Taxes:** Minimization Strategy—Utilizing a tax efficient protocol as well as tax-deferred accounts (i.e., IRA contributions) for wealth compounding.

- ✔ **Time Horizon:** Moderate- to Long-Term

- ✔ **Unique:** Exploring estate planning issues as well as business succession planning is of the utmost importance.

Institutional　　So the Investment Policy Statement below is geared toward an institutional client rather than the small business owner or individual as shown above.

Prepared for

The XYZ Association of Anytown, USA

By

Joe Advisor

February 2009

INVESTMENT POLICY DISCUSSION

What is an Investment Policy?　An investment policy outlines and prescribes a prudent and acceptable individualized investment philosophy and sets out the investment management procedures and long-term goals for the investor.

The Need for a Written Policy　The purpose of this *Investment Policy Statement (IPS)* is to establish a clear understanding between the Investor and the Advisor as to the investment goals and objectives and management policies applicable to the Investor's investment portfolio ("Portfolio").

This Investment Policy Statement will:

- Establish reasonable expectations, objectives, and guidelines in the investment of the Portfolio's assets.
- Create the framework for a well-diversified asset mix that can be expected to generate acceptable long-term returns at a level of risk suitable to the Investor, including:
  - Describing an appropriate risk posture for the investment of the Investor's Portfolio; specifying the target asset allocation policy; diversification of assets; specifying the criteria for evaluating the performance of the Portfolio's assets and encouraging effective communication between the Advisor and the Investor.
- This IPS is not a contract. This investment policy has not been reviewed by any legal counsel, and the Advisor and Investor use it at their own discretion. This IPS is intended to be a summary of an investment philosophy and the procedures that provide guidance for the Investor and the Advisor. The investment policies described in this IPS should be dynamic. These policies should reflect the Investor's current status and philosophy regarding the investment of the Portfolio. These policies will be reviewed and revised periodically to ensure they adequately reflect any changes related to the Portfolio, to the Investor or the capital markets.
- A written investment policy allows you to clearly establish your investment time horizon and goals, your tolerance for risk, and the prudence and diversification standards that you want the

investment process to maintain. A written investment policy also helps identify your need to take risk in light of such factors as your financial objectives and income stability.

✔ Articulating a long-term investment policy explicitly and in writing, offers significant assistance to both our clients and their investment advisors in protecting the portfolio from ad hoc revisions of a well-reasoned policy based on important personal considerations. Studies have shown that investors all too often act on emotional responses, generally to their detriment. A written policy helps to ensure that rational analysis is the primary basis for important investment decisions.

Introduction   The purpose of this Investment Policy Statement (IPS) is to establish a clear understanding between The XYZ Association ("Investor") and Joe Advisor ("Advisor") as to the investment objectives and policies applicable to the Investor's investment portfolio. This IPS will:

✔ Establish reasonable expectations, objectives, and guidelines for the investment of the Portfolio's assets.

✔ Set forth an investment structure detailing permitted asset classes and the desired allocation among asset classes.

✔ Encourage effective communication between the Advisor and the Investor.

✔ Create the framework for a well-diversified asset mix that can be expected to generate acceptable long-term returns commensurate with the level of risk suitable to the Investor.

✔ Serve as a reference over time to provide long-term discipline for an established investment plan.

✔ Describe constraints that the Investor chooses to place on the investment strategy.

✔ This IPS is intended to be a summary of an investment philosophy that provides guidance for the Investor and the Advisor.

Investment Objectives   The Investor's objective for the investment assets of the accounts, set forth in the following sections of this Investment Proposal, is *growth and income*, accompanied by a *conservative level of risk*. The Investor has no expected immediate need of the assets in this account, except as noted below, and is willing to accept a measured amount of short-term volatility in order to achieve higher expected rates of return over the long run. The Investor's performance objective is to equal or exceed the performance of the S&P 500 Index, the EAFE (International) Index, and the Barclays Aggregate Bond Index, allocated in a ratio of approximately 65/35 percent (stocks/bonds) including an international equity allocation of 15 percent. However, no guarantees can be given about future performance and nothing contained in this IPS shall be construed as offering such a guarantee.

Liquidity and Income Needs   The Investor has determined that sufficient disposable income and liquidity is available from other sources so that the Investor is not expecting a significant annual invasion from this portfolio. However, the Investor's income need from the investment portfolio may be approximately $50,000 per year, subject to an annual cost of living/inflation adjustment if necessary. Income will be distributed only upon request, and is to be achieved on a total return basis (i.e., interest, dividends, and capital appreciation). The size of the required annual distribution relative to the size of the account may necessitate a withdrawal of principal (assets as they were valued on 12/31 of the prior year), depending on capital market performance.

Diminution of portfolio value due to prolonged periods of poor market performance may require an alteration of investment policy.

Time Horizon   The investor's time horizon for these investments, given the nature of the portfolio ("endowment"), is greater than 20 years. The Investor does anticipate withdrawing a portion of the portfolio prior to that time. Such anticipated needs are noted above. Capital values do fluctuate and the Investor recognizes that the possibility of capital loss does exist. Historical asset-class return data suggest the shorter the holding period the greater the risk of the Investor's objective not being achieved.

Risk Tolerance   The Investor recognizes that seeking increased returns generally involves accepting greater volatility and risk. The Investor understands that risk is inherent in investing in marketable securities and results could be better or worse than indicated above in the future. The Investor is prepared to tolerate negative performance in order to meet the Investor's longer-term objectives as a result of expected long-term returns.

The statement of the Investor's risk tolerance is an indication that the investor is unlikely to abandon the investment strategy set forth in this IPS if negative performance is no worse than indicated. The Investor understands that maintaining a consistent strategy during good and bad markets is an important factor in achieving longer-term objectives.

The Portfolio will be managed in a manner that seeks to minimize principal fluctuations within realistic market expectations consistent with the stated objectives and the chosen asset allocation over the established horizon. Financial research has demonstrated that risk is best minimized by holding assets over time, and through diversification across low correlating assets, including international investments. The Investor recognizes that inherent in this strategy is the likelihood that portfolio performance will differ over various time periods from any particular asset class or popular index (e.g., S&P 500, Wilshire 5000, etc.). The Investor accepts the likelihood of such tracking errors as an acceptable condition of this strategy. The Investor recognizes, however, that performance results cannot be guaranteed and historical performance is not indicative of future performance.

Asset Allocation   Academic research suggests that the decision of how to allocate total assets among various asset classes will have far greater impact upon portfolio performance than security selection and market timing. Increased weighting to higher risk asset classes like small cap or value, as compared to a total market weighting (e.g., Wilshire 5000) is expected to provide a higher expected return and more effective diversification. International asset class funds have historically also provided more effective diversification. Increasing allocation to fixed income typically decreases the volatility risk of a portfolio.

Deciding on the Investor's appropriate asset allocation should be based on a review of the Investor's personal circumstances. This review may include the Investor's assets not included in accounts covered by this IPS, the Investor's income sources, and the investor's or business holdings; and their sensitivity to factors which may impact individual asset classes specifically, or markets generally. After reviewing both personal circumstances and the long-term performance and risk characteristics of various asset classes, and balancing the risks and rewards of market behavior, the asset allocation model offered in this proposal was selected to achieve the objectives of the Investor's Portfolio.

Investment Constraints and/or Preferences   Given the nature of the entity, a federally tax-exempt not-for-profit, the tax issues with respect to his portfolio are currently minimized.

The Investor has not, as of yet, made clear if there are any issues with investments in certain industries or sectors (i.e., alcohol companies, defense and healthcare sectors, tobacco companies).

Investment Strategy and Review

Diversification   Investment of the funds shall be limited, in general, to passively managed mutual funds or direct fixed income obligations in the following categories:

- ✔ Cash and cash equivalents (including money market funds and bank certificates of deposit);
- ✔ Bonds (corporate, U.S. government, municipal, or foreign government);
- ✔ Stocks (U.S. and foreign-based companies);
- ✔ Real Estate (REITs) and alternatives (commodities).

Investment Management   Passively managed and actively managed asset-class mutual funds and investment managers shall be chosen. This strategy—*The Core/Satellite Strategy*—is employed to capture the return behavior of an entire asset class and to complement that with an eye toward outperforming the index through extensive research and analysis. The passive management approach is based upon the major tenets of Modern Portfolio Theory which states that markets are "efficient" and that investors' returns are determined principally by asset allocation decisions, not market timing or selection of specific securities. In the Active Management approach, evident in the annals of phenomenal returns by the likes of Buffett, Longleaf Partners, The Sequoia Fund and scores of others, the thinking is that strong, disciplined research coupled with a contrarian profile will yield extraordinary returns. Asset classes with historically demonstrated low correlation and different risk/return profiles are combined together in an attempt to both lower the volatility of the overall portfolio and enhance returns.

Portfolio Review and Rebalancing Procedures   From time to time, market conditions are likely to cause the Portfolio's investment in various asset classes to vary from the established allocation guidelines established by this IPS. Each asset class in which the Portfolio is invested shall be reviewed on a quarterly basis by the Advisor and may, with the Investor's approval, be rebalanced back to the recommended weighting, when appropriate. Rebalancing will be advised if either the weighting of an individual asset class varies by 25 percent, plus or minus, of its recommended weighting, or if the major components (domestic equity, international equity, total equity, and total fixed income) vary by 10 percentage points, plus or minus, from those components' recommended weighting. When necessary and/or available, cash flows will be deployed or withdrawals will be made in a manner consistent with rebalancing the asset allocation. In the absence of cash flows, the advisor may effect transactions to rebalance the portfolio. In many cases, although not yours given the tax-exempt nature of your portfolio, income tax considerations may influence the appropriateness of rebalancing activity.

Adjustment in the Target Allocation   The approved asset allocation set out above indicates an initial target allocation for each asset class. From time to time, based on the Investor's changing economic or life circumstances or new academic research, it may be desirable to make changes in the target allocation. Such changes should not, however, be made due to expectations of the relative performance of individual asset classes. The Investor must approve any proposed changes in the form of a written amendment to this IPS.

Investment Strategy Performance   The Investor recognizes that asset class investment performance is cyclical and, therefore, the Investor may experience periods of time in which investment objectives are not met. In addition, unless there are extenuating circumstances, patience will often prove appropriate when performance has been disappointing for a particular asset class, or the overall portfolio.

For the overall portfolio, the Investor should allow a five-year time period or longer for achieving the stated investment return objectives. Shorter time frames contradict the principles of long-term investing. Under no circumstances, however, can results be guaranteed.

In the following case study, the Investment Policy Statement is demonstrated in a potentially real life circumstance. *Do you have an Investment Policy Statement for your investment account? Why not?* As will be seen later in this chapter, a well-defined IPS will go a long way to optimize a portfolio's return objectives without impeding on its constraints. This case study will teach the fundamentals of developing an Investment Policy Statement from which an investor could formulate an asset allocation model (AAM) that is best suited to his individual needs. The AAM is the crux of the modern portfolio theory and is crucial to the individual investor who seeks the highest risk-adjusted return.

Case Study: Investment Policy Statement for Susan Fairfax[1]

Introduction

Susan Fairfax is president of Reston Industries, a U.S.-based company whose sales are entirely domestic and whose shares are listed on the New York Stock Exchange. The following are additional facts concerning her current situation.

✔ Fairfax is single, aged 58. She has no immediate family, no debts, and does not own a residence. She is in excellent health and covered by Reston-paid health insurance that continues after her expected retirement at age 65.

✔ Her base salary of $500,000/year, inflation-protected, is sufficient to support her present lifestyle, but can no longer generate any excess for savings.

✔ She has $2,000,000 of savings from prior years, held in the form of short-term instruments.

✔ Reston awards key employees through a generous stock-bonus incentive plan, but provides no pension plan and pays no dividend.

✔ Fairfax's incentive plan participation has resulted in her ownership of Reston stock worth $10 million (current market value). She will likely hold the stock, which she received tax-free but subject to a 35-percent tax rate (on entire proceeds) if sold, at least until her retirement.

✔ Her present level of spending and the current annual inflation of 4 percent are expected to continue after her retirement.

✔ Fairfax is taxed at 35 percent on all salary, investment income, and realized capital gains. Assume her composite tax rate will continue at this level indefinitely.

Fairfax's orientation is patient, careful, and conservative in all things. She has stated that an annual after-tax real total return of 3 percent would be completely acceptable for her if she could achieve it in a context where an investment portfolio created from her accumulated savings was not subject to a decline of more than 10 percent in nominal terms in any given 12-month period. To obtain the benefits of professional assistance, she has approached two investment advisory firms—HH Counselors ("HH") and Coastal Advisors ("Coastal")—for recommendations on allocation of the investment portfolio to be created from her existing savings assets (the "Savings Portfolio") as well as for advice concerning investing in general.

Case Study Question   Create and justify an Investment Policy Statement for Fairfax based *only* on the information provided in the Introduction. Be specific and complete as to objectives and constraints. (An asset allocation is *not* required in answering this question.)

Guideline Answer

Case Study Question   An Investment Policy Statement for Fairfax based only on the information provided in the Introduction is shown below.

Overview. Fairfax is 58 years old and has seven years to go until a planned retirement. She has a fairly lavish lifestyle but few money worries: Her large salary pays all current expenses, and she has accumulated $2 million in cash equivalents from savings in previous years. Her health is excellent, and her health insurance coverage will continue after retirement and is employer paid. While Fairfax's job is a high-level one, she is not well versed in investment matters and has had the good sense to connect with professional counsel to get started on planning for her investment future—a future that is complicated by ownership of a $10 million block of company stock that, while listed on the NYSE, pays no dividends and has a zero-cost basis for tax purposes. All salary, investment income (except interest on municipal bonds), and realized capital gains are taxed to Fairfax at a 35 percent rate; this tax rate and a 4 percent inflation rate are expected to continue into the future. Fairfax would accept a 3 percent real, after-tax return from the investment portfolio to be formed from her $2 million in savings (Savings Portfolio) if that return could be obtained with only modest portfolio volatility (i.e., less than a 10-percent annual decline). She is described as being conservative in all things.

Objectives

✔ *Return requirement.* Fairfax's need for portfolio income begins seven years from now, at the date of retirement, when her salary stops. The investment focus for her Savings Portfolio should be on growing the portfolio's value in the interim in a way that provides protection against loss of purchasing power. Her 3-percent real, after-tax return preference implies a gross total return requirement of at least 10.8 percent, assuming her investments are fully taxable (as is the case now) and assuming 4 percent inflation and a 35 percent tax rate. For Fairfax to maintain her current lifestyle, she would have to generate $500,000 × $(1.04)^7$, or $658,000, in annual income, inflation-adjusted, when she retires. If the market value of Reston's stock does not change, and if she has been able to earn a 10.8 percent return on the Savings Portfolio (or 7 percent nominal after-tax return = $2,000,000 × $(1.07)^7 = \$3,211,500$), she should accumulate $13,211,500 ($10 million in stock plus $3,211,500) by retirement age. To generate $658,000, a return on $13,211,500 of 5.0 percent would be needed.

✔ *Risk tolerance.* From the information provided, Fairfax is quite risk averse, indicating she does not want to experience a decline of more than 10 percent in the value of the Savings Portfolio in any given year. This would indicate that the portfolio should have below-average risk exposure to minimize its downside volatility. In terms of overall wealth, she could afford to take more than average risk, but because of her preferences and the nondiversified nature of the total portfolio, a below-average risk objective is appropriate for the Savings Portfolio. It should be noted, however, that truly meaningful statements about the risk of Fairfax's total portfolio are tied to assumptions about the volatility of Reston's stock, if it is retained, and about when and at what price the Reston stock will be sold. Because the Reston holding constitutes 83 percent of Fairfax's total portfolio, it will largely determine the risk she actually experiences as long as it remains intact.

Constraints

✔ *Time horizon.* Two time horizons are applicable to Fairfax's situation. The first is the medium- or intermediate-term between now and when she plans to retire, which is seven years. The second is the long-term horizon between now and the expected end of Fairfax's life, perhaps 25 to 30 years from now. The first time horizon represents the period during which Fairfax should set up her financial situation in preparation for the balance of the second time horizon, her retirement period of indefinite length. Of the two horizons, the longer term to the expected end of her life is the dominant horizon because it is over this period that the assets must fulfill their primary function of funding her expenses, in an annuity sense, in retirement.

✔ *Liquidity.* With liquidity defined either as income needs or as cash reserves to meet emergency needs, Fairfax's liquidity requirement is minimal. Her salary of $500,000 is available annually, health cost concerns are nonexistent, and we know of no planned needs for cash from the portfolio.

✔ *Taxes.* Fairfax's taxable income (salary, taxable investment income, and realized capital gains on securities) is taxed at a 35-percent rate. Careful tax planning and coordination of tax policy with investment planning is required. Investment strategy should include seeking income that is sheltered from taxes and holding securities for periods long enough to produce larger after-tax returns. Sale of the Reston stock will have sizable tax consequences because Fairfax's cost basis is zero; special planning will be needed for this. Fairfax may want to consider some form of charitable giving, either during her lifetime or at death. She has no immediate family, and we know of no other potential gift or bequest recipients.

✔ *Laws and regulations.* Fairfax should be aware of and abide by any securities (or other) laws or regulations relating to her "insider" status at Reston and her holding of Reston stock. Although there is no trust instrument in place, if Fairfax's future investing is handled by an investment advisor, the responsibilities associated with Prudent Expert Rule will come into play, including the responsibility for investing in a diversified portfolio. Also, she has a need to seek estate planning legal assistance, even though there are no apparent gift or bequest recipients.

✔ *Unique circumstances and/or preferences.* Clearly, the value of the Reston stock dominates the value of Fairfax's portfolio. A well-defined exit strategy needs to be developed for the stock as soon as is practical and appropriate. If the value of the stock increases, or at least does not decline before it is liquidated, Fairfax's present lifestyle can be sustained after retirement with the combined portfolio. A significant and prolonged setback for Reston Industries, however, could have disastrous consequences. Such circumstances would require a dramatic downscaling of Fairfax's lifestyle, or generation of alternate sources of income to maintain her current lifestyle. A worst-case scenario might be characterized by a 50-percent drop in the market value of Reston's stock and a sale of that stock to diversify the portfolio, where the sale proceeds would be subject to a 35-percent tax rate. The net proceeds of the Reston part of the portfolio would be $10,000,000 \times 0.5 \times (1 - 0.35) = \$3,250,000$. When added to the Savings Portfolio, total portfolio value would be $5,250,000. For this portfolio to generate $658,000 in income, a 12.5-percent return would be required.

Synopsis. The policy governing investment in Fairfax's Savings Portfolio shall put emphasis on realizing a 3-percent real, after-tax return from a mix of high-quality assets aggregating less-than-average risk. Ongoing attention shall be given to Fairfax's tax planning and legal needs, her progress toward retirement, and the value of her Reston stock. The Reston stock holding is a unique circumstance of decisive significance in this situation: Developments should be monitored closely, and protection against the effects of a worst-case scenario should be implemented as soon as possible.

Now that we have gotten our arms around the IPS, we can turn our attention to some other facets of the first step in the investment management process. Using the IPS as a template, the personality aspects of the investor would be documented under the "unique" constraint in the IPS, because they are important in realizing the investor's needs. While honest self-evaluation may be difficult for someone in this circumstance (What kind of investor are you? Analytical or passive—or both?), it is important to attempt to get a handle on your needs. I recommend seeking the counsel of a financial services provider (FSP) and then take it from there. Or perhaps just talking with someone else will provide you with the necessary information to make a decision.

The Psychographics of the Individual Investor

Psychographics describes psychological characteristics of people and involves the somewhat fuzzy process of classifying people based on their personalities and needs. While much market research is done via demographic approaches, it is also known that any two individual investors can have very different psychological needs in the way their money is invested.

The most popular method of "psychographic labeling" in the financial services industry is the Barnwell two-way model, which studies various occupational groups and develops a superficially simple, yet surprisingly useful model of passive and active investors. A passive investor is defined as that investor who has become wealthy passively (e.g., by inheritance or by risking the capital of others rather than his own). Passive investors have a greater need for security and less tolerance for risk. Occupational groups that tend to be passive investors include corporate executives, CPAs and attorneys in large firms, medical and dental non-surgeons, politicians, bankers, and journalists. An active investor is defined as that individual who has earned his own wealth in his lifetime by being actively involved in wealth creation, and by risking his own capital in achieving wealth objectives. Active investors have a high tolerance for risk and a lesser need for security. Related to their high tolerance for risk is the fact that active investors prefer to maintain control of their own investments. By their involvement and control, they feel that they reduce the risk to an acceptable level. Occupationally, active investors are typically small business owners, entrepreneurs, and self-employed consultants.

In addition to this two-way methodology, a quadrant methodology has a growing following among the financial advisor community. The four types of investors in this methodology are:

1. *The In-Control Investor.* These investors are typically entrepreneurs and consequently earn their investment capital by making their own decisions and taking risks. In-control investors usually adopt a tactical asset allocation (versus a strategic asset allocation) strategy—constantly changing their allocation to take advantage of perceived opportunities in the capital markets. This book could be of particular assistance to these proactive investors in the assembling and organizing of research data, the understanding of the capital markets, and the valuing of financial securities.

2. *The Followers.* This group of investors is typically dominated by wealthy, non-business individuals (e.g., medical and dental professionals) who, for fear of "missing the market," choose their investments by seeking the most fashionable, currently "hot" ideas. Typically, however, what is hot on Wall Street today is also quite expensive (read: has high valuation) and tends to correct (decrease in price) in the short run. While this group of investors could be quite profitable for an investment counselor, they usually tend to "burn themselves up" within a short period of time and are destined to the mantra "I am the best reverse indicator on Wall Street—when I buy you should sell short!"

   In this case, my advice is simple: Attempt to be a free thinker when it comes to your investment portfolio. Many times, I query my clients to find some of my best investment ideas: What is going on in your industry? Who are the major players? Has demand for the company's goods recently picked up due to an external force that is expected to remain intact for an extended period? When my wife comes home from the store, we go through a similar line of questioning to understand what is happening in the malls and shopping centers (which a fortuitous strain of virus prevents me from ever visiting). This type of investment analysis was popularized by Peter Lynch (former manager of Fidelity's Magellan Fund), who would only buy what he understood and used in his daily life. Once an investor can divorce himself from the emotions involved with the stock itself and boil things down to this rudimentary foundation, investing in equities is simply determining whether you want to buy the "business" at the stated (share) price.

3. *Do-It-Yourselfers.* This investor always brings to mind the commercial featuring a fellow who is attempting to save the $20 on a haircut by giving himself a trim (if you haven't seen it, he is forced, by the end of the spot, to wear a hat). The do-it-yourselfers are curious characters who may seek as much information as possible, only to make the final decisions themselves. The brokerage community refers to these investors as "professional seminar goers" or "information gatherers." While as an educator, as well as a financial services provider, I am in full support of this investor, I believe that investors who fall into this category owe it to themselves to seek professional advice from time to time, in addition to their self-managed portfolio. My advice to these investors: Open more than one account (there is usually no fee or obligation to open an account), one with a professional adviser and one with a discount firm (or for those who are "mouse literate," a computer-linked account) for the self-managed portfolio. Furthermore, a competition (Wall Streeters love a good game) should emerge between the two accounts, the winner being rewarded with a greater commitment in the next period.

4. *The Scared.* These are your certificate of deposit, passbook savings account investors. They may know that the return they are receiving, on an after-tax, real basis is probably negative, but they cannot make a move. These investors (I use the term loosely) have an unmanageable fear of loss of principal, even though they may have a long-term time horizon. These investors are destined to mediocrity, and unless they have significant wealth (unusual

for this group because the wealthy usually get rich by investing), they will be burdened in their retirement with concerns about outliving their assets. It is difficult to suggest a remedy for this type of investor, for there is no panacea to cure the fainthearted. Nor would I ever attempt to convert a scared investor; the ramifications to such an act could be severe. However, I would use every possible means (seminars, face-to-face discussions, books, magazine articles, TV broadcasts), to educate this investor in the hope that he will begin to see the light.

In addition to the demographics of wealth and the psychographics of individual investors, there are the demographics of age or, more appropriately, of stages in the life cycle of an investor (see Figure 8.7). These stages are important to understand because of their impact on an individual's risk and return preferences. It is useful to break up this continuous life cycle into four different phases in which individuals exhibit one dominant motif in viewing their wealth: the accumulation (early career), consolidation (mid- to late-career), spending (period of financial independence), and gifting (individual realizes he has more assets than he will ever need for personal security and spending) phases.

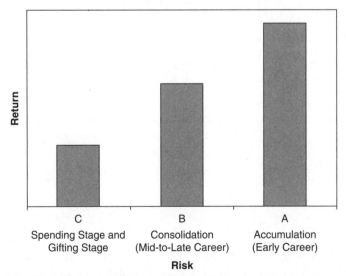

FIGURE 8.7 Risk/Return Position at Various Life Cycle Stages.

Life Cycle of Investors

Phase 1. Accumulation Phase Typically, these investors have these qualities:

- ✔ They are 25–40 years old.
- ✔ They are spending capital to build home and career.
- ✔ They have a high level of debt and live slightly beyond their means.

In this phase, growth would be the most favored investment objective. The greatest asset that this investor has is the great number of years of compounding ahead. It is the power of this mechanism that is truly the investor's greatest resource. One is reminded of the Rule of 72 (the mathematical construct that permits the determination of the number of years it would take for capital to double by simply dividing the expected rate of growth into 72). See Figure 8.8 as an illustration of what Albert Einstein referred to as "the greatest invention of all time"—compound interest.

Phase 2. Consolidation These investors generally have the following characteristics:

- ✔ They are 40–55 years old.
- ✔ Career growth is strong; household income tends to rise at a faster rate than in any other phase.
- ✔ Spending becomes less of a major commitment of total income.
- ✔ Household debt is reduced as savings (for children's education and retirement) takes a front seat.

Here again, growth of capital is probably best suited; however, there may be a greater liquidity need due to children's education expenses, a cost that is quickly becoming more pervasive than retirement. At least in retirement, there is (or is there?) the prospect of Social Security benefits.

Phase 3. Spending These investors follow this pattern:

- ✔ They are 55–70 years old.
- ✔ Career and income have peaked and are beginning to decline as retirement sets in.

To find out how long it will take an amount of money to double, divide 72 by the rate of return.

For example, a $10,000 investment earning a fixed 2.5 percent will take 28.8 years to double to $20,000 (72 divided by 2.5 is 28.8). If the $10,000 earns 10 percent a year, it will take only 7.2 years to double your money (72 divided by 10).

You can also determine the rate of return if you divide the number of years it took to double your money into 72. For example, if it took 12 years for you to double your investment, that means you were earning 6 percent.

To determine how long it will take you to double your money or figure out the rate of return you received on your investment, refer to the chart below.

The chart assumes that the investment earns a fixed rate of return, and is not subject to principal fluctuations. Many investments will fluctuate in value, and this chart is for instructional purposes only and does not depict or predict the return on any specific investment.

Rate of Return	Years	Rate of Return	Year
2.00%	36.0	2.50%	28.8
3.00	24.0	2.50	20.5
4.00	18.0	4.5	16.0
5.00	14.4	5.5	13.0
6.00	12.0	6.5	11.0
7.00	10.3	7.5	9.6
8.00	9.0	8.5	8.5
9.00	8.0	9.5	7.6
10.00	7.2	10.5	6.9
11.00	6.5	11.5	6.3
12.00	6.0	12.5	5.8
13.00	5.5	13.5	5.3
14.00	5.1	14.5	5.0
15.00	4.8	15.5	4.6
16.00	4.5	16.5	4.4
17.00	4.2	17.5	4.1
18.00	4.0	18.5	3.9
19.00	3.8	19.5	3.7
20.00	3.6	20.5	3.5
21.00	3.4	21.5	3.3
22.00	3.3	22.5	3.2
23.00	3.1	23.5	3.0
24.00	3.0	24.5	2.9
25.00	2.8	25.5	2.8

FIGURE 8.8 Applying the Rule of 72.

✔ Big-ticket spending typically increases as vacation homes and other recreational activities are acquired.

This is the stage where growth is replaced by fixed income as the majority weight in a portfolio. Because much of the investor's assets have been acquired by this time, there is a larger pool of funds from which an income can be generated and subsequently drawn.

Phase 4. Gifting In this phase, investors fit the following description:

✔ They are 70–85 years old.
✔ They are preoccupied with reduction of estate taxes through the process of gifting away assets.

✔ Potential charity and philanthropic activities may begin to gain importance.

✔ Realization sets in that one's accumulated assets might not be fully spent during the remaining lifetime.

In this stage, the growth/income decision is really based on the final disposition of the assets. Due to estate planning, much of the wealth in the United States is being passed on to younger generations much earlier than ever before. Because of this phenomenon, the investment horizon is not definitive; is the time horizon the gifter's or the giftees' (possibly the children or even the grandchildren)? Prudent investment counsel is required in this all-important stage.

Vignettes of Investors

These fictional accounts are intended to help investors identify their own investment requirements. I also hope that some entertainment value will be a by-product of this exercise.

Doc Medical professionals typically go through a life cycle fraught with high debt loads. The average physician has gone through 4 years of undergraduate studies, 4 years of medical school, and then 3 to 4 years of residency and/or specialty program. Unlike other professionals who may also go through an extensive academic apprenticeship, the physician usually can't earn a living outside his chosen profession until this coursework is completed. Few med students would feel comfortable working in their Uncle Joe's insurance office during the summer between their second and third year. Furthermore, the medical professional must witness his contemporaries mature in their respective fields—move up the ladder, start 401(k) plans, take vacations, get married, buy homes while they are still "in school." When the doctor finally begins to make money, he has a lot of catching up to do and spends (read: debt increases) accordingly (see earlier discussion of Followers). Lenders will be knocking on the Doc's door, granting the best rates with the most credit without a qualm of default; after all, who could be a better credit risk than a physician? In my experiences, these are unfortunate freedoms; the typical young physician is so mired in debt (especially given school loans) that he is unable to save adequately for his future (not to mention the very real threat of managed care that has altered the profitability of the medical profession).

Moral. With regard to personal finances, always plan for the unexpected, do not live beyond your means, and always put some (even a tiny amount) to work in investments. For the young and thriving physician, perhaps a disciplined investment program in a tax-deferred retirement account would go a long way to satisfy tax savings as well as investment performance. Here again, due to the age of the investor, growth is the overwhelming investment objective and equities, consequently, are the favored asset class. Fortunately, in my practice, I've come in contact with many medical professionals who understand their predisposition (as illustrated above), and consequently have established investment programs for the long term.

The Timer   Here is the story about Timmy the Timer. Timmy, an avid ice-skater, makes a valiant (and often successful) effort to time the market. Although we are not privy to his methods, rumor has it that much of it is based on the occult and witchcraft. Timmy's contention remains that by pinpointing the perfect time to buy a particular security or sector of the market, he is able to profit in the short run. Unfortunately for Timmy, academically he has been proven wrong: It has been shown that by attempting to time entry (bottoms) and exit (tops) points of the market, an investor would be prone to miss a majority of the entire move. A recent study conducted by various organizations and often bandied about at brokerage firm seminars suggests an investor who missed only 40 trading sessions out of 10 years (about 2,200 sessions) would have earned a return equal to a mere fraction of the total period return—a shortfall that could mean the difference between a retirement sloop and a rowboat.

Moral. While Timmy's ice-skating may be worthy of Olympic play, his timing of the market is bound to slip up. My advice? To employ a disciplined investment program that allows for dollar-cost averaging (the procedure of investing a stated amount into the portfolio periodically) so that the volatility of the capital markets can be put to the investor's advantage. Is dollar-cost averaging a perfect policy that should be adopted by all investors? Probably not, for the jury is still out on the true, quantifiable benefits to such a program (if the markets were to go straight up, the "averager" would be behind the bold and brazened "full amount investor"); however, given the alternative (market timing), dollar-cost averaging, in my estimation, is probably a good practice. Investors should realize that many of us are, and have been for some time, employing dollar-cost averaging in our retirement plans—salary deductions to 401(k) plans and the like.

The Gambler   Always looking for the next big "hit." Putting his entire investment portfolio on one idea and sticking to it no matter how bad it gets. Meet Donny, the kind of investor who treats brokers as if they are bookies instead of investment professionals. Don makes investment decisions on a whim, without a modicum of research or analysis. When he inquires about the last quote on the stock (as he will every 30 minutes or so), he asks, "What is the score?" as if he were really playing a game. Such clients are more detrimental to an FSP's practice than they are profitable.

Moral. My advice to the Gambler: Risk money at the tables; invest capital seriously and most effectively for your future.

The Do-It-Yourselfer   My colleague, Jack Sullivan, tells of an incident that brings this issue of "do-it-yourself" to center stage. It seems a few years ago, Jack and his lovely family were playing host to a family gathering, and Mrs. Sullivan decreed that the driveway repair (including a new border) was tantamount to the success of the party. So Jack (his real name is John, I just call him Jack) did the perfunctory suburban exercise of seeking estimates for this project. While the estimates ranged from "might-ever-pay-you-that much" to "too-cheap-to-be-good-quality," the overriding similarity was the additional cost involved for laying a Belgian block border. So Jack decided to go with the median estimate (a fellow of good reputation in such matters), but only for the driveway; Jack was going to "knock out the border over a couple of weekends" and therefore, as he then estimated, save a considerable sum. Jack's calculations, however, failed to include that he was unable to play golf for the next four weeks, was forced to leave work early, and incurred sizable chiropractor bills for his aching back (which to this day is still not right). In the end, Jack had spent more money in doing the job himself than it would have cost him to have it done professionally.

Moral. Leverage the capabilities of those professionals who have a "comparative advantage" in certain areas, and focus your time and attention on those areas where your advantage is known.

Step 2. The Capital Markets—Managing Expectations

Understanding the historical interrelationships of the stock and bond markets is necessary to develop an appropriate investment strategy. It is also important to recognize that inflation can impact investment returns and erode purchasing power. As mentioned, it is probably best to view inflation as a parasite, eating away the purchasing power of all capital market investments. If an investment makes a return of 5 percent before inflation (nominal), and if inflation is approximately at 4 percent, then the inflation-adjusted return is 1 percent (real return). While this 1 percent may be keeping your investment portfolio above the inflationary tide, that is, permitting level buying power, are you really meeting your investment needs?

Using the most dramatic example (60 years), as shown in the typical chart—the mountain chart, as it is known, you can see that an investment in 90-day T-bills just kept pace with inflation and resulted in no gain in purchasing power, while an investment in long-term government bonds yielded returns only slightly greater than inflation's growth. Bear in mind, too, that income taxes paid on the returns from these investments further impair their suitability as inflation hedges. The only asset class to outpace inflation consistently over long time periods is equities.

In all five periods, the annualized returns for the stock market dramatically outpaced inflation. The point, then, is that investors with a long-term view may want to consider equities as a component of their portfolio to enhance returns and, as history illustrates, protect their wealth from dangers of inflation.

The history of the capital markets relates the returns of each major asset class with respect to a long-term time horizon. As illustrated, again, equities are the best performing of all asset classes, but this outperformance comes with a price—notice the variation of returns in this asset class. While in any 10-year period, the chance of a capital loss in the equity market is quite insignificant, that chance is greatly enhanced in a

1- or 3-year time horizon. As discussed, the issue of time horizon is one of the most critical in the application of an investment policy statement. If an investor came into my office seeking counsel and I learned while interviewing him that his time horizon was "about one year because we are looking to buy our first home by then," the advised asset allocation model (AAM) would be quite different from the investor who is investing for his newborn's college education (the AAM, in this case, should consist of at least 80 percent equities).

Looking at a long-term chart of the asset classes has a greater, more personal meaning for me. During the summer of 1929, my grandfather (age 22 and fresh out of college) was debating his twin brother, Harry, over the state of the stock market at a family dinner in their hometown of Hartford, Connecticut. Uncle Harry, the wide-eyed optimist, had just invested his share of their father's inheritance into the stock market, while Papa kept his share in cash. Furthermore, Papa sold all his previously purchased holdings in the stock market and committed this capital to cash and cash equivalents. As any student of history could already figure out— my grandfather called the Crash of 1929; however, his prowess in the investment field has never earned any recognition since then. When the brothers got back together at Thanksgiving, Papa certainly had the bragging rights over his brother. But Harry, rather than conceding defeat, boldly explained that he had recently begun a program to "save" $20 per month of his newfound job's salary into the market. Well, my grandfather was outraged, he remembers telling Harry that he was crazy and should not be so naive but rather try to become a more "rational" investor. Nevertheless my brothers and I, when we were young, would always wonder why Harry's grandkids seemed to have the most expensive toys and, as we got older, the Porsches, speedboats, and Yale degrees.

Different asset classes and portfolio management strategies produce varying levels of risk. Generally, as the potential for reward increases, so does the likelihood of increased risk. Equities, therefore, though potentially rich in terms of reward, will almost always be riskier than bonds or T-bills. Think of risk as the degree of certainty with which future returns can be predicted. The less predictable a return, the more risk (uncertainty) it engenders.

While there are different types of risk—the risk of an outcome not occurring, reinvestment risk, credit risk, political risk, purchasing power risk, career risk—the one that is typically used in investment finance is volatility. Financial service providers will typically attempt to measure risk through a series of questionnaires focusing around the fundamental questions: If your portfolio underperforms for two to four quarters, could you tolerate it? Could you tolerate six to eight quarters of under-performance (versus some stated benchmark) if, as compensation for this risk, you had a chance of a greater upside?

Volatility around the mean (standard deviation of return) is the benchmark that is used in the investment industry. As a review of the dis-cussion of statistics in Chapter 4, examine the following portfolios:

Portfolio A	Portfolio B
Return on portfolio (year 1): 0%	Return on portfolio (year 1): 8%
Return on portfolio (year 2): 20%	Return on portfolio (year 2): 12%

While both portfolios have the identical mean (for illustration purposes—arithmetic) return (10 percent), Portfolio A is quite a bit more volatile than B. In terms of statistics, Portfolio A's standard deviation (or movement around the mean) is greater than that of Portfolio B:

Standard deviation A = Square root of $\{(0 - 10)^2 + (20 - 10)^2\}$ = 14.14

Standard deviation B = Square root of $\{(8 - 10)^2 + (12 - 10)^2\}$ = 2.82

As discussed in Chapter 4, the greater the standard deviation the higher the probability for negative performance. For example, there is a 95 percent chance that the return of Portfolio A would be between −18 percent (10 percent minus 2 standard deviations or 2 × 14, or 28 percent) and + 38 percent (10 percent plus 2 standard deviations or 2 × 14, or 28 percent). In Portfolio B, the range is much "tighter": +4.35 percent (10 percent minus 2 standard deviations or 2 × 2.8, or 5.6 percent) and +15.6 percent (10 percent plus 2 standard deviations or 2 × 2.8, or 5.6 percent).

To effectively manage this risk or volatility, investment professionals typically prescribe the use of diversification for smoothing out the returns of different asset classes. As explained in the Modern Portfolio Theory section earlier in this chapter, this "volatility management" process is crit-ical to the success of the entire portfolio. It is through the effective use of different investment styles (see box: "Investment Styles") that an invest-ment manager hopes to insulate a portfolio from serious declines. We can think of the asset class decision as a macro one and the style decision as a micro one, both with a common goal of reducing the volatility of a given portfolio.

Investment Styles

Different investment management styles and various investments utilized within these styles produce different results in terms of growth, income, and risk. Your goal in evaluating investment styles is to understand how the approach used for your portfolio will impact overall return without exceeding your risk tolerance. To allow you to differentiate among four common investment management styles, some of their characteristics are presented here.

1. **Value Style.** Appropriate for investors seeking superior long-term total return. Value managers tend to perform better than the market when the market is trending down, while providing close-to-market (plus or minus) returns in a rising equity market. Over a market cycle, the objective is to equal or exceed market returns with less risk. These investment managers are searching through the rubble for the company whose stocks have been irrationally "sold off" and currently present an outstanding "value." Only patient investors, however, need to apply to this school.

2. **Contrarian Style.** Appropriate for investors seeking superior long-term total return and high current dividend yield. Contrarian managers expect to perform very well in down markets and should participate well in up markets.

3. **Growth Style.** Appropriate for investors seeking superior long-term total return, mostly through capital appreciation, growth managers must be able to tolerate a higher degree of risk. In this camp, the investment manager is looking for the next "hot" company—one whose earnings are growing at an unsustainably high rate. The growth investor expects to benefit from this earning growth (through increased share price), and will "get off the train" right before the growth ends (so he hopes).

4. **Aggressive Growth Style.** Appropriate for investors with an extremely high tolerance for risk while seeking superior long-term returns through capital appreciation. This style can perform very well in up markets but poorly in down markets.

Step 3. Portfolio Construction and Implementation

Step 1 suggests what determines the investment decision—from objective/risk tolerance to mind-set and even lifestyle. Step 2 shows how the capital markets work (the risk and reward paradigm, effects of inflation, different asset classes, etc.), as well as current expectations for capital markets (managing expectations). In this third step, we attempt to use both of the first two steps to formulate an efficient portfolio (in the words of Dr. Markowitz—"optimized") at a given level of risk.

Included in this step are the expenses involved in the efficient management of a portfolio—a critical red flag. As most investors now realize, almost every investment comes along with certain expenses and fees. With mutual funds, direct money managers and even individual equities have some charges (be it expense ratios, management fees, or bid/offer spreads). The investor should make certain that these fees are not out of line, but are reasonable and competitive. Some investments (in certain sectors) require more fees and expenses (e.g., international and small-cap investments) than others (long-term, core holdings or passive portfolios).

Fundamental to the efficient construction of an investment portfolio is the asset allocation model, which details the commitment of resources to each market sector. It has been proven (Brinson, Beebower, & Hood, *The Determinants of Portfolio's Return*, 1991) that an effective asset allocation model accounts for 91.5 percent of any account's stated return. All other considerations (market timing, federal reserve intervention, security selection, etc.) have an insignificant effect on the total return of any particular portfolio. What is an asset allocation model? The term is often bandied about in the investment community as being of critical importance to today's investor: "Does your asset allocation make sense?" "Which firm's AAM has been the most profitable over the past several months?" Asset allocation is simply the art (or, as some academics would postulate, the science) of positioning your capital in the asset classes that most reflect your needs without ignoring your constraints; in its most simplistic form, asset allocation is "not investing all of your eggs in one basket." The exercise of deploying one's assets to optimize a return is far from the simplistic, agrarian definition stated here. Asset allocation is of the utmost importance and should not

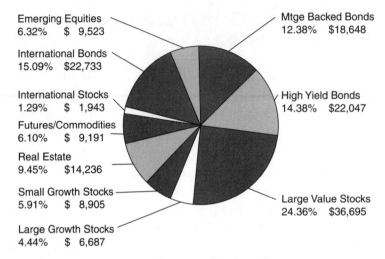

Emerging Equities
6.32% $ 9,523

International Bonds
15.09% $22,733

International Stocks
1.29% $ 1,943

Futures/Commodities
6.10% $ 9,191

Real Estate
9.45% $14,236

Small Growth Stocks
5.91% $ 8,905

Large Growth Stocks
4.44% $ 6,687

Mtge Backed Bonds
12.38% $18,648

High Yield Bonds
14.38% $22,047

Large Value Stocks
24.36% $36,695

FIGURE 8.9 Proposed Asset Allocation for Growth Investor.

be compromised for the "investment-du jour," nor should it be the sole ingredient in an investment portfolio. Does the asset allocation model assure you success in investing? Perhaps not—there never have been any guarantees in equities—but evidence in the long-term return charts is convincing.

Figure 8.9 depicts a typical asset allocation model for a conservative growth investor (an investor whose objectives require growth of capital and constraints that permit slightly more volatility of returns and a somewhat longer time horizon). As illustrated, there is the importance of style differentiation as well as asset class diversification. Investment history is rich in examples of the importance of style differentiation to the long-term investment performance of a growth-oriented portfolio—perhaps as important as an asset allocation model. Most prominently, the periods of outperformance shift between the growth and value style of equity investing. While one style may prevail for a year or two, typically the other style comes back to outperform.

Step 4. Monitoring the Portfolio

The investment management process is not nearly complete until a careful and extensive review is orchestrated on a continued basis. This review will look to find any changes to the Investment Policy Statement that might have taken place, which would deem it crucial to revise this plan and act accordingly. This is an important step in the process and requires prudence and diligence. Typically, investors should consider it appropriate to have quarterly discussions with their advisors to determine whether any personal changes have occurred and to review the account's performance (vs. a benchmark).

Ethics in the Financial Services Industry

Ethics is difficult to teach because most people adhere to these beliefs intuitively; those who don't grasp the meaning of ethical concepts often reveal a character flaw deeply embedded in their subconscious. The financial services industry has gone to great lengths to remove any stigmas of unethical dealings that have damaged their reputation in the past (and to a certain extent still do).

The CFA Institute's Code of Ethics provides a basis for the understanding of the ethical broad stroaks within the financial services industry. It is this code that each chartered financial analyst, candidate (currently enrolled in the CFA Program) for the CFA, and member of the CFA Institute, must uphold. Once again, it should be clear just how seriously ethics is taken within this organization, and consequently by its members. While much of this may seem like fluff, we assure you that it is anything but; this fact is further evidenced by AIMR's CFA Institute's Professional Standards Program. As the language in this extract illustrates, chartered financial analysts are definitely held to a high ethical standard.

Why is any of this information of consequence to the individual investor? Today's investor needs to be aware of the mechanisms that are in place to protect the efficiency and integrity of capital markets. Investors should understand the legal, policy, and ethical constraints that govern the industry they are trusting to preserve, and appreciate their hard-earned capital. This is not to say that fraud and deceit are not present in the financial markets, but it is comforting to know that, for the most part, this behavior is in the minority and most likely will be weeded out in the short run. This is the essence of an efficient market—a fair game for each participant if he invests his resources wisely and prudently.

Code of Ethics

The following serves as an outline of the areas comprising The CFA Institute's Code of Ethics:

Members of the CFA Institute shall:

- Act with integrity, competence, dignity, and in an ethical manner when dealing with the public, clients, prospects, employers, employees, and fellow members.
- Practice and encourage others to participate in a professional and ethical manner that will reflect credit on members and their profession.
- Strive to maintain and improve their competence and the competence of others in the profession.
- Use reasonable care and exercise independent professional judgment.

The following serves as a basis for the Standards of Professional Conduct adhered to by members of the CFA Institute:

I. Obligation to inform employer of code and standards

II. Compliance with governing laws and regulations

III. Research reports, investment recommendations, and actions are required to have a reasonable basis and representatives

IV. Priority of transactions whereby transactions for customers, clients, and employer have priority over personal transactions, and so that his personal transactions do not operate adversely to their interests

V. Disclosure of conflicts

VI. Compensation disclosure of additional compensation arrangements and referral fees

VII. Preservation of confidentiality and independence, objectivity, and maintaining fiduciary duties

Insider Trading

The ethics of inside information is an important topic in the financial services industry. As purveyors of research, the financial analyst community often comes in contact with information that they, because of their position, are trusted with. In most cases, the analyst who comes in contact with nonpublic information will not be explicitly warned about the confidential nature of such information. It is incumbent upon the analyst to be aware of what material nonpublic information is and to make every effort to seek its public disclosure.

Firms may, for strategic reasons, decide to keep this information nonpublic until such time that it is required to be public. The analyst should "divorce" himself or herself from any dealings with the security, and cease any trading in this security. Furthermore, the analyst also has a duty to inform his firm of any lax policies with regard to the disclosure of nonpublic information. There should be firm policies with regard to material nonpublic information. There should also be educational programs to inform employees of these policies. Watch lists and restricted lists should be used. Different departments in the firm should be separated, to some degree, by an information barrier (called a Chinese Wall or firewall).

The legal issues surrounding trading in material nonpublic information has evolved over the last 50 years or so. Has a breach of fiduciary duty been consummated? Under the classical theory, this breach of fiduciary duty is defined as being between the company and their investment bankers, accountants, and lawyers. If XYZ Company tells their accountant of a lucrative new contract and the accountant then buys shares in anticipation of such an announcement, the accountant is clearly breaching the fiduciary duty between himself and the company. The same thing applies for the company's attorneys and investment bankers—a breach of fiduciary duty results in violations of inside information.

Now consider the employee of XYZ's financial printer who, through his work, comes into contact with material, nonpublic information. He trades on this information. Is this an insider trading violation? As illustrated in the *Chiarella vs. United States* case, the employees of the printer do not have a fiduciary relationship (as required by the Classical Theory) with XYZ, and therefore cannot breach such a relationship. Enter the Misappropriation Theory; it was this theory that sanctioned the illegality of the use of material, nonpublic information for any breach—not just those of a fiduciary nature. According to the Misappropriation Theory, if a person misappropriates material, nonpublic information and uses or conveys this information to someone else, then that person has breached a duty that then imposes an illegal act.

Definitions

Material Information. Information that would (with a high degree of certainty) upon its dissemination, cause a significant effect on the price of the securities involved. In addition, materiality can be illustrated if a knowledgeable investor would expect this information to affect his or her trading in this security.

Nonpublic Information. Information that is not in the public domain; that is, it has not yet been disseminated and made available to all investors who seek it.

Fiduciary. One who has a special relationship of trust with someone (person or institution) else. This fiduciary has a duty to this counterparty to serve in a manner that is fair and honest, and to keep the counterparty's best interests as the sole beneficiary of the fiduciary's actions. Simply put, a fiduciary must put the interests of the beneficiaries before his own or those of his firm.

Misappropriation Theory. Pertains to violations of 10-b(5) that occur when material, nonpublic information is misappropriated in a breach of duty or similar relationship of trust and confidence. The breach need not be one of fiduciary nature (as in the Classical Theory) but only a breach of duty (as in the case of an employee to an employer). Further, this information is then used in transactions or is communicated to others for their use. This theory is the basis of insider trading laws.

The Chinese Wall (or the Firewall). While all confidential information must be handled in accordance with the policies and procedures set forth by the firm's compliance handbook, the securities laws require more specific procedures to separate the disparate business activities of the firm. These procedures, known collectively as the Chinese Wall, are reasonably designed to restrict the flow of inside information and to prevent those employees engaged in research, sales, trading, portfolio management, and administrative activities (marketing) from gaining access to inside information that the firm may have acquired or developed in connection with investment or merchant banking activities of other employees of the firm (banking side), except pursuant to specific wall-crossing procedures. In general, banking employees must obtain prior authorization (usually written) on a project-by-project and person-by-person basis from a senior banking employee before contacting the marketing employee to bring him across the Wall.

Mosaic Theory. Pertains to the act of researching, through the use of public and nonpublic information, nonmaterial information about a company's history and business dealings. This research may allow the analyst to "piece together" (hence the term mosaic) facts that lead to conclusions that are the basis of material, nonpublic information. The analyst, for his own protection, is expected to keep detailed records of his research that allowed him to build the mosaic and the consequent conclusions.

Watch List. A confidential list of securities about which the firm may have received or may expect to receive inside information. These lists are ordinarily used to monitor sales, trading (especially that of employees), and research activities in these securities and to monitor compliance with the Chinese Wall.

Legal Restricted List. A confidential list of securities that are subject to restrictions in handling customer orders, trading for proprietary accounts, trading for discretionary accounts, trading for employee and related accounts, and other activities. The restricted list refers to those securities that the firm may have or expect to have a fiduciary relationship with in the near future.

Employee Education. A firm has a duty to educate its employees about the internal compliance procedures, especially those dealing with inside information. There are several methods that Wall Street firms use to increase the awareness of ethical and legal violations, including courses on ethics, firm-wide retreats, and policy manuals.

Insider Trading Laws

Insider Trading & Securities Fraud Enforcement Act (ITS-FEA)–1988. Increased criminal penalties for securities law violations (maximum jail term increased from 5 to 10 years, maximum individual fine increased from $100,000 to $1,000,000, maximum fine for business entities increased from $500,000 to $2,500,000); allows the SEC to pay bounties to informants of up to 10 percent of penalty imposed; authorizes the SEC to exchange information with foreign governments; and establishes joint liability for "contemporaneous traders" (total damages may be assessed against any and all users of insider information).

Securities Enforcement Remedies & Penny Stock Reform Act (SERP-SRA)–1990. Provides the SEC with additional remedies including civil penalties in administrative proceedings; penalties can be assessed by the SEC in its own hearings or by the courts in civil cases; the SEC can issue permanent or temporary cease-and-desist orders after finding that a person or entity is or will violate securities laws. Allows the SEC to bar brokers, investment advisors and dealers (firms) from participating in the INDUSTRY for any period of time, including lifetime.

Epilogue

The financial world has certainly experienced its fair share of turmoil in the time between the first edition of this book (1998) and this second edition, 11 years later. We have seen the rise and fall of the Internet bubble, the growing importance of emerging market economies like Brazil, Russia, India, and China, and a vast War on Terror, with significant fiscal consequences for the United States. The start of the twenty-first century brought with it an explosion of home building in places like Las Vegas, NV and Phoenix, AZ; a vast (and ultimately unsustainable) run-up in home prices; and a subsequent economic collapse like few the industrialized world has ever seen before.

The mortgage meltdown of 2007–2008 set off a period of extreme financial calamity and brought an inglorious end to former stalwarts of the financial community (gone are Lehman Brothers, Merrill Lynch, Bear Stearns, and Washington Mutual, among others). Governments across the world responded with unprecedented measures such, as lowering interest rates toward zero and taking ownership interests in large, private corporations like GM and AIG. At the time of this writing, the ultimate results of such measures are as yet unknown.

What is an investor to do in the face of such turmoil? Looking back at the volatility in the financial markets over the past decade, it might seem as though the safest bet is to simply sock money away under the mattress. Between mid-1999 and mid-2009, the S&P 500 stock market index *declined* in value by over 25 percent. The price of oil ranged from a low of less than $30 per barrel to a high of more than $130 per barrel before plummeting back toward $30 once again. The yield on 10-year U.S. Treasury notes was once over 5 percent, but almost dipped below 2 percent in early 2009.

Throughout all this turmoil and change, however, the fundamental elements of security analysis have stayed the same. Of course, this is not to say that security analysis is a purely static endeavor—accounting rules change from time to time, government regulations come and go, and complex new securities require complex new valuation techniques. But the underlying principles of finance—like the time value of money, discounted cash flows, the calculation of credit liquidity ratios, or the measures of supply and demand in the real estate market—retain their meaning. Be it a bull market, bear market, mortgage meltdown, or economic recovery, an understanding of these basic principles will serve you well.

Our advice, then, is not to hide money under your mattress, but to put the techniques you have learned in this book to good use to make more informed investment decisions. Perhaps you are saving for retirement, paying for a child's college education, or planning to start a new career. Whatever your goals may be, you will be able to go more confidently in the direction of your financial dreams armed with the principles of security analysis at your side.

Selected Tables

TABLE A.1 Present Value of $1

$$PVIF = 1/(1 + k)^t$$

Period	1%	2%	3%	4%	5%	6%	7%	8%	9%	10%	12%	14%	15%	16%	18%	20%	24%	28%	32%	36%
1	.9901	.9804	.9709	.9615	.9524	.9434	.9346	.9259	.9174	.9091	.8929	.8772	.8696	.8621	.8475	.8333	.8065	.7813	.7576	.7353
2	.9803	.9612	.9426	.9246	.9070	.8900	.8734	.8573	.8417	.8264	.7972	.7695	.7561	.7432	.7182	.6944	.6504	.6104	.5739	.5407
3	.9706	.9423	.9151	.8890	.8638	.8396	.8163	.7938	.7722	.7513	.7118	.6750	.6575	.6407	.6086	.5787	.5245	.4768	.4348	.3975
4	.9610	.9238	.8885	.8548	.8227	.7921	.7629	.7350	.7084	.6830	.6355	.5921	.5718	.5523	.5158	.4823	.4230	.3725	.3294	.2923
5	.9515	.9057	.8626	.8219	.7835	.7473	.7130	.6806	.6499	.6209	.5674	.5194	.4972	.4761	.4371	.4019	.3411	.2910	.2495	.2149
6	.9420	.8880	.8375	.7903	.7462	.7050	.6663	.6302	.5963	.5645	.5066	.4556	.4323	.4104	.3704	.3349	.2751	.2274	.1890	.1580
7	.9327	.8706	.8131	.7599	.7107	.6651	.6227	.5835	.5470	.5132	.4523	.3996	.3759	.3538	.3139	.2791	.2218	.1776	.1432	.1162
8	.9235	.8535	.7894	.7307	.6768	.6274	.5820	.5403	.5019	.4665	.4039	.3506	.3269	.3050	.2660	.2326	.1789	.1388	.1085	.0854
9	.9143	.8368	.7664	.7026	.6446	.5919	.5439	.5002	.4604	.4241	.3606	.3075	.2843	.2630	.2255	.1938	.1443	.1084	.0822	.0628
10	.9053	.8203	.7441	.6756	.6139	.5584	.5083	.4632	.4224	.3855	.3220	.2697	.2472	.2267	.1911	.1615	.1164	.0847	.0623	.0462
11	.8963	.8043	.7224	.6496	.5847	.5268	.4751	.4289	.3875	.3505	.2875	.2366	.2149	.1954	.1619	.1346	.0938	.0662	.0472	.0340
12	.8874	.7885	.7014	.6246	.5568	.4970	.4440	.3971	.3555	.3186	.2567	.2076	.1869	.1685	.1372	.1122	.0757	.0517	.0357	.0250
13	.8787	.7730	.6810	.6006	.5303	.4688	.4150	.3677	.3262	.2897	.2292	.1821	.1625	.1452	.1163	.0935	.0610	.0404	.0271	.0184
14	.8700	.7579	.6611	.5775	.5051	.4423	.3878	.3405	.2992	.2633	.2046	.1597	.1413	.1252	.0985	.0779	.0492	.0316	.0205	.0135
15	.8613	.7430	.6419	.5553	.4810	.4173	.3624	.3152	.2745	.2394	.1827	.1401	.1229	.1079	.0835	.0649	.0397	.0247	.0155	.0099
16	.8528	.7284	.6232	.5339	.4581	.3936	.3387	.2919	.2519	.2176	.1631	.1229	.1069	.0930	.0708	.0541	.0320	.0193	.0118	.0073
17	.8444	.7142	.6050	.5134	.4363	.3714	.3166	.2703	.2311	.1978	.1456	.1078	.0929	.0802	.0600	.0451	.0258	.0150	.0089	.0054
18	.8360	.7002	.5874	.4936	.4155	.3503	.2959	.2502	.2120	.1799	.1300	.0946	.0808	.0691	.0508	.0376	.0208	.0118	.0068	.0039
19	.8277	.6864	.5703	.4746	.3957	.3305	.2765	.2317	.1945	.1635	.1161	.0829	.0703	.0596	.0431	.0313	.0168	.0092	.0051	.0029
20	.8195	.6730	.5537	.4564	.3769	.3118	.2584	.2145	.1784	.1486	.1037	.0728	.0611	.0514	.0365	.0261	.0135	.0072	.0039	.0021
25	.7798	.6095	.4776	.3751	.2953	.2330	.1842	.1460	.1160	.0923	.0588	.0378	.0304	.0245	.0160	.0105	.0046	.0021	.0010	.0005
30	.7419	.5521	.4120	.3083	.2314	.1741	.1314	.0994	.0754	.0573	.0334	.0196	.0151	.0116	.0070	.0042	.0016	.0006	.0002	.0001
40	.6717	.4529	.3066	.2083	.1420	.0972	.0668	.0460	.0318	.0221	.0107	.0053	.0037	.0026	.0013	.0007	.0002	.0001	*	*
50	.6080	.3715	.2281	.1407	.0872	.0543	.0339	.0213	.0134	.0085	.0035	.0014	.0009	.0006	.0003	.0001	*	*	*	*
60	.5504	.3048	.1697	.0951	.0535	.0303	.0173	.0099	.0057	.0033	.0011	.0004	.0002	.0001	*	*	*	*	*	*

*The factor is zero to four decimal places.

TABLE A.2 Present Value of an Annuity of $1 Per Period for n Periods

$$\text{PVIFA} = \sum_{t=1}^{n} \frac{1}{(1+k)^t} = \frac{1 - \dfrac{1}{(1+k)^n}}{k}$$

	1%	2%	3%	4%	5%	6%	7%	8%	9%	10%	12%	14%	15%	16%	18%	20%	24%	28%	32%
1	0.9901	0.9804	0.9709	0.9615	0.9524	0.9434	0.9346	0.9259	0.9174	0.9091	0.8929	0.8772	0.8696	0.8621	0.8475	0.8333	0.8065	0.7813	0.7576
2	1.9704	1.9416	1.9135	1.8861	1.8594	1.8334	1.8080	1.7833	1.7591	1.7355	1.6901	1.6467	1.6257	1.6052	1.5656	1.5278	1.4568	1.3916	1.3315
3	2.9410	2.8839	2.8286	2.7751	2.7232	2.6730	2.6243	2.5771	2.5313	2.4869	2.4018	2.3216	2.2832	2.2459	2.1743	2.1065	1.9813	1.8684	1.7663
4	3.9020	3.8077	3.7171	3.6299	3.5460	3.4651	3.3872	3.3121	3.2397	3.1699	3.0373	2.9137	2.8550	2.7982	2.6901	2.5887	2.4043	2.2410	2.0957
5	4.8534	4.7135	4.5797	4.4518	4.3295	4.2124	4.1002	3.9927	3.8897	3.7908	3.6048	3.4331	3.3522	3.2743	3.1272	2.9906	2.7454	2.5320	2.3452
6	5.7955	5.6014	5.4172	5.2421	5.0757	4.9173	4.7665	4.6229	4.4859	4.3553	4.1114	3.8887	3.7845	3.6847	3.4976	3.3255	3.0205	2.7594	2.5342
7	6.7282	6.4720	6.2303	6.0021	5.7864	5.5824	5.3893	5.2064	5.0330	4.8684	4.5638	4.2883	4.1604	4.0386	3.8115	3.6046	3.2423	2.9370	2.6775
8	7.6517	7.3255	7.0197	6.7327	6.4632	6.2098	5.9713	5.7466	5.5348	5.3349	4.9676	4.6389	4.4873	4.3436	4.0776	3.8372	3.4212	3.0758	2.7860
9	8.5660	8.1622	7.7861	7.4353	7.1078	6.8017	6.5152	6.2469	5.9952	5.7590	5.3282	4.9464	4.7716	4.6065	4.3030	4.0310	3.5655	3.1842	2.8681
10	9.4713	8.9826	8.5302	8.1109	7.7217	7.3601	7.0236	6.7101	6.4177	6.1446	5.6502	5.2161	5.0188	4.8332	4.4941	4.1925	3.6819	3.2689	2.9304
11	10.3676	9.7868	9.2526	8.7605	8.3064	7.8869	7.4987	7.1390	6.8052	6.4951	5.9377	5.4527	5.2337	5.0286	4.6560	4.3271	3.7757	3.3351	2.9776
12	11.2551	10.5753	9.9540	9.3851	8.8633	8.3838	7.9427	7.5361	7.1607	6.8137	6.1944	5.6603	5.4206	5.1971	4.7932	4.4392	3.8514	3.3868	3.0133
13	12.1337	11.3484	10.6350	9.9856	9.3936	8.8527	8.3577	7.9038	7.4869	7.1034	6.4235	5.8424	5.5831	5.3423	4.9095	4.5327	3.9124	3.4272	3.0404
14	13.0037	12.1062	11.2961	10.5631	9.8986	9.2950	8.7455	8.2442	7.7862	7.3667	6.6282	6.0021	5.7245	5.4675	5.0081	4.6106	3.9616	3.4587	3.0609
15	13.8651	12.8493	11.9379	11.1184	10.3797	9.7122	9.1079	8.5595	8.0607	7.6061	6.8109	6.1422	5.8474	5.5755	5.0916	4.6755	4.0013	3.4834	3.0764
16	14.7179	13.5777	12.5611	11.6523	10.8378	10.1059	9.4466	8.8514	8.3126	7.8237	6.9740	6.2651	5.9542	5.6685	5.1624	4.7296	4.0333	3.5026	3.0882
17	15.5623	14.2919	13.1661	12.1657	11.2741	10.4773	9.7632	9.1216	8.5436	8.0216	7.1196	6.3729	6.0472	5.7487	5.2223	4.7746	4.0591	3.5177	3.0971
18	16.3983	14.9920	13.7535	12.6593	11.6896	10.8276	10.0591	9.3719	8.7556	8.2014	7.2497	6.4574	6.1280	5.8178	5.2732	4.8122	4.0799	3.5294	3.1039
19	17.2260	15.6785	14.3238	13.1339	12.0853	11.1581	10.3356	9.6036	8.9501	8.3649	7.3658	6.5504	6.1982	5.8775	5.3162	4.8435	4.0967	3.5386	3.1090
20	18.0456	16.3514	14.8775	13.5903	12.4622	11.4699	10.5940	9.8181	9.1285	8.5136	7.4694	6.6231	6.2593	5.9288	5.3527	4.8696	4.1103	3.5458	3.1129
25	22.0232	19.5235	17.4131	15.6221	14.0939	12.7834	11.6536	10.6748	9.8226	9.0770	7.8431	6.8729	6.4641	6.0971	5.4669	4.9476	4.1474	3.5640	3.1220
30	25.8077	22.3965	19.6004	17.2920	15.3725	13.7648	12.4090	11.2578	10.2737	9.4269	8.0552	7.0027	6.5660	6.1772	5.5168	4.9789	4.1601	3.5693	3.1242
40	32.8347	27.3555	23.1148	19.7928	17.1591	15.0463	13.3317	11.9246	10.7574	9.7791	8.2438	7.1050	6.6418	6.2335	5.5482	4.9966	4.1659	3.5712	3.1250
50	39.1961	31.4236	25.7298	21.4822	18.2559	15.7619	13.8007	12.2335	10.9617	9.9148	8.3045	7.1327	6.6605	6.2463	5.5541	4.9995	4.1666	3.5714	3.1250
60	44.9550	34.7609	27.6756	22.6235	18.9293	16.1614	14.0392	12.3766	11.0480	9.9672	8.3240	7.1401	6.6651	6.2492	5.5553	4.9999	4.1667	3.5714	3.1250

TABLE A.3 Future Value of $1 at the End of n Periods

$$FVIF_{k,n} = (1 + k)^n$$

Period	1%	2%	3%	4%	5%	6%	7%	8%	9%	10%	12%	14%	15%	16%	18%	20%	24%	28%	32%	36%
1	1.0100	1.0200	1.0300	1.0400	1.0500	1.0600	1.0700	1.0800	1.0900	1.1000	1.1200	1.1400	1.1500	1.1600	1.1800	1.2000	1.2400	1.2800	1.3200	1.3600
2	1.0201	1.0404	1.0609	1.0816	1.1025	1.1236	1.1449	1.1664	1.1881	1.2100	1.2544	1.2996	1.3225	1.3456	1.3924	1.4400	1.5376	1.6384	1.7424	1.8496
3	1.0303	1.0612	1.0927	1.1249	1.1576	1.1910	1.2250	1.2597	1.2950	1.3310	1.4049	1.4815	1.5209	1.5609	1.6430	1.7280	1.9066	2.0972	2.3000	2.5155
4	1.0406	1.0824	1.1255	1.1699	1.2155	1.2625	1.3108	1.3605	1.4116	1.4641	1.5735	1.6890	1.7490	1.8106	1.9388	2.0736	2.3642	2.6844	3.0360	3.4210
5	1.0510	1.1041	1.1593	1.2167	1.2763	1.3382	1.4026	1.4693	1.5386	1.6105	1.7623	1.9254	2.0114	2.1003	2.2878	2.4883	2.9316	3.4360	4.0075	4.6526
6	1.0615	1.1262	1.1941	1.2653	1.3401	1.4185	1.5007	1.5869	1.6771	1.7716	1.9738	2.1950	2.3131	2.4364	2.6996	2.9860	3.6352	4.3980	5.2899	6.3275
7	1.0721	1.1487	1.2299	1.3159	1.4071	1.5036	1.6058	1.7138	1.8280	1.9487	2.2107	2.5023	2.6600	2.8262	3.1855	3.5832	4.5077	5.6295	6.9826	8.6054
8	1.0829	1.1717	1.2668	1.3686	1.4775	1.5938	1.7182	1.8509	1.9926	2.1436	2.4760	2.8526	3.0590	3.2784	3.7589	4.2998	5.5895	7.2058	9.2170	11.703
9	1.0937	1.1951	1.3048	1.4233	1.5513	1.6895	1.8385	1.9990	2.1719	2.3579	2.7731	3.2519	3.5179	3.8030	4.4355	5.1598	6.9310	9.2234	12.166	15.916
10	1.1046	1.2190	1.3439	1.4802	1.6289	1.7908	1.9672	2.1589	2.3674	2.5937	3.1058	3.7072	4.0456	4.4114	5.2338	6.1917	8.5944	11.806	16.060	21.647
11	1.1157	1.2434	1.3842	1.5395	1.7103	1.8983	2.1049	2.3316	2.5804	2.8531	3.4785	4.2262	4.6524	5.1173	6.1759	7.4301	10.657	15.112	21.199	29.439
12	1.1268	1.2682	1.4258	1.6010	1.7959	2.0122	2.2522	2.5182	2.8127	3.1384	3.8960	4.8179	5.3503	5.9360	7.2876	8.9161	13.215	19.343	27.983	40.037
13	1.1381	1.2936	1.4685	1.6651	1.8856	2.1329	2.4098	2.7196	3.0658	3.4523	4.3635	5.4924	6.1528	6.8858	8.5994	10.699	16.386	24.759	36.937	54.451
14	1.1495	1.3195	1.5126	1.7317	1.9799	2.2609	2.5785	2.9372	3.3417	3.7975	4.8871	6.2613	7.0757	7.9875	10.147	12.839	20.319	31.691	48.757	74.053
15	1.1610	1.3459	1.5580	1.8009	2.0789	2.3966	2.7590	3.1722	3.6425	4.1772	5.4736	7.1379	8.1371	9.2655	11.974	15.407	25.196	40.565	64.359	100.71
16	1.1726	1.3728	1.6047	1.8730	2.1829	2.5404	2.9522	3.4259	3.9703	4.5950	6.1304	8.1372	9.3576	10.748	14.129	18.488	31.243	51.923	84.954	136.97
17	1.1843	1.4002	1.6528	1.9479	2.2920	2.6928	3.1588	3.7000	4.3276	5.0545	6.8660	9.2765	10.761	12.468	16.672	22.186	38.741	66.461	112.14	186.28
18	1.1961	1.4282	1.7024	2.0258	2.4066	2.8543	3.3799	3.9960	4.7171	5.5599	7.6900	10.575	12.375	14.463	19.673	26.623	48.039	85.071	148.02	253.34
19	1.2081	1.4568	1.7535	2.1068	2.5270	3.0256	3.6165	4.3157	5.1417	6.1159	8.6128	12.056	14.232	16.777	23.214	31.948	59.568	108.89	195.39	344.54
20	1.2202	1.4859	1.8061	2.1911	2.6533	3.2071	3.8697	4.6610	5.6044	6.7275	9.6463	13.743	16.367	19.461	27.393	38.338	73.864	139.38	257.92	468.57
21	1.2324	1.5157	1.8603	2.2788	2.7860	3.3996	4.1406	5.0338	6.1088	7.4002	10.804	15.668	18.822	22.574	32.324	46.005	91.592	178.41	340.45	637.26
22	1.2447	1.5460	1.9161	2.3699	2.9253	3.6035	4.4304	5.4365	6.6586	8.1403	12.100	17.861	21.645	26.186	38.142	55.206	113.57	228.36	449.39	866.67
23	1.2572	1.5769	1.9736	2.4647	3.0715	3.8197	4.7405	5.8715	7.2579	8.9543	13.552	20.362	24.891	30.376	45.008	66.247	140.83	292.30	593.20	1178.7
24	1.2697	1.6084	2.0328	2.5633	3.2251	4.0489	5.0724	6.3412	7.9111	9.8497	15.179	23.212	28.625	35.236	53.109	79.497	174.63	374.14	783.02	1603.0
25	1.2824	1.6406	2.0938	2.6658	3.3864	4.2919	5.4274	6.8485	8.6231	10.835	17.000	26.462	32.919	40.874	62.669	95.396	216.54	478.90	1033.6	2180.1
26	1.2953	1.6734	2.1566	2.7725	3.5557	4.5494	5.8074	7.3964	9.3992	11.918	19.040	30.167	37.857	47.414	73.949	114.48	268.51	613.00	1364.3	2964.9
27	1.3082	1.7069	2.2213	2.8834	3.7335	4.8223	6.2139	7.9881	10.245	13.110	21.325	34.390	43.535	55.000	87.260	137.37	332.95	784.64	1800.9	4032.3
28	1.3213	1.7410	2.2879	2.9987	3.9201	5.1117	6.6488	8.6271	11.167	14.421	23.884	39.204	50.066	63.800	102.97	164.84	412.86	1004.3	2377.2	5483.9
29	1.3345	1.7758	2.3566	3.1187	4.1161	5.4184	7.1143	9.3173	12.172	15.863	26.750	44.693	57.575	74.009	121.50	197.81	511.95	1285.6	3137.9	7458.1
30	1.3478	1.8114	2.4273	3.2434	4.3219	5.7435	7.6123	10.063	13.268	17.449	29.960	50.950	66.212	85.850	143.37	237.38	634.82	1645.5	4142.0	10143.
40	1.4889	2.2080	3.2620	4.8010	7.0400	10.285	14.974	21.724	31.409	45.259	93.050	188.88	267.86	378.72	750.37	1469.7	5455.9	19426.	66520.	*
50	1.6446	2.6916	4.3839	7.1067	11.467	18.420	29.457	46.901	74.357	117.39	289.00	700.23	1083.6	1670.7	3927.3	9100.4	46890.	*	*	*
60	1.8167	3.2810	5.8916	10.529	18.679	32.987	57.946	101.25	176.03	304.48	897.59	2595.9	4383.9	7370.1	20555.	56347.	*	*	*	*

*FVIFA > 99.999

TABLE A.4 Future Value of an Annuity of $1 Per n Periods

$$FVIFA_{k,n} = \sum_{t=1}^{n}(1+k)^{t-1} = \frac{(1+k)^n - 1}{k}$$

n	1%	2%	3%	4%	5%	6%	7%	8%	9%	10%	12%	14%	15%	16%	18%	20%	24%	28%	32%	36%
1	1.0000	1.0000	1.0000	1.0000	1.0000	1.0000	1.0000	1.0000	1.0000	1.0000	1.0000	1.0000	1.0000	1.0000	1.0000	1.0000	1.0000	1.0000	1.0000	1.0000
2	2.0100	2.0200	2.0300	2.0400	2.0500	2.0600	2.0700	2.0800	2.0900	2.1000	2.1200	2.1400	2.1500	2.1600	2.1800	2.2000	2.2400	2.2800	2.3200	2.3600
3	3.0301	3.0604	3.0909	3.1216	3.1525	3.1836	3.2149	3.2464	3.2781	3.3100	3.3744	3.4396	3.4725	3.5056	3.5724	3.6400	3.7776	3.9184	4.0624	4.2096
4	4.0604	4.1216	4.1836	4.2465	4.3101	4.3746	4.4399	4.5061	4.5731	4.6410	4.7793	4.9211	4.9934	5.0665	5.2154	5.3680	5.6842	6.0156	6.3624	6.7251
5	5.1010	5.2040	5.3091	5.4163	5.5256	5.6371	5.7507	5.8666	5.9847	6.1051	6.3528	6.6101	6.7424	6.8771	7.1542	7.4416	8.0484	8.6999	9.3983	10.146
6	6.1520	6.3081	6.4684	6.6330	6.8019	6.9753	7.1533	7.3359	7.5233	7.7156	8.1152	8.5355	8.7537	8.9775	9.4420	9.9299	10.980	12.135	13.405	14.799
7	7.2135	7.4343	7.6625	7.8983	8.1420	8.3938	8.6540	8.9228	9.2004	9.4872	10.089	10.730	11.066	11.413	12.141	12.915	14.615	16.533	18.695	21.126
8	8.2857	8.5830	8.8923	9.2142	9.5491	9.8975	10.259	10.636	11.028	11.435	12.299	13.232	13.726	14.240	15.327	16.499	19.122	22.163	25.678	29.732
9	9.3685	9.7546	10.159	10.582	11.026	11.491	11.978	12.487	13.021	13.579	14.775	16.085	16.785	17.518	19.085	20.798	24.712	29.369	34.895	41.435
10	10.462	10.949	11.463	12.006	12.577	13.180	13.816	14.486	15.192	15.937	17.548	19.337	20.303	21.321	23.521	25.958	31.643	38.592	47.061	57.351
11	11.566	12.168	12.807	13.486	14.206	14.971	15.784	16.645	17.560	18.531	20.654	23.044	24.349	25.732	28.755	32.150	40.237	50.398	63.121	78.998
12	12.682	13.412	14.192	15.025	15.917	16.869	17.888	18.977	20.140	21.384	24.133	27.270	29.001	30.850	34.931	39.580	50.894	65.510	84.320	108.44
13	13.809	14.680	15.617	16.626	17.713	18.882	20.140	21.495	22.953	24.522	28.029	32.088	34.351	36.786	42.218	48.496	64.109	84.852	112.30	148.47
14	14.947	15.973	17.086	18.291	19.598	21.015	22.550	24.214	26.019	27.975	32.392	37.581	40.504	43.672	50.818	59.195	80.496	109.61	149.23	202.93
15	16.096	17.293	18.598	20.023	21.578	23.276	25.129	27.152	29.360	31.772	37.279	43.841	47.580	51.659	60.965	72.035	100.81	141.30	197.99	276.98
16	17.257	18.639	20.156	21.824	23.657	25.672	27.888	30.324	33.003	35.949	42.753	50.980	55.717	60.925	72.939	87.442	126.01	181.86	262.35	377.69
17	18.430	20.012	21.761	23.697	25.840	28.212	30.840	33.750	36.973	40.544	48.884	59.117	65.075	71.673	87.068	105.93	157.25	233.79	347.30	514.66
18	19.614	21.412	23.414	25.645	28.132	30.905	33.999	37.450	41.301	45.599	55.749	68.394	75.836	84.140	103.74	128.12	195.99	300.25	459.44	700.94
19	20.810	22.840	25.116	27.671	30.539	33.760	37.379	41.446	46.018	51.159	63.439	78.969	88.211	98.603	123.41	154.74	244.03	385.32	607.47	954.28
20	22.019	24.297	26.870	29.778	33.066	36.785	40.995	45.762	51.160	57.275	72.052	91.024	102.44	115.37	146.62	186.68	303.60	494.21	802.86	1298.8
21	23.239	25.783	28.676	31.969	35.719	39.992	44.865	50.422	56.764	64.002	81.698	104.76	118.81	134.84	174.02	225.02	377.46	633.59	1060.7	1767.4
22	24.471	27.299	30.536	34.248	38.505	43.392	49.005	55.456	62.873	71.402	92.502	120.43	137.63	157.41	206.34	271.03	469.05	811.99	1401.2	2404.6
23	25.716	28.845	32.452	36.617	41.430	46.995	53.436	60.893	69.531	79.543	104.60	138.29	159.27	183.60	244.48	326.23	582.62	1040.3	1850.6	3271.3
24	26.973	30.421	34.426	39.082	44.502	50.815	58.176	66.764	76.789	88.497	118.15	158.65	184.16	213.97	289.49	392.48	723.46	1332.6	2443.8	4449.9
25	28.243	32.030	36.459	41.645	47.727	54.864	63.249	73.105	84.700	98.347	133.33	181.87	212.79	249.21	342.60	471.98	898.09	1706.8	3226.8	6052.9
26	29.525	33.670	38.553	44.311	51.113	59.156	68.676	79.954	93.323	109.18	150.33	208.33	245.71	290.08	405.27	567.37	1114.6	2185.7	4260.4	8233.0
27	30.820	35.344	40.709	47.084	54.669	63.705	74.483	87.350	102.72	121.09	169.37	238.49	283.56	337.50	479.22	681.85	1383.1	2798.7	5624.7	11197.9
28	32.129	37.051	42.930	49.967	58.402	68.528	80.697	95.338	112.96	134.20	190.69	272.88	327.10	392.50	566.48	819.22	1716.0	3583.2	7425.6	15230.2
29	33.450	38.792	45.218	52.966	62.322	73.639	87.346	103.96	124.13	148.63	214.58	312.09	377.16	456.30	669.44	984.06	2128.9	4587.6	9802.9	20714.1
30	34.784	40.568	47.575	56.084	66.438	79.058	94.460	113.28	136.30	164.49	241.33	356.78	434.74	530.31	790.94	1181.8	2640.9	5873.2	12940	28172.2
40	48.886	60.402	75.401	95.025	120.79	154.76	199.63	259.05	337.88	442.59	767.09	1342.0	1779.0	2360.7	4163.2	7343.8	22728	69377.	*	*
50	64.463	84.579	112.79	152.66	209.34	290.33	406.52	573.76	815.08	1163.9	2400.0	4994.5	7217.7	10435.	21813.	45497.	*	*	*	*
60	81.669	114.05	163.05	237.99	353.58	533.12	813.52	1253.2	1944.7	3034.0	7471.6	18535	29219.	46057.	*	*	*	*	*	*

*FVIF > 99.999

Bibliography

Allen, Franklin, Richard A. Brealey, and Stewart C. Myers. *Principles of Corporate Finance.* New York, NY: McGraw-Hill, 2005.

Association for Investment Management and Research. *Standards of Practice Handbook.* Charlottesville, VA: AIMR, 1993.

Association for Investment Management and Research. *Standards of Practice Casebook.* Charlottesville, VA: AIMR, 1996.

Billingsley, R. S. "Equity Securities Analysis Case Study: Merck & Company." In *Equity Securities Analysis and Evaluation.* Charlottesville, VA: AIMR, 1993.

Bodie, Z., A. Kane, and A. J. Marcus. *Investments* (2nd ed.). Burr Ridge, IL: Irwin, 1993.

Caccese, M. S. "Compliance Guidelines: Introduction." In *Good Ethics: The Essential Element of a Firm's Success.* Charlottesville, VA: AIMR, 1994.

Casey, J. L. *Ethics in the Financial Marketplace.* New York: Scudder, Sterns, & Clark, 1998.

Clayman, M. "In Search of Excellence: The Investor's Viewpoint," *Financial Analyst's Journal* (May/June, 1987).

Cohen, J. B., E. D. Zinbarg, and A. Zeikel. *Investment Analysis and Portfolio Management* (5th ed.). Homewood, IL: Irwin, 1987.

Der Hovanessian, A. "Guide to Evaluating Sovereign Credits," *Fixed Income Credit Research* (Nov. 1992), Morgan Stanley & Co.

DiCola, Annemarie. A Fundamental CMBS Overview (2008), www.cmsaglobal.org (last accessed December 17, 2008).

Fabozzi, F. J. *Bond Markets, Analysis and Strategies* (2nd ed.). Englewood Cliffs, NJ: Prentice Hall, 1993.

Fabozzi, F. J., T. D. Fabozzi, and I. M. Pollack (Eds.). *The Handbook of Fixed Income Securities* (3rd ed.). Homewood, IL: Irwin, 1991.

Frumkin, N. *Tracking America's Economy.* Armonk, NY: ME Sharpe, 1987.

Geffen, David. "Shocks in Commercial Mortgage Trigger Selloff in REIT Stocks," *Wall Street Journal,* November 5, 2008.

Gillis, J. G., and G. J. Ciotti. "Insider Trading Update," *Financial Analyst's Journal* (Nov./Dec. 1992).

Gordon, Mark. *The Complete Guide to Investing in Real Estate Investment Trusts: How to Earn High Rates of Return Safely.* Ocala, FL: Atlantic Publishing Company, 2008.

Hakkio, C. S. "Is Purchasing Power Parity a Useful Guide to the Dollar?" *Economic Review* (1992), Federal Reserve Bank of Kansas City (Third Quarter).

Harvard Business School. The Congruence Model (2009), www.people.hbs.edu/rdornin/draft-fifteen.html (last accessed February 13, 2009).

Higgins, R. C. *Analysis for Financial Management* (2nd ed.). Burr Ridge, IL: Business One Irwin, 1993.

Hillman, Michelle. "Boston Properties a Textbook Case of REIT's Struggles," *Boston Business Journal* (November 14, 2008).

Kritzman, M. "The Portable Financial Analyst," *Financial Analyst's Journal.* Charlottesville, VA: AIMR, 1995, pp. 3–5.

Lewis-Beck, M. S. *Applied Regression, An Introduction.* Thousand Oaks, CA: Sage Publications, 1980.

Longstreth, B. "The Prudent Man Rule Today—Variations on a Single Theme." In *Modern Investment Management and the Prudent Man Rule.* New York: Oxford University Press, 1987.

Magnin, J. L., and D. L. Tuttle. *Managing Investment Portfolios: A Dynamic Process* (2nd ed.). New York: Warren, Gorman & Lamont, 1990.

McNees, S. K. "The Accuracy of Macroeconomic Forecasts." In *Improving the Investment Decision Process—Better Use of Economic Inputs in Securities Analysis.* Charlottesville, VA: AIMR, 1991.

The National Association of Real Estate Investment Trusts. Glossary of REIT Terms, What is a REIT, REIT Characteristics, REIT FAQs (2009), www.REIT.com (last accessed January 19, 2009).

The National Association of Real Estate Investment Trusts. "REIT Watch: A Monthly Statistical Report on the Real Estate Investment Trust Industry" (June 2009).

Nelson, C. *The Investor's Guide to Economic Indicators.* New York: John Wiley & Sons, 1987.

Peters, Thomas J. and Robert H. Waterman. In *Search of Excellence: Lessons from America's Best Run Corporations.* New York: Random House, 1982.

Poorvu, William J. and Samuel Plimpton. *Financial Analysis of Real Property Investments.* Boston, MA: Harvard Business School Publishing, 2003.

Porter, M. E. "Competitive Strategy: The Core Concepts." In *Competitive Advantage: Creating and Sustaining Superior Performance.* New York: The Free Press/Macmillan, 1985.

Reilly, F. K. *Investment Analysis and Portfolio Management* (4th ed.). Fort Worth, TX: The Dryden Press, 1994.

Rubin, Joseph, and Richard Schlenger. Originating and Underwriting Commercial Mortgages for CMBS (2008), www.cmsaglobal.org (last accessed December 17, 2008).

Shapiro, A. C. *Multinational Financial Management* (4th ed.). Needham Heights, MA: Allyn & Bacon, 1992.

Siegel, J. J. "Does It Pay Stock Investors to Forecast the Business Cycle?" *Journal of Portfolio Management* (Fall, 1991).

Solnik, B. *International Investments* (2nd ed.). Reading, MA: Addison-Wesley, 1991.

"S&P's Corporate Finance Criteria." *Standard & Poor's Debt Ratings.* New York: Standard & Poor's Corporation, 2009.

Tracy, J. A. *How to Read a Financial Report* (4th ed.). New York: John Wiley & Sons, 1994.

Van Duyn, Aline. "Securitisation sector braced for a long, painful haul," *Financial Times,* December 5, 2008.

White, G. I., A. C. Sondhi, and D. A. Fried. *The Analysis and Use of Financial Statements.* New York: John Wiley & Sons, 1994.

Index

Absorption, 214
Accounting, 17
  documents, footnote section (fine print), 18
  financial analysis tool, 13
  policies, 132, 142
    importance, 5
  science, 14
  statements, understanding, 31–34
Account receivable turnover, 141–142
Accounts payable, 20
Accounts receivable
  balance sheet component, 19
  collection period, 128, 180
  turnover, 128–129
Accretive acquisition, 247–248
Accrued expenses, 20
Acid test, equation, 180
Acquisitions/dispositions, 143
Active management approach, 280
Adjustable rate loans, 224
Adjustable rate mortgages (ARMs), 225
Adjusted funds from operations (AFFO), 249
Agency mortgage-backed security (AMBS), 232
Aggressive growth style, 298
Air pollution, impact (example), 109
Alpha, positive level, 264
Alt-A loans, 224
Amortization, expense, 24
Analyst, term (interchangeability), 3
Annuities, 87–92
  future value, table, 313
  present value, 89–90
    table, 311
  problem set, 94–95
Arithmetic mean, 98
Assessment process, 138–139
Asset Allocation Model (AAM), 264, 296, 299
Asset-backed security (ABS), 226
Asset market approach, 67
Assets, 8, 18–20. *See also* People Assets Technology
    International strategy Return Operations
    Cost-effective management
  allocation

  defining, 278–279
  example, 263
  classes, risk level, 296
  correlation, 267
  hounds, 8
  liquidation, 186
  mix, framework, 275
  risk/return, example, 262f
  sale, 254
  target allocation, adjustment, 280
Asset turnover (ATO), 128
Automobile sales, 47
Average growth, exhibition, 153–154
Average workweek of production workers in
    manufacturing, 55–56

Bad debt reserve, 208
Balance of payments method, 67
Balance sheet, 18
  examination, 18
  examples, 19, 140, 196, 198
  factor, 5
  strength, 8
Barclays Aggregate Bond Index, performance, 277
Barrier to entry, 212
Benchmarking, 158
Bond market, timing, 39
Bonds
  basics, 171–176
  components, 172–173
  definition, 171–172
  seniority, 185–186
Borrowers
  characteristics, 223
  credit score, 223
Bridge loans, 225–226
Building
  improvements, 208
  permits/starts/completions, 213
  price per square foot, 215
Build-to-suit development, 216
Burden, 22
Business, scriptures, 14

Business cycle/investments, 59–60
Buyers
  bargaining power, 137
  power, 145

Capital
  appreciation, 250
  commitment, 119
  expenditures, 208–209
  markets, 295–298
  raising, 147
  risk, 261–262
  structure, 252
Capital allocation line, example, 263
Capital asset line (CAL), 263
Capital Asset Pricing Model (CAPM), 121,
    154–155, 269–270
  assumptions, 264
  equation, 269
  problems, sample, 155
  theoretical construct, 162
  usage, 159
Capitalization rate, 251
Cap (maximum interest rate), 225
Career risk, 296–297
Cash, balance sheet component, 19
Cash available for distribution (CAD), 249
Cash flow after financing (CFAF), 209
Cash flow before financing (CFBF), 209
Cash flow from financing activities, 25, 29–34
Cash flow from investing activities, 25
Cash flow from operating activities, 27
Cash flow from operations, 25, 26
Cash flows
  alignment, 254
  constraint, 129
  diagram, NPV calculation (process), 86–87
  sensitivity, 221–222
  streams, production, 233–234
Cash flow statement, 5, 25–26
  development, 34
  direct method, 25, 26–28
  example, 34
  indirect method, 25, 28
Cash inflows/outflows, 18
Cash ratio, equation, 180
Central Business District (CBD) property, 205
Central tendency, measures, 97–101
CFA Institute
  Code of Ethics, 301
  Professional Standards Program, 301
Chiarella vs. United States, 303
Chinese Wall (Firewall), 304–305
Client diagnosis/interview, importance, 271

Closing costs, 219
Coca-Cola, product/service duplication, 10
Code of Ethics (CFA Institute), 301
Coefficient of determination (R-squared), 111
Coincident index, 59
Collateral, 186
Commercial mortgage-backed security (CMBS),
    226–227
Commissions, impact, 209
Common-size financial statements, 126
  example, 127
Company
  acquisition exercise, competitive advantage, 10
  business fundamentals, 182
  capital structure, 185
  creditworthiness, 186
  international strategy, implementation, 9
  leverage, amount, 178–179
  liquidity position, determination, 179–180
  market share, 139
  morale, true test, 7
  operating/financial performance, determinants, 6
  position, importance, 3
  sales, VFII examination, 24
Comparable rents, 215
Comparable sales, 214–215, 247
Comparative valuation, 188
Compounded annual growth rate (CAGR), 107
  calculation, 100
Conference Board, LEI release/usage, 54, 57–58
Confidence limits, 103–105
Consumer basket differences, measurement
    difficulties, 68
Consumer expectations, index, 57
Consumer goods, new orders, 47
Consumer goods/materials, average initial weekly
    claims, 56
Consumer price index (CPI), 62
Contrarian investment style, 298
Conversion ratio, 175
Convertible bond issue, 175
Core real estate assets, long-term cash flow stability,
    215–216
Core/Satellite Strategy, 279–280
Corporate bonds, fixed income security, 173
Correlation, 111
  coefficient, 266
  measure. See Variables
Cost-effective management, 11–12. See also People
    Assets Technology International strategy
    Return Operations Cost-effective management
Cost of goods sold (COGS), 30
  definition, 22
  division, 129

Counterparties, 176
Coupon, bond component, 172
Covariance, 110–111
Covenant lite loans, 223
Coverage, 187
  ratios, calculation, 181
Credit analysis, 117–118, 165
  function, ratios (impact), 178
  problem set, 195–201
  tools, 176–188
Credit default swaps (CDS), 176
Credit enhancers, 230
Credit line, 254
Credit ratings, 188–201
  actions, 194
  changes, 193–195
  credit statistics, impact, 195
  downgrade, threat, 194
  issuance, 189–190
  key metrics, relationship, 195–201
  securing, 192–193
Credit risk, 296–297
Credit score, 223
Cultures, differences, 68
Current assets, balance sheet component, 18–20
Current liabilities, balance sheet component,
    20–21
Current ratio, equation, 180
Current supply, 213
Current yield, bond component, 172–173

Days to sell inventory, 129
  equation, 180
Debt
  issue, creditworthiness, 188
  maturities, schedule, 132, 182
  tranches, 185
Debt service, 170, 209
  affordability, 180–182
Debt service coverage ratio (DSCR), 222, 253
Default, 219, 234
  cushion, 170–171
  rate, 235
  risk, 234–235
Deficit data, 44–45
Degrees of freedom, 111
Delinquency
  rate, 235
  risk, 234–235
Depreciation
  expense, 24
  operating earnings, relationship, 24
Derivatives, 176
  usage, 131

Determinants of Portfolio's Return
    (Brinson/Beebower/Hood), 299
Development capital budget, 209–210
Dilutive acquisition, 247–248
Discounted cash flow (DCF), 159
  valuation, 216–218
Discounted cash flow model, 165–167
  usage, 159
Discount rate
  calculation, 165–166
  change, 43, 44
  usage, 269
Dispersion, measures, 101–103
Diversifiable risk, 267
Dividend Discount Model, 6, 159
Dividend payout ratio, 146
Dividend per share, 249
Dividends
  record/policy, 5
  yield, 249–250
Do-It-Yourselfers, investor type, 288, 294–295
Dollar
  pound, exchange rate, 64
  value
    decrease, 66
    increase, 64–65
Domestic importers, economic incentives (increase),
    64–65
Domestic inflation, impact, 65
Dow Jones REIT Composite Index, 255
Duff & Phelps, rating agency, 189
DuPont Derivation Equation, 132
DuPont Method. *See* Return on Equity Equation

Earnings, 21–22
Earnings before interest, taxes, depreciation and
    amortization (EBITDA), 24
  EBITDA/interest expense ratio, 181
Earnings before interest and taxes (EBIT), 165
  EBIT/interest expense ratio, 181
  ROE definition, 124
  usage, 128
Earnings per share (EPS), 156, 164–165
Economic activity, Fed restriction, 43–44
Economic releases
  calendar, 48–52
  uncertainty, importance, 45
Economics
  determination, 42
  financial analysis tool, 13
  tenets, understanding, 36
Economy
  evaluation, 42–43
  health, determination, 36–39

Efficiency measure, 268
Efficient frontier, 263
example, 262
Efficient portfolios, calculation, 265–266
8-K, SEC filing, 122
Electronic accounting, action, 9
Employee education, 305
Employee Retirement Income Safety Act (ERISA), 273
Employment cost index, 53
Employment situation, 53–54
indicator, 54
Endogenous variable, 108
Enterprise Value (EV), 157
Enterprise Value-to-EBITDA ratio, 157, 165
calculations, 166–167
Equity
analysis/valuation, 119
Problem set, 151–154
REITs, 241–242
sale, 147
valuation, 156–163
case study, 163
problems, sample, 162–163
Ethics. *See* Financial services industry
code, 302
Exchange-traded funds, 242
Ex-dividend date, 250
Existing home sales, 214
Exogenous variable, 108
Exotic real estate loans, 224–226
Expectations, management, 295–298
Explained variable, 108
Explanatory variable, 108

Face value, 172
Federal funds rate, change, 43–44
Federal Open Market Committee (FOMC)
activities, 43, 44
Federal Reserve, function, 43–44
Fiduciary, 304
Finance mathematics, financial analysis tool, 13
Financial analysis
assistance, 126
tools, 13
valuation models, 121
Financial instruments (valuation), economic events
(impact), 14
Financial metrics, analysis, 248–252
Financial performance, 183–184
Financial projections, 216–218
Financial ratios, tweaking, 125
Financial security analysis, 117
problem set, 140–143
Financial service provider (FSP), advice, 39

Financial services industry, ethics, 301–302
Financial statements
examination, 14
footnotes, usage, 130–133
understanding, 22–23
usage, 140–141
Financing costs, 209
Financing transaction costs, 209
Firms
book value, calculation, 21
rivalry, 139, 145
Firm-specific risk, 267
First in-first out (FIFO), 30
Fitch Investors Service, rating agency, 189, 229
Fixed assets (noncurrent assets), 20
Fixed charges, 181–182
Fixed cost, definition, 22
Fixed income security, 171
review, 194
types, 173–176
Fixed-rate loan, 220–221
Floor (minimum interest rate), 225
Followers (investor type), 287–288
Forward P/E ratio, 157
Forward rate, 67
Franchise value, 10
FTSE NAREIT U.S. Real Estate Index Series, 255
Full recourse, 223
Funds from operation (FFO), 248–249
yield, 248
Future earnings (projected earnings), 22
Future performance, projection, 149–154
Future value, tables, 312–313
Future Value Factor (FVF), 80–81
correspondence, 83–84
Future Value Factor of an Annuity (FVFA), 88, 94
Future value (FV)
investment, 92
mathematical equation, 80

Gamblers, investor type, 294
Generally accepted accounting principle (GAAP), 131
guidelines, 179
measurement, 248
standards, application, 184
General obligation (BO) bonds, 174, 201
Geometric mean, 99–100, 107
Geometric mean (average), 99
Goodness of fit, 111
Goods, real cost (inflation-adjusted cost), 68
Goods/services, U.S. international trade, 61
Gordon's Constant Growth Model, 159
Government entities, impact, 232
Government policymakers, forecast usage, 69
Government releases/indicators, 40–47

Great Depression, 232, 296
Gross domestic income (GDI), 62–63
Gross domestic product (GDP), 62–63
  industry contribution, 52–53
Gross national income (GNI), 63
Gross national product (GNP), 63
Gross profit, definition, 23
Growth, 182–183. *See also* Sustainable growth
  acquisition, 149
  drivers, 149
  evaluation, 145
  forecasts, 163–164
  investment style, 298
  investor, asset allocation (example), 300
  strategies, 148–149

Hard assets, 210–218
  fundamentals, 223
Hard costs, 209–210
Healthcare facilities, real estate, 206
Hewlett-Packard (HP) 12C financial calculator,
  usage, 90–92
High-risk subprime loan, 229
High-yield bonds, fixed income security, 174–175
High-yield tranches, 229
Historical trends, 188
  analysis, 149–154
H Model, 159–160
Home loans, prepayments (commonness), 234
Housing completions, reference, 218
Housing market
  activity level, 213–214
  average time, 214
  rents, 215
Housing permits, 218
Hybrid REITs, 242
Hybrid security, 175

Illiquid, term (usage), 254
Import taxes, 68
Income
  guarantee, 187–188
  stability, 182
Income-producing real estate, 240
Income statement
  examples, 23, 140, 196, 198
  factor, 5, 21–25
Income tax
  expense, 25
  payable, 20–21
In-control investor, 287
Indenture, 172
Index of Leading Economic Indicators (LEI), 54–59
  indicator composite, 55–57
Individual investor, psychographics, 286–289

Industrial real estate, 205–206
Industry
  analysis, 137–145, 184
  considerations, 3
Inflation
  defining, 40–41
  rate, 67
Information
  gatherers, 288
  sources, 122–123
In-place rents, 246
Insider ownership, 7
Insider trading, 302–303
  laws, 305–306
Insider Trading & Securities Fraud Enforcement Act
  (ITS-FEA), 305
Institute for Supply Management (ISM)
  PMI measurement, 53
  PMI report, VFII Study, 52
  report, 47, 52–53
Institutional client, IPS (usage), 274–279
Interest burden, 128
Interest expense, 24–25
Interest-only loans, 225
Interest rate arbitrage, 71–75
  quick math method, 72–75
Interest rate parity (IRP), 67, 70–71
  mathematical notation, 71
  quick math method, 71
Interest rates, 67, 219
  differentials, 67
  fluctuations, 41
  inflation, impact, 40
Interest-rate-sensitive securities, price decline, 38
Internal rate of return (IRR), 83–87
  analysis, 161–162
  defining, 85
  discount rate, 162
  examples, 95–96
  financial calculator, usage, 86
Internal Revenue Service (IRS), debt due,
  20–21
International Fisher Parity Condition, 40–41
International investing, 63–66
International parity conditions, 67
International strategy, 9. *See also* People Assets
     Technology International strategy Return
     Operations Cost-effective management
Internet, information source, 123
Inventories, 47
Inventory
  balance sheet component, 19
  control, 9
  turnover, 129, 142–143
Inventory on market, 213

Investment
account, IPS (presence), 281
constraints, 279
definition, 119
dispositions, 132–133
expectations, management, 295–298
grade, 194
management, 261, 270
methodology/process, 270, 271
objectives, 274, 276–277
parties, relationship, 169–170
policy, defining, 275
report checklist, 3–6
review, 279
strategy, 279
performance, 280–281
styles, 298
time horizon/goals, establishment, 275–276
Investment analysis
importance, 1–2
quantitative approach, 15
Investment finance
knowledge, 77–78
study, 14–15
Investment-grade tranches, 228–229
Investment mathematics, 14–15
problem set, 92–93
Investment Policy Statement (IPS), 272
case study, 281–286
constraints, 273
example, 284–285
contract, difference, 275
guideline answer, 282–286
objectives, 272, 276–277
example, 283–284
overview, example, 283
purpose, 276
versions, differences, 274–281
writing, 272–273
written policy, necessity, 275–276
Investors
accumulation phase, 290
consolidation phase, 290
diagnosis, 271–295
examples, 292–295
gifting phase, 291–292
life cycle, 290–292
psychographics, 286–289
spending pattern, 290–291
term, interchangeability, 3
types, 287–288
Items, breakdown, 142–143

Junior bond, 185
Junk bonds, 174–175

Lagging index, 59
Land, fixed assets, 20
Last in-first out (LIFO), 30
Leading coincident and lagging (LCL) classification, 59
Leading economic indicators, formation, 58
Leading index, 59
Lease expiration schedule, 246
Legal fees, impact, 209
Legal issues, constraint, 273
Legal restricted list, 305
LEI. *See* Index of Leading Economic Indicators
Lender
growth, impact, 183
legal protections, 184
Lender, perspective, 219–220
Leverage, 129, 187
amount, 178–179
determination, 253
analysis, 252–255
ratios, 178
NAREIT usage, 253
usage, reasons, 252–255
Liabilities, 20–21
Lien, 218
Life cycle stages, risk/return position, 289
Linear regression, 108
Liquidation, 185–186
Liquidity
access, 254
constraint, 273, 274
example, 284
income needs, relationship, 277
position, determination, 179–180, 254–255
Loans
covenants, 223
origination, 227
payments, financing cost, 209
pool, creation, 228
repayment, 177
servicing, 230–231
subordination, 225
terms, 220
Loan-to-value (LTV), 222
Lock-out period, 234
Lodging, real estate, 205
London Interbank Offered Rate (LIBOR), 225
Long-run growth rate, usage, 166
Long-term debt, balance sheet component, 21
Long-term debt/total equity ratio, 178
Long-term growth rate, impact, 161
Long-term investment policy, articulation, 276
Lower of cost or market (LCM), 19
Low-risk investment-grade tranche, 229

Macroeconomic relationships, tenets
   (understanding), 37
Macroeconomic releases, dynamics, 3
Management
   analysis, 133, 184
   policy/style, understanding, 14
Mandatory covenants, 187
Manufacturer's new orders, 55
Manufacturer's shipments, 47
Manufacturing, average workweek of production
   workers, 56
Margin squeeze, creation, 170–171
Market indices, analysis, 255
Market portfolio risk/return, 264
Market rents, 215, 246
Market risk, 121
   premium, 155
Markowitz, Harry, 263, 265, 299
Markowitz diversifiers, 269
Material information, 304
McDonald's, product/service duplication, 10
McNees, Stephen, 37
Mean equation, scientific notation, 98–99
Mean-variance diversifiers, 269
Mean-variance portfolios, 263
Measures of central tendency, 97–101
Median, 100
Medical professionals, investor type,
   292–293
Mento machines, 143–145
Merchandise trade balance, 61
Mezzanine tranches, 229
Minimization strategy, 274
Misappropriation Theory, 303, 304
Mode, 100–101
Modern Portfolio Theory (MPT), 261–270
   basis, 279–280
Monetary shocks, impact, 41
Money
   future value, 79–81
   present value, 81–82
Money supply (M2), 57
Moody's, rating agency, 188–189, 229
Morgan Stanley Europe Asia Far East (MS EAFE),
   63–64
   Index, performance, 277
Mortgage
   broker, 227
   constant, 220–221
     calculation formula, 221
   definition, 218–219
   meltdown, 307
   problem set, 238–240
   REITs, 242
Mortgage-backed security (MBS), 226

analysis, 232–237
   bond analysis, 233–237
   B-piece, 231
   creation, 227–232
   definition, 226–227
   problem set, 238–240
   secondary market, 230
   tranches
     creation, 228–230
     investor sale, 230
     risk levels, tailoring, 229
   underlying loans analysis, 233
   underlying property analysis, 233
Mosaic Theory, 305
Multi-family real estate, 204
Multinational businesses, forecast usage, 69
Multinational corporation (MNC), currency
   exposure, 66
Multiple regression, 114
Multistage Model (2-Stage Model), 160–161
Municipal bonds
   advantage, 174
   fixed income security, 173–174

National Association of Real Estate Investment
   Trusts (NAREIT)
   leverage ratio usage, 253
   REITWatch information, 253
NCREIF Property Index, 255
Net asset value (NAV), 251–252
Net capital expenditures, 159
Net cash flow from investing activities, 29
Net income, 25
   ROE definition, 124
Net operating income (NOI), 208, 222, 252
Net present value (NPV), 21, 83–87
   calculation, 85, 95
   determination, 83
   equation, cash flow quantification, 78
   examples, 95–96
   framework, 84
Net result, determination, 83
Net return on equity, 130
Network environments, complexity, 143
New businesses, formation, 55
New entrants, threat, 138, 144–145
New home sales, 213–214
New housing, permits, 55
New private housing units, building permits, 56
New product development, 149
Nominal interest rate, 40–41
Non-cash charges, factors, 24
Non-core assets, focus, 216
Noncurrent assets. *See* Fixed assets
Non-exchange-traded REITs, 242

Nonfinancially interested individuals (NFIIs), 2–3, 35, 89
Non-operating costs, 208–209
Non-performing loans, 231
Nonpublic information, 304
Non-recourse, 223
Normally distributed data sets, 103–104

Obligation, 189–190
    rating, 190–192
Occupancy, trends, 245
Off-balance sheet liabilities, 131, 142
Office building, quality (classes), 205
Office real estate, 204–205
Operating cash flow/fixed charges, 181
Operating earnings, depreciation (relationship), 24
Operating expenses, 208
    definition, 23–24
Operating leverage, 250
Operating margin, 128
Operating statement (set-up), 207–209
Operational performance, 183–184
Operations, 10. *See also* People Assets Technology International strategy Return Operations Cost-effective management
Opportunistic, term (usage), 216
Ordinary annuity, 87
Overcollateralization, 230
Overhead, 22
Ownership, rental (contrast), 207

Parity condition, factors, 68
Par value, 172, 236
Passive management approach, basis, 279–280
Payment-in-kind (PIK) option, 225
Payout ratio, 250
    increase, 147–148
    reduction, 147
People, 7–8
People Assets Technology International strategy Return Operations Cost-effective management (PATIROC), 6
    characteristics, 11–12
PepsiCo, product/service duplication, 10
Periodic tests, 223
Permitting process, 212
Personal consumption expenditures, 60
Personal income/expenditures, 60
Plant and equipment, contracts/orders, 55, 56
Pledged assets, 186
Political risk, 296–297
Pooling & Service Agreement (PSA), 230–231
Porter, Michael E., 120–121, 137
    five competitive forces, 121, 212
Portfolio. *See* Mean-variance portfolios

construction/implementation, 299–300
lenders, 227
management, 259
    definitions, 304–305
    strategies, risk levels, 296
monitoring, 300–306
return rate, (estimation), CAPM (usage), 269–270
review, 280
risk, reduction, 267–268
selection theory, 265–268
standard deviation, 266–267
Practitioner, term (interchangeability), 3
Predicted variable, 108
Pre-leased real estate, 216
Premium to par, 172
Prepaid expenses, balance sheet component, 20
Prepayment risk, 233–234
    level, increase, 234
Present Value Factor of an Annuity (PVFA), 89, 94
Present Value Factor (PVF), 92–93
Present value (PV)
    defining, 81
    tables, 310–311
Pretax income, ROE definition, 124
Price, bond component, 172
Price-FFO multiple, 249
Price-to-book value, 157
Price-to-earnings ratio (P/E), 156, 164–165
    calculations, 166–167
    inequality, 158
    usage, 10
Price-to-sales ratio, 157
Primary servicer, 230–231
Prime loans, 224
Principal, 219
Private REITs, 242
Problem set format, 14–15
Producer price index (PPI), 61–62
Product analysis, example, 98
Product duplication, 10
Product line growth, 148
Profitability conditions, determination, 139
Profit sharing, 208
Prohibitive covenants, 187
Property
    foreclosure, 219
    NOI, 222
    value, 222
Property, plan, and equipment (fixed assets), 20
Psychographic labeling, 286–287
Publicly traded REITs, 241, 242
Public Securities Association (PSA) Standard Prepayment Model, 234

Purchasing power parity (PPP), 35, 67–69
  equation, calculation, 73
  mathematical notation, 70
  quick math method, 70
  usage, benefits, 69
Purchasing power risk, 296–297

Quadrant methodology, 287–288
Quantitative analysis, 97, 118
  financial analysis tool, 13
  statistics, 97
Quantitative easing (QE), 44
Quick ratio, 180

Rating agencies, 188–189, 229
Rating process, 192–193
Ratios
  analysis, 164–165
  heuristics, 156
  standardization, 158
  usage, 157–158
Real estate
  absorption, 214
  area amenities, 211–212
  assets, long-term cash flow stability, 215–216
  DCF valuation, 216–218
  demographics, 211
  economic conditions, 211
  financial projections, 216–218
  financial statements, 207–210
  infrastructure, 212
  investment, 210–218
    strategies, 215–216
  legal terms, 223
  location, importance, 210–212
  market
    activity level, 213–214
    average time, 214
  new supply, pipeline, 213
  operating statement (set-up), 207
  ownership, rental (contrast), 207
  physical attributes, 211
  political circumstances, 212
  price levels, 214–215
  price per square foot, 215
  problem set, 217–218
  revenue, 207–208
  supply and demand statistics, 212–215
  taxes, 208
  types, 204–207
Real estate investment trusts (REITs), 240
  analysis, 243
  business lines, 244–245
  capitalization rate, 251
  creation, 241

  debt payments, affordability, 253
  definition, 240–241
  dividends, 249–250
  financial metrics, analysis, 248–252
  funds from operations (FFO), 248–249
  growth strategy, 248
  in-place rents, 245
  investment strategy, 243–244
  investment vehicles, 242–243
  lease expiration schedule, 246
  leasing activity, 246
  leverage, analysis, 252–255
  liquidity position, determination, 254–255
  market indices, analysis, 255
  market rents, 246
  mutual funds, 242
  net asset value, 251–252
  occupancy/vacancy, 245
    trends, 245
  operating leverage, 250
  operating metrics, 245–247
  operations, analysis, 243–248
  pipeline, 247–248
  portfolio composition, 244
  problem set, 255–258
  replacement cost, 252
  stability/timing, 243
  types, 241–243
Real estate loans. *See* Exotic real estate loans
  analysis, 222–223
  cash flows, analysis, 219–222
  categories, 224
  financial terms, 219
  investment, 218–226
Real rate, 40–41
Rebalancing, procedures, 280
Regression analysis, 108–110
  problem set, 114–116
Regression coefficients, 113
Regression data, example, 113
Reimbursements, real estate, 207
Reinvestment risk, 296–297
Release-of-concern, 44–45
Rental income, 207
Replacement cost, 252
Replacement reverse, 253
Reputation fear, 1
Research and development (R&D), dedication, 9
Residential loans, prepayment risk, 234
Residential mortgage-backed security (RMBS), 226–227
Residential real estate, 204
Resorts, real estate, 205
Retail real estate, 205
Retained earnings, 21

Retention ratio, 146
  increase, 147
Return, 10. *See also* People Assets Technology
    International strategy Return Operations
    Cost-effective management
  objective, 272
  rate, 269–270
  requirement, 283
  standard deviation, 297
Return on assets (ROA), 120, 124, 129–130
Return on Equity Equation, DuPont Method, 6
Return on equity (ROE), 120, 124–130, 182. *See
    also* Net return on equity
  asset turnover, 128
  definitions, 124–127
  derivations, 129–130
  equation, 127–129
  interest burden, 128
  operating margin, 128
  tax burden, 127–128
  usage, 183–184
Revenue
  definition, 22
  issue, 201
  ROE definition, 124–125
Revenue bonds, 174
Revenue per available room (RevPAR), 215
Risk
  allocation, 228–229
  conservative level, 277
  evaluation, 154–155
  management, 297
  objective, 272
  reduction, securities (addition), 267
  tolerance, 274
    defining, 277–278
    example, 284
  types, 296–297
Risk-free assets, asset allocation (example), 263
Risk-free investments, 237
Risk-free rate, 155
Risk/return quarters, example, 265
Risk-return trade-off, understanding, 2
Rollover schedule, 246
Router industry, 144
R-squared, 111
Rule of 72, 93
  application, 291

Sales, general, and administrative expenses (SG&A),
    24
Sales/average accounts receivable, 141–142
Sales comps, 214–215
Sales income, 207
Scared (investor type), 288–289

Secured bond, 186
Securities
  addition, impact, 267–268
  correlation, 266–267
  portfolio risk (calculation), 265–266
  return rate (estimation), CAPM (usage),
    269–270
  weightings, assumption, 266
Securities and Exchange Commission (SEC) filings,
    122
Securities Enforcement Remedies & Penny Stock
    Reform Act (SERP-SRA), 306
Securitization, 226
Securitized lenders, 227
Security, nature, 5
Security analysis checklist, 4–5
Security Market Line (SML), 264
Security price record, 5
Self-storage, real estate, 206
Senior bond, 185
Senior securities, 185
Sensitivity analysis, 161–162, 167
Sensitivity table, 161
Service duplication, 10
Set-up (operating statement), 207–209
Sharpe Ratio, 263, 268
Short-term money market instruments, 8
Simple regression, example, 111–116
Soft costs, 210
Solnik, Bruno, 68
Special servicer, 231
Speculative development, 216
Spot rate, 67
Spreads, 188
  widening, 237
  yields, relationship, 236–237
Stability, 182–183
Standard deviation, 103
  measure, usage, 105
  scientific equation, 103
Standard & Poor's (S&P)
  issue, credit rating definitions, 189–192
  rating agency, 188–189, 229
Standard & Poor's 500 (S&P500) Index,
    performance, 277
Statement of Financial Accounting Concepts
    (SFAC) 5, 124–125
State unemployment insurance, average initial
    weekly claims, 56
Statistical deviations (noise), 62
Statistics. *See* Quantitative analysis; Summary
    statistics
  problem set, 106–108
Stock compensation plan, 132
Stockholder equity, 21